W9-BJM-439

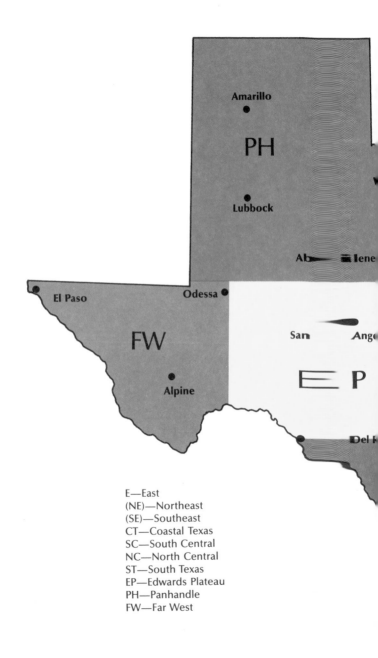

Amarillo

PH

Lubbock

Ab≡lene

El Paso   Odessa

FW   San   Ang

Alpine   E P

Del

E—East
(NE)—Northeast
(SE)—Southeast
CT—Coastal Texas
SC—South Central
NC—North Central
ST—South Texas
EP—Edwards Plateau
PH—Panhandle
FW—Far West

WILDFLOWERS *of* TEXAS

by Geyata Ajilvsgi

SHEARER PUBLISHING
FREDERICKSBURG, TEXAS

Copyright © 1984 by Geyata Ajilvsgi

*No part of this book may be used or
reproduced in any manner whatsoever
without written permission except in the
case of brief quotations embodied in
critical articles and reviews.*

Library of Congress Catalog Card Number 84-50025

ISBN 0-940672-46-4

Designed by Whitehead & Whitehead.

Production by Phoenix Offset, Hong Kong
Printed in China

Published by   Shearer Publishing
                406 Post Oak Road
                Fredericksburg, Texas 78624

Unless otherwise indicated, all photographs are by the author.

CONTENTS

CONTRIBUTING PHOTOGRAPHERS

Scooter Cheatham, *Austin*
Sandra J. Darby, *Plano*
Doris and Doug Evans, *Big Bend National Park*
Madge Lindsay Gatlin, *Richardson*
Martha S. Henschen, *Houston*
Robert (Bob) Hill, *Portland*
Marshall C. Johnston, *Austin*
Tony Keeney, *Uvalde*
John M. Koros, *Humble*
William F. Mahler, *Dallas*
George Oxford Miller, *Austin*
Stephan Myers, *Houston*
Benny J. Simpson, *Dallas*
John L. Tveten, *Baytown*
Bonnie E. Wenk, *New Stanton, Pennsylvania*
Vernon L. Wesby, *Kerrville*
Theron A. Wilbanks, *Arlington*
Burr Williams, *Midland*
Doug Williams, *Houston*
Frances C. Williams, *Midland*
Richard D. Worthington, *El Paso*
Tom R. Young, *Dallas*

MAJOR VEGETATION ZONES
OF TEXAS

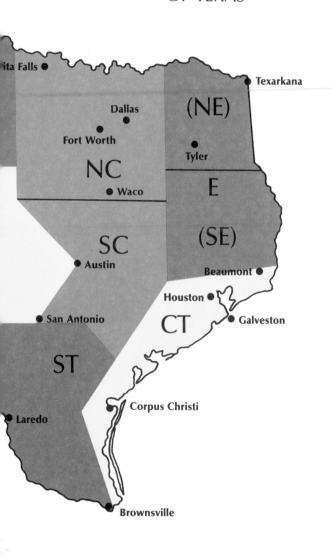

Wildflowers of Texas

ACKNOWLEDGMENTS

No book of this type is possible without the support and encouragement of many individuals. I have depended heavily upon, and received help of all kinds, not only from perfect strangers or acquaintances but also from some very special friends. In my attempt to select some of the most common wildflowers of the state, many people were helpful. To all those who methodically reviewed various lengthy lists, and for their astute suggestions for specific inclusion or deletion, I am most grateful.

The response from photographers in my search for slides was overwhelming. I feel that I have had the choice of topnotch work, and final selection from among the thousands submitted was most difficult. Some photographers, such as John Tveten, Stephan Myers and Richard Worthington, made a special effort to submit material. Vern and Marie Wesby traveled many miles over the state to obtain specially needed species. Mere words of thanks for all their efforts are hardly enough.

Dr. William F. Mahler and Barney Lipscomb of the Southern Methodist University Herbarium spent many hours with me going over specimens and unraveling identification problems. For their time, patience and consideration, I am deeply indebted. I particularly wish to thank Jesús Valdés at Texas A & M University for the translation of Spanish names for the wildflowers, and Dr. Paul Fryxell, USDA, also at Texas A & M, for information and help in dealing with numerous and varied problems.

Without the constant enthusiasm and positive attitude of my friend and publisher, William Shearer, I would never have made it through another wildflower book. To my most competent editor, Jean Hardy, and to Fred and Barbara Whitehead for their excellent layout and design, I offer a most profound thanks. The illustrations were skillfully rendered by Tina K. Forster, based on originals by Martha Bell.

Appreciation is extended to the Texas A & M University Press for permission to use certain photos, portions of the glossary and occasional passages from the text of my book *Wild Flowers of the Big Thicket*. I am most grateful to the Biology Department of Texas A & M, and especially to Dr. Hugh Wilson, Associate Professor of Biology and Curator of the Herbarium, for their patience and support during the compiling of this book.

As in the compilation of almost any work of this sort, I have met many new and interesting people— some of whom have become friends, making my life richer. To all those who have shared their books, their knowledge, their "hear-say" and "notions," I thank you. And to all my "old" friends who have patiently and consistently given advice, encouragement and moral support during this eventful period, I extend my most humble appreciation and gratitude.

College Station, Texas   *Geyata Ajilvsgi*

This book is dedicated to my people, the Cherokee, whose reverence, knowledge and usage of plants enabled them to live as one with the land.

INTRODUCTION

Texas is a vast and varied state. Encompassing some 267,339 square miles, it reaches 773 miles from east to west and 860 miles from north to south. In the eastern portion of the state, dense pine and hardwood forest slowly give way to fertile blackland prairies, while the flat, unbroken plains of the Panhandle drop southward to the semitropical Rio Grande Valley. Waters of the Gulf of Mexico pile stretches of white sand along the southern coastline, leaving shifting dunes and long, narrow beaches. In the middle west rise the sharp, craggy cliffs of the Edwards Plateau, with outcroppings of limestone and granite. Far west Texas is a land of tall mountains, purple-shadowed valleys and flat stretches of scorched sands.

Within an area of such sharp natural contrasts, a wide diversity of plant life is to be expected. From early March until the end of October, the state is covered with blooms. These wildflower months produce landscapes of brilliant colors: undulating expanses of bluebonnets spreading across the Hill Country, patches of bluebells quilting the prairies, and large mounds of fragrant heliotrope clinging tenaciously to the ever-shifting dunes of the Trans-Pecos. Long ribbons of constantly changing colors border the roadsides, as one species after another comes into bloom.

Vegetation Zones

The range maps on the end papers of this book divide the state into seven major ecological or vegetation zones. Two of these, East Texas and Central Texas, have been further divided into two sections. These zones or regions are a simplified version of the regions outlined by Frank Gould in his *Texas Plants, A Checklist and Ecological Summary*.

The Northeastern zone (NE) is an area of gently rolling to hilly land interspersed with open farmlands, while the Southeastern area (SE), known generally as the Big Thicket, is relatively flat and forested in pine and hardwoods. The entire eastern section has ample rainfall, high humidity and high summer temperatures. Soils are mostly light-colored acid sands or sandy loams with occasional deposits of clay, especially in alluvial bottomland soils. Some widespreading flowering plants of this mostly forested region include spring beauties (*Claytonia virginica*), brown-eyed Susans (*Rudbeckia hirta*), Philadelphia fleabane (*Erigeron philadelphicus*), self-heal (*Prunella vulgaris*), the goldenrods (*Solidago* spp.) and ironweeds (*Vernonia* spp.).

Cross Timbers and Prairies, the Blackland Prairies and the Post Oak Savannahs comprise what is defined as the Central zone of the state in this work. The northern section (NC) is comprised generally of the Cross Timbers and Prairies and Blackland Prairies. The topography is hilly to gently rolling to nearly level. Annual rainfall averages from 40 inches or more in the east to 25 inches in the west, with the highest occurring in April, May and June. While soils of the Cross Timbers and Prairies are brownish, neutral to slightly acid sandy or clay loams, the Blackland soils are fairly uniform, dark-colored calcareous clay usually interspersed with some gray acid sandy loams.

The Post Oak Savannahs of the South Central zone (SC) are periodically dissected by the Blackland Prairies, mainly the San Antonio and Fayette prairies.

Various grasses dominate the vegetation of the prairies, which are interspersed with occasional areas of dense brush. In some places "improved" pasturelands have replaced the native vegetation, but still the prairies bloom with a touch of their former splendor. The prairies are not noted for many *different* species of wildflowers, but for the *abundance* of some species. Here, the wine-cups (*Callirhoë* spp.), showy primroses (*Oenothera speciosa*), bluebells (*Eustoma grandiflorum*), Texas squaw-weed (*Senecio ampullaceus*) and snow-on-the-prairie (*Euphorbia bicolor*) cover large areas and form masses of color.

The Coastal Texas region (CT) is made up of prairies, marshes, beaches and islands. The nearly level, slowly draining prairies in the northern portion of this area are dissected by streams flowing into the Gulf and by narrow belts of low, wet, saline marshlands. These in turn give way to the deep, white, Gulf–deposited sands of the beaches and islands. Rainfall varies from more than 50 inches in the east to less than 20 inches in the west, with warm temperatures and relatively high humidity. The spring season is short, lasting only through March and April, when the hot temperatures of summer take over. Soils of the coastal prairies are generally heavy acid clays or clay loams with occasional sandy loams. The marshes are composed of acid sands, sandy loams and clays.

Both the prairies and marshes are grazed, with some farming in the better soils of the prairies. Native vegetation of the prairies is predominantly grasses interspersed with post oak savannah or live oak mottes. Wildflowers of these areas are salt-tolerant species such as salt marshmallow (*Kosteletzkya virginica* var. *althaefolia*), sea oxeye (*Borrichia frutescens*), sea lavender (*Limonium nashii*) and salt-marsh morning glory (*Ipomoea sagittata*). Beach morning glory (*Ipomoea stolonifera*) and goat-foot morning glory (*I. pes-caprae*) along with beach evening primrose (*Oenothera drummondii*) are dominants of the deep sands of the beaches and dunes.

The Panhandle (PH) includes both the Rolling Plains and the High Plains and is an area of gently rolling to moderately rough terrain and a high, relatively level plateau. Seasonal precipitation is highly variable, with most of the annual 15 to 30 inches occurring in the spring and fall. The summers are generally dry, with high temperatures and high evaporation rates. Soils vary from sandy to clays or shale. In some areas surface soils are underlaid with caliche, a "chalky" formation. Vegetation occurring on each soil type in this zone is fairly distinct and more easily defined than in other areas of the state. In the western portion numerous playa lakes occur, providing moist habitats that support various plant species different from surrounding vegetation.

Native vegetation is predominantly prairie grasses, but much of the area is under cultivation or is grazed. Some of the more common wildflowers of this region include spectacle-pod (*Dithyrea wislizenii*), paper-flower (*Psilostrophe* spp.), plains zinnia (*Zinnia grandiflora*) and common sunflower (*Helianthus annuus*).

The Edwards Plateau (EP), commonly referred to as the "Hill Country," is located in west central Texas. Rainfall varies from more than 30 inches in the eastern portion to less than 15 inches in the western portion. Humidity is generally low, with gentle but almost constant winds during the warmer months. Soils are generally shallow and laid over limestone or caliche, or in some places over granite. Several rivers and numerous streams traverse the area, with narrow, adjacent belts of alluvial deposits. The region is predominantly rangeland with a wide mixture of vegetation. Spanish oak (*Quercus texana*) and cedar (*Juniperus ashei*) are dominant overstory species. The western portion of the area is more typically prairielands or semidesert grasslands.

In the EP region the bluebonnets (*Lupinus* spp.) are a major springtime attraction, and when at the peak of bloom, are truly spectacular. Also highly visible but blooming in less profusion are Indian paintbrush (*Castilleja* spp.), Indian blanket (*Gaillardia pulchella*) and coreopsis (*Coreopsis* spp.). During the warmer summer and early fall months mountain pink (*Centaurium beyrichii*), hairy wedelia (*Wedelia hispida*) and woolly ironweed (*Vernonia lindheimeri*) form bright splashes of color on steep, rocky slopes.

The area designated as South Texas (ST) includes the South Texas Plains, chaparral brushland, and the Rio Grande Valley. Most published sources also include some of the coastal marshes and beaches. For this book only the marshes and beaches of this area are included in the Coastal Texas (CT) habitat.

Topography of the South Texas region is gently rolling to level, with a wide mixture of soils ranging from deep sands to sandy loams to clays. Annual precipitation varies from 16 to 35 inches, decreasing from east to west. Most rainfall is during May and June. High temperatures during the summer months cause extremely high evaporation rates, especially along the western border.

Originally the climax vegetation of South Texas was grassland or savannah. Over the years, grazing has altered much of the grasslands in the northern portion and the area is now being invaded with brush that is competitive with the original species. In the warmer Valley area, most of the land has been cleared of its former vegetation and is now under cultivation. In areas where native vegetation still exists, distinct differences in plant communities are quite evident. Many interesting species more commonly found in Mexico grow well in the extreme southern tip of Texas. The best and easiest places to find the wildflowers in this highly disturbed area are along roadsides, in state parks, and in wildlife refuges. In their seasons, baby blue-eyes (*Nemophila phacelioides*), phacelia (*Phacelia congesta*), tropical sage (*Salvia coccinea*) and Dakota vervain (*Verbena bipinnatifida*) are quite showy.

The Far West (FW) region includes the Trans-

Pecos, Mountains and Basins. This is an area of extreme variability with high mountains, plateaus, wooded slopes and arid valleys. Annual precipitation is usually less than 20 inches with highest rainfall usually occurring during July and August. Soils are generally calcareous with accumulations of alkali where drainage is poor. Due to the extremes of terrain, surface sites range from sands, hard-packed clay, saline, gypsum flats and gravelly or rocky soils to solid rock.

Surprisingly, numerous species of wildflowers occur in this harsh terrain. Often the plants themselves are small, but the flowers are large and showy or in colorful clusters. Because of the sparse rainfall, plants put most of their energy into flowering instead of plant growth, producing large flowers which are easily seen by their insect pollinators. Also, the flowering period for each species is usually very short, for they must quickly produce mature seed from the small amount of available moisture. With rainfall so uncertain, seeds often lie dormant for many years, and certain species of wildflowers may be seen only once in a lifetime, if at all.

How Wildflowers Were Chosen

With over 5,000 species of flowering plants listed for the state, the task of choosing 370 or so from among the most common was no easy task. Obviously, certain criteria had to be established.

Basically, only the most common and the showiest herbaceous species were chosen, leaving out all trees, shrubs, cacti and woody vines. A few herbaceous vines were included. Some plants not native to the United States such as chicory (*Cichorium intybus*), common dandelion (*Taraxacum officinale*) and henbit (*Lamium amplexicaule*) are included because they have become naturalized and are self-perpetuating outside cultivation.

To be considered common, a plant must occur

over a large portion of the state, cover a long bloom period, or be very common in its area. For example, the beach morning glory can be found only in the coastal sands, but it blooms all summer and is a prominent component of the beach flora. This book makes no claim to have included *all* the common wildflowers of the state—an impossible chore, since the definition of "common" is truly ambiguous and arbitrary. "Showy" does not always mean bigness of flower—often it is used to describe large areas of plants. Frequently the individual flowers of a plant are small, but the plants occur en masse, so the effect is quite spectacular.

Format

The approach taken in the organization and writing of this book has been one of simplicity. Since the most obvious thing about a plant usually is the color of the flowers, the species chosen for reproduction here have been divided into four color groups: white-green, yellow-orange, pink-red and blue-purple. Since one color often shades into another, the color cream or ivory for instance, the two closest color sections should be consulted—in this case, both the white and yellow sections. Where more than one color is common for a species, the color most commonly encountered is illustrated, with the other colors mentioned in the text.

Within each color section, the plants are listed alphabetically by family, then by genus and species. This follows no scientific order and is done purely for ease of use by the layperson.

Within each plant description the common name is followed in parentheses by the scientific name. In most cases, the orthography of common names follows *Webster's Third International Dictionary*. The bloom periods given for each plant should be considered typical but not absolutely limiting, as many of the flowers continue to bloom sporadically long after the last given date. The range of most of these plants is so large, and weather conditions so variable, that it is impossible to predict bloom periods with certainty.

The description of each plant includes general notes on growth form, followed by a description of the flower, the inflorescence and the leaves. Measurements have been expressed in feet and inches followed in parentheses by the nearest metric equivalencies. This was done to satisfy the preferences of both the general public and the more botanically experienced. The exact conversion of one measurement into the other was often impossible without becoming tedious; in these instances, the closest reasonable measurement was chosen and used consistently thereafter.

The "Habitat" entry for each plant describes what soil types a species most commonly grows in, as well as any other habitat limitations. Then the geographic range of each plant is expressed in terms of its vegetation zones (NC, EP, ST, etc.) within the state (see end maps).

For the most part, terms used to describe the plants, their parts and various other characteristics have been taken from the vernacular. Sometimes, for the sake of clarity, it has been necessary to use somewhat technical terms. The glossary should help clear up any confusion caused by these terms.

The color photographs were chosen not only to help in the identification of the flowers, but for their composition, depiction of naturalness of growth, flower form and color, and to emphasize the beauty, often overlooked, in our more common species.

A Final Word

This book has been prepared as a general guide for teachers and students, but especially for the amateur naturalist and the tourist. It should prove particularly useful to those interested in natural history but not having the time, resources or desire for extensive botanical training.

A major intent of this book is to enhance public awareness and knowledge of our beautiful wildflowers. As more and more people begin to learn the plants and flowers by name, perhaps they will remember to appreciate the flowers in their natural settings and *leave them there*. The wildflowers are a common heritage of our state and one of our most significant natural resources; we wish to encourage their preservation, not their destruction.

Those wishing to incorporate wildflowers into their home gardens can buy seeds from a variety of commercial suppliers. Plants from seeds will be more likely to adapt to somewhat less favorable habitats. Often plants may be readily obtained where they are being destroyed to make way for highways or other types of construction. Such plants usually will transplant only to similar habitats, however, and then only moderately successfully, depending upon the species. In any case, indiscriminant digging of our native plants is to be discouraged if we wish to preserve our wealth of wildflowers for future generations of Texans.

WHITE FLOWERS

WATER-WILLOW (Wesby)

WAPATO

WATER-WILLOW (*Justicia americana*)
Acanthus Family (Acanthaceae)

Bloom Period: May–October

Description: Upright, smooth perennial herb to 30 in. (76 cm); stems angled, slender, branched in upper portion, usually rooting in lower portion. Plants form colonies by rooting at the joints of underground stems. **Flower** ⅜–½ in. (10–13 mm) long, white or occasionally violet, dotted with purple, 2-lipped; upper lip notched or 2-lobed, turned backward; lower lip deeply 3-lobed, occasionally turned under. Flowers few, in cluster at tip of long stalk from leaf axils. **Leaves** 3–6 in. (7.6–15 cm) long, narrow, opposite, stalkless or almost so, narrowed at both ends; margins entire.

Habitat: Mud or shallow water along shores or margins of streams, lakes, ponds or marshes. In all except SC, PH, ST, FW.

Note: Linnaeus named this genus for James Justice, a Scottish botanist and horticulturist of the 18th century. This plant has a place in every water planting and is easily propagated by root cuttings.

WAPATO (*Sagittaria latifolia*)
Water-Plantain Family (Alismataceae)

Bloom Period: May–August

Description: Upright to sprawling, coarse, smooth aquatic perennial 1–4 ft. (3–12 dm) high from tuber-bearing roots; herbage contains milky juice. Plants form large colonies. **Flower** ¾–1½ in. (2–3.8 cm) across; white; petals 3, soon falling. Flowers few to numerous, stalked, in whorls of 3 around elongated terminal spike; spike slender, angled, occasionally branched from lower flower whorls; female flowers in lower portion of spike; male flowers in upper portion. **Leaves** basal, upright, conspicuously large, long-stalked, growing either above or below water; stalk to 40 in. (10 dm) long; blade prominently veined, rounded or sharp-pointed at tip, sharply lobed at base; portion above lobes to 10 in. (25 cm) long and 10 in. wide; basal lobes one-half as long to longer than upper portion.

Habitat: In water, mud or muck along edges of streams or lakes and in marshes, swamps, canals or ditches. In all except ST.

Note: The starchy tubers buried beneath the mud were once an important food source for Indians. They were eaten raw or were stored and later boiled or dried and pounded into a flour used in making gruel or bread. These tubers are eaten by various forms of wildlife, especially ducks, and hence another common name, *duck potato*.

3

ROWHEAD

A SNAKE-COTTON

DELTA ARROWHEAD (*Sagittaria platyphylla*)
Water-Plantain Family (Alismataceae)

Bloom Period: April–October

Description: Upright, smooth perennial 1–3 ft. (3–9 dm) high from small tubers formed at tips of thick roots; herbage contains milky juice. Plants usually form dense colonies. **Flower** about 1 in. (25 mm) across, white; petals 3, falling early. Flowers few to numerous, stalked, in whorls of 3 at joints in terminal portion of weak, leafless stem; lower whorls of female flowers with thick, soon-recurving stalks; upper whorls of male flowers with erect or spreading stalks. **Leaves** to 7½ in. (19 cm) long, to 3½ in. (8.9 cm) wide, frequently smaller, from tuber, long-stalked, base of blade sheathing flowering stem; blade usually unlobed at base, prominently veined.

Habitat: In mud or shallow water of streams, ponds, sloughs, swamps, marshes, canals and ditches. In all except FW.

Note: The name *Sagittaria* was given this genus for the prevailing shape of the leaves, *sagitta* being Latin for "arrow." In some specimens, such as the one at left, the leaves are not lobed at the base, and in some species the distinction between stalk and blade is practically nonexistent.

ARIZONA SNAKE-COTTON (*Froelichia arizonica*)
Amaranth Family (Amaranthaceae)

Bloom Period: July–October

Description: Rather stiffly upright, slender, hairy perennial 16–48 in. (4–12 dm) high; stems usually several, stout, unbranched or few-branched. Plant covered with long, silky hairs. **Flower** very small, pale yellowish or whitish; petals absent; sepals tubular, 5-lobed. Flowers congested in dense, elongated, woolly spikes along stem. **Leaves** to 4 in. (1 dm) long, ¼–1⅛ in. (6–29 mm) wide, opposite, short-stalked, mostly crowded at base of stem; upper leaves mostly reduced to a pair beneath the flower clusters.

Habitat: Dry, rocky or gravelly soils in grassy plains, along arroyos, hillsides and slopes. In western portion of PH, FW.

Note: Individual flowers of snake-cotton are not showy, but the plants with their woolly fruiting clusters are quite conspicuous. The plants are relished by livestock and are rarely found in grazed areas. Sometimes called *cotton-weed*.

SNAKE-COTTON (Tveten)

EVENING-STAR RAIN-LILY (Wilbanks)

SNAKE-COTTON (*Froelichia floridana*)
Amaranth Family (Amaranthaceae)

Bloom Period: March–November
Description: Stiffly upright, stout-stemmed, hairy annual 1½–5 ft.
(4.5–15 dm) high; stem solitary, branching in upper portion, the
branches slender and wandlike. Plant covered with short, often
sticky whitish or brownish hairs. **Flower** to ³⁄₁₆ in. (5 mm) long,
whitish or pinkish; petals absent; sepals united to form tube, 5-
lobed at rim, densely woolly outside, becoming flattened and
enlarged in fruit. Flowers several, densely clustered in short,
woolly, sometimes branched spikes at end of slender stalks.
Leaves 1⅛–4 in. (3–10 cm) long, to ¾ in. (2 cm) wide, opposite,
short-stalked, widely spaced on stem; blades thick, pale, usually with pinkish midrib. Upper leaves even fewer and much
smaller.
Habitat: Deep sands in prairies, rangelands, disturbed areas and
woodland edges and openings. Throughout.
Note: Snake-cotton usually forms large colonies and is quite conspicuous, with the long white hairs covering the plant giving it a
"woolly" or "cottony" appearance. At night the plants become
silver-colored, and they are especially interesting in wildflower
plantings. Cultivated members of this family include princess
feather, cockscomb and globe amaranth. Plants of snake-cotton
are wind-pollinated and are considered a major cause of hay
fever.

EVENING-STAR RAIN-LILY (*Cooperia drummondii*)
Amaryllis Family (Amaryllidaceae)

Bloom Period: May–September
Description: Upright, smooth perennial to 12 in. (3 dm), from
deep bulb. **Flower** white, sometimes pink-tinged on outer surface, fragrant, solitary, terminal on leafless stem; petallike segments 6, the slender tube 3⅛–7¼ in. (8–18 cm) long. The
flowers open in the evening and last up to 4 days before turning
pinkish and withering. **Leaves** from bulb, elongating after
flowering and becoming to 12 in. (3 dm) long, smooth, gray-
green, very slender and grasslike.
Habitat: Generally clayey or sandy soils in lawns, pastures, prairies, open woodlands and on hills and slopes. In all except
PH, FW.
Note: This is the most widely distributed of the *Cooperias*, with
its greatest frequency in Texas. While it may bloom in the
spring, the most frequent flowering is in late summer and fall.
The plants almost always appear a day or so after a rain. It is also
called *Drummond rain-lily* and *cebolleta*. The similar but larger-
flowered giant rain-lily (*C. pedunculata*) blooms more often in
spring and early summer.

7

SPIDER LILY

PRAIRIE BISHOP'S-WEED

SPIDER LILY (*Hymenocallis liriosme*)
Amaryllis Family (Amaryllidaceae)

Bloom Period: March–May

Description: Upright, smooth, fleshy or succulent perennial herb to 40 in. (10 dm) high from large, onionlike bulb; stems solitary or several in clump, thick and spongy, sharply 2-edged. **Flower** to 7 in. (17.5 cm) across, snowy-white tinged with yellow in center, intensely fragrant; petallike segments 6, very narrow; stamens 6, the lower portion connected by thin, membranous tissue to form large, spreading cup then extending from rim of cup as very narrow segments; anthers golden-yellow, conspicuous. Flowers 4–6, in cluster at top of leafless stalk. **Leaves** to 30 in. (76 cm) long, to 1½ in. (38 mm) wide or less, from bulb, pale green and shiny with midrib forming conspicuous groove.

Habitat: Various soils in periodically inundated bottomlands, marshes, along stream banks and ditches. In NE, SE, SC.

Note: The spider lily gets its genus name from the Greek words *kallos* meaning "beautiful" and *hymen* meaning "membrane." Hymen was also the name of the Greek god of marriage.

PRAIRIE BISHOP'S-WEED (*Bifora americana*)
Parsley Family (Apiaceae)

Bloom Period: April–May

Description: Upright, slender, delicate, smooth annual herb 8–24 in. (2–7 dm) high; stem solitary, few-branched in upper portion. **Flower** about ⅛ in. (3 mm) across; petals 5, white, spreading flat. Flowers 4–14 in small, stalked clusters, the clusters again congested into larger terminal cluster. **Leaves** ¾–2 in. (2–5 cm) long, to 1⅛ in. (3 cm) wide, alternate, smooth, dark green, the blade finely divided into widely spaced threadlike segments.

Habitat: Sandy, clayey or limestone soils in prairies, abandoned pastures, rocky hillsides, edges and openings of woodlands. In NC, SC, EP, PH.

Note: Prairie bishop's-weed is the only member of this genus in North America; the other three occur in the Mediterranean region. This plant is very similar to other members of the parsley family, but differs in the flower clusters, which are generally flat instead of rounded, with one cluster opening above the other.

QUEEN ANNE'S LACE

BUTTON SNAKEROOT

QUEEN ANNE'S LACE (*Daucus carota*)
Parsley Family (Apiaceae)

Bloom Period: April–May, sporadically in fall

Description: Upright, coarse, hairy-stemmed biennial to 4 ft. (12 dm) from stout, fleshy taproot; stem solitary, usually branched in upper portion. **Flower** very small, white, 5-petaled. Flowers numerous and forming a lacy terminal cluster. One scarlet, dark wine or blackish-colored flower is often found in center of cluster. Cluster flat to rounded in full bloom becoming deeply cupped in fruit and forming "bird's-nest." **Leaves** 2–8 in. (5–20 cm) long, to 2¾ in. (7 cm) wide, alternate, stalked, the blade finely divided into numerous opposite, narrow segments, appearing fernlike.

Habitat: Various soils of abandoned areas, fields, prairies and plains. In NE, SE, NC, SC, ST.

Note: A native of Europe, Queen Anne's lace is generally considered a "weed" because of its invasive capability. It is an ancestor of the garden carrot, and its taproot can be cooked and eaten. Eastern Indian tribes brewed a tea from the plant, using it as a bath for swelling. Butterflies are attracted to the flowers for the nectar. The black swallowtail lay their eggs on the foliage, which the larvae use as a food source.

BUTTON SNAKEROOT (*Eryngium yuccifolium*)
Parsley Family (Apiaceae)

Bloom Period: May–August

Description: Stiffly upright, stout, smooth perennial 1–4 ft. (3–12 dm) high; stem slender, solitary, usually branching in upper portion. **Flower** minute, white or greenish; petals 5, styles exserted. Flowers numerous, subtended by tiny, sharp-pointed leaflike bracts and tightly congested in rounded spike. Spike to 1 in. (2.5 cm) across, subtended by short, sharp-pointed bracts, with several spikes in terminal cluster. **Leaves** to 40 in. (10 dm) long but usually much shorter, to 1¼ in. (3.2 cm) wide, rigid, unlobed but occasionally with bristles along margins, sharp-pointed at tip. Leaves becoming fewer and smaller in size toward upper portion of stem.

Habitat: Sandy or clayey soils in prairies, thickets and mixed pine-hardwood forests. In NE, SE, SC.

Note: The Cherokee made a decoction from this plant and gave it to their children to ward off whooping cough. While the root is supposedly a strong stimulant, it also was used as a remedy for snakebite, hence another common name, *rattlesnake-master*.

MOCK BISHOP'S-WEED

MOCK BISHOP'S-WEED (*Ptilimnium nuttallii*)
Parsley Family (Apiaceae)

Bloom Period: April–July

Description: Upright, slender, delicate herbaceous annual 12–24 in. (3–6 dm) high; stem solitary, ribbed, commonly widely branched, the branches upright. **Flower** to ¼ in. (6 mm) across; petals 5, white. Flowers numerous, in stalked clusters, the clusters again congested into larger terminal cluster. **Leaves** to 3½ in. (9 cm) long, to 1⅝ in. (4.1 cm) wide, usually 2 at a joint (node), the blade twice divided into threadlike segments.

Habitat: Moist sandy or silty soils in prairies, open areas, edges of fields and woodlands, and roadside ditches. In NE, SE, SC.

Note: Many of the white-flowered members of the parsley family are difficult to differentiate from one another, and usually the fully mature fruit is required. Mock bishop's-weed is one of the most common and is usually seen in extensive colonies, often covering entire pastures or stretches of roadside for several miles. As an addition to the wildflower garden these plants are excellent, the flower clusters adding a wonderfully lacy effect. This plant is a major larval food source for the beautiful black swallowtail butterfly.

ANTELOPE-HORNS (*Asclepias asperula*)
Milkweed Family (Asclepiadaceae)

Bloom Period: March–November

Description: Low, upright to widely sprawling herbaceous perennial 8–24 in. (2–6 dm) high; stems usually several from base, rather stout, unbranched. Plants contain milky sap. **Flower** ⅞ in. (22 mm) or more long, pale greenish-yellow, deeply 5-lobed, the lobes erect, somewhat cupped. Flowers numerous and rather crowded, forming rounded, solitary terminal clusters. **Leaves** 4-8 in. (1–2 dm) long, ⅜–1⅛ in. (1–3 cm) wide, opposite or almost so, short-stalked, firm, thick, the edges often folded together.

Habitat: Sandy or rocky soils in prairies, pastures, plains, desert swales, hillsides, brushlands and open woodlands. In NC, PH, EP, FW.

Note: Almost all of the *Asclepias* are considered very poisonous, yet they constitute some of the major medicinal herbs. Another common name is *immortal plant* in reference to their many medicinal uses. Some species are boiled and eaten when young as potherbs, or the young pods are boiled like okra. The dried stems of some species can be chewed for gum.

WHITE-FLOWERED MILKWEED

(Tveten)

GREEN MILKWEED

WHITE-FLOWERED MILKWEED (*Asclepias variegata*)
Milkweed Family (Asclepiadaceae)

Bloom Period: April–July

Description: Upright, stout, herbaceous perennial to 3½ ft. (10.5 dm) high, often lower, containing milky juice; stems usually solitary (or sometimes few and forming clump), slender, unbranched. **Flower** less than ½ in. (1.3 cm) across, to ½ in. (1.3 cm) long, white, the 5 petals curved backward; anthers 5, purple. Flowers numerous, in rounded clusters to 3 in. (7.6 cm) wide, terminal or from upper leaf axils. **Leaves** 3–6 in. (7.6–15 cm) long, 1½–3½ in. (3.8–8.9 cm) wide, opposite, stalked; blade thick, leathery, dark green on upper surface, paler beneath; lowest pair of leaves smaller.

Habitat: Sandy or rocky soils in openings and along margins of woodlands and thickets. In NE, SE, NC.

Note: This is perhaps our most beautiful milkweed. The generic *Asclepias* comes from *Asklepios*, the Greek god of medicine and healing. Appropriately named, the milkweeds have been an important medicinal source for centuries. They also have been a source of cordage obtained from the tough fibers of its stems and of a rubbery glue from the milky latex. Young shoots and seedpods of some species were boiled and eaten for food.

GREEN MILKWEED (*Asclepias viridis*)
Milkweed Family (Asclepiadaceae)

Bloom Period: March–September

Description: Upright to somewhat widely spreading, essentially smooth perennial to 2 ft. (6 dm); stems solitary or several from base, rather stout, unbranched. Plants contain a sticky, milky sap. **Flower** to ⅝ in. (16 mm) high, pale green, purple in center, deeply 5-lobed, the lobes upright, broad and somewhat cupped. Flowers several to many, stalked, crowded in clusters at tip of stalks and from upper leaf axils. **Leaves** 1½–5⅛ in. (3.8–13 cm) long, ⅜–2⅜ in. (1–6 cm) wide, usually alternate, short-stalked, yellowish-green, thick, firm; margins entire.

Habitat: Various soils but especially silty or clayey soils in prairies, pastures, disturbed areas, ditch banks, hillsides and woodland edges. In all except PH, FW.

Note: The silky fluff from the seed of milkweed was formerly used in the making of candle wicks. The silk was carded and spun much in the manner of cotton or wool. In the burning, it was far superior to cotton, giving a cleaner light and producing a less offensive smoke after the candle was blown out. This fluff is used by goldfinches to line their nests.

MILFOIL

ARKANSAS LAZY DAISY

MILFOIL (*Achillea millefolium*)
Sunflower Family (Asteraceae)

Bloom Period: April–June

Description: Stiffly upright, tough, hairy perennial 8–40 in. (2–10 dm) high, with soft, gray-green, aromatic foliage; stems one to several from base, unbranched or forking in upper portion. Plants form clumps or small colonies. **Flower** head about ¼ in. (6 mm) across; ray flowers 5–12, white or sometimes pink; disk flowers few, whitish or yellowish. Heads 10–20, forming a dense cluster, with several clusters forming large terminal mass. **Leaves** ¾–6 in. (2–15 cm) long, to 1⅝ in. (4.1 cm) wide, alternate, 2 or 3 times parted and finely divided into threadlike segments and appearing almost fernlike. Basal leaves often stalked.

Habitat: Various soils in mostly disturbed areas, old fields, edges of woodlands and thickets. In all except ST.

Note: Introduced from Europe, milfoil is now naturalized almost throughout North America. It is an excellent plant for the yard and is extensively cultivated. A tea from the leaves is said to be good for fever and restful sleep. Many other medicinal uses are made of this plant. Milfoil is also referred to as *yarrow*, especially in the old herbals.

ARKANSAS LAZY DAISY (*Aphanostephus skirrhobasis*)
Sunflower Family (Asteraceae)

Bloom Period: February–November

Description: Low, upright to sprawling, soft-hairy annual to 20 in. (5 dm), usually much lower; stem solitary, branching in upper portion. **Flower** head ¾–1⅜ in. (2–3.5 cm) across, solitary, terminal on leafy branches; ray flowers white above, reddish or purplish beneath, 40 or more; disk flowers yellow, more than 250. Bases of both ray and disk flowers become swollen, hardened and whitened in age. **Leaves** 1–4 in. (2.5–10 cm) long, alternate, stalkless or almost so, wedge-shaped or tapering at base; margins entire, toothed or lobed.

Habitat: Sandy soils in open areas, prairies, old fields, pastures and woodland edges. In all except NE.

Note: Another common name for this plant is *doze-daisy*; both common names refer to the flower's habit of remaining closed until about midday. The buds droop, slowly becoming upright as the flowers open.

HEATH ASTER (Wenk)

MEXICAN DEVIL-WEED (Cheatham)

HEATH ASTER (*Aster ericoides*)
Sunflower Family (Asteraceae)

Bloom Period: October–December

Description: Upright, arching or reclining, much-branched perennial to 3 ft. (1 m). Plants spread from underground stems (rhizomes) and form colonies. **Flower** head to ½ in. (13 mm) across; ray flowers white, about 15; disk flowers yellow. Heads numerous, short-stalked, arranged along one side of short, leafy, upright branches. **Leaves** ⅜–¾ in. (1–2 cm) long along midstem, but these usually withered away by flowering time; leaves on flowering branches much smaller, numerous and crowded, stiff and heathlike.

Habitat: Various soils in abandoned areas, pastures, edges of woodlands, and open lowlands. Throughout.

Note: Flower heads reach their maximum size on plants growing in the western portion of the state. The abundance of flowers makes this aster an attractive and desirable addition to the garden.

MEXICAN DEVIL-WEED (*Aster spinosus*)
Sunflower Family (Asteraceae)

Bloom Period: June–December

Description: Stiffly upright, smooth, herbaceous perennial to 7½ ft. (2.5 m); stems woody at base, slender, bright green, leafless for most of year, occasionally spiny especially near base, usually much branched. Plants often form extensive colonies. **Flower** head to ⅝ in. (16 mm) wide, scattered or in small, loose terminal clusters; ray flowers white; disk flowers yellow. **Leaves** very small, smooth, entire, dropping from branches early and usually absent.

Habitat: Various soils in ditches, swales, depressions, bottomlands and along lowland stream- and riverbanks. In all except NE, SE.

Note: Mexican devil-weed is especially attractive when used as a hedge along banks or ravines. It is an excellent plant to use for erosion control. It can easily be started by root division, is quite hardy and multiplies rapidly.

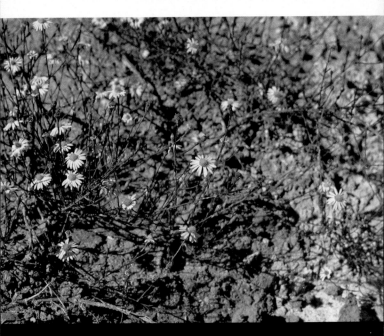

ANNUAL ASTER (Wenk)

TEXAS ASTER (Miller)

ANNUAL ASTER (*Aster subulatus*)
Sunflower Family (Asteraceae)

Bloom Period: August–December

Description: Upright to widely sprawling, robust, smooth annual to 3 ft. (1 m); stems solitary or several, often zigzag, much-branched, the branches slender, wiry, dark green. **Flower** head ½–⅝ in. (13–16 mm) across; ray flowers 20–30, white to lavender or purplish; disk flowers yellow. Heads usually solitary, at ends of branches, numerous on plant. **Leaves** mostly ⅜–4 in. (1–10 cm) long, to 5⁄16 in. (8 mm) wide, alternate, narrow; upper leaves much smaller.

Habitat: Various moist soils along edges of ponds, lakes and streams, but especially in swales and roadside ditches. Throughout.

Note: Annual aster is the most abundant aster occurring in the state. Each individual flower is not particularly showy, but the plants often grow in masses that are quite noticeable. Annual aster is common in lawns, blooming profusely even when mowed quite short.

TEXAS ASTER (*Aster texanus*)
Sunflower Family (Asteraceae)

Bloom Period: September–November

Description: Rather stiffly upright perennial 12–32 in. (3–8 dm) high; stems slender, much-branched in upper portion, the branches wide-spreading. **Flower** head to ⅞ in. (22 mm) across; ray flowers 8–15, whitish to pale blue or purplish; disk flowers several, yellow. Heads solitary, terminal on short stalks, the stalks numerous along upper portion of branches. **Leaves** 2–5 in. (5–12.5 cm) long, alternate, stalked, lobed at base and extending down stem as narrow wings, becoming thick, brittle and crumbly in age. Leaves in flowering portion much smaller.

Habitat: Rich, shaded, loamy or well-drained clay soils in prairies, open woodlands, along creek banks and rocky slopes. In NE, SE, NC, SC, EP.

Note: The late-blooming asters may be planted with blue mistflower (*Eupatorium coelestinum*), gayfeather (*Liatris* spp.), and goldenrod (*Solidago* spp.) for a spectacular show in the fall wildflower garden. The asters are best started from root divisions in late fall or early spring.

PRAIRIE PLANTAIN (Tveten)

PRAIRIE PLANTAIN (*Cacalia plantaginea*)
Sunflower Family (Asteraceae)

Bloom Period: April–June

Description: Rather stiffly upright, coarse, smooth perennial to 3 ft. (1 m); stem usually solitary, grooved, stout, branched only in flowering portion. **Flower** head to ½ in. (1.3 cm) long; ray flowers absent; disk flowers creamy-white, few, surrounded by about 5 upright, narrow, leaflike bracts (phyllaries) with each bract winged or keeled on midrib. Heads numerous, long-stalked, the whole forming large, loose, rather flat-topped terminal mass. **Leaves** 4–8 in. (10–20 cm) long, 1–3 in. (2.5–7.6 cm) wide, thick, prominently 5–7 veined; lower leaves very long-stalked, clustered near base of plant; upper leaves alternate, stalkless or almost so, much smaller.

Habitat: Various soils in prairies, abandoned fields, pastures, woodland openings and edges. In NE, SE, NC, SC, EP.

Note: Prairie plantain blooms most abundantly in the spring but will appear again sporadically in early fall if rains are sufficient. A similar species was used by the Cherokee as a poultice for cuts, bruises, tumors and infections.

PLAINS FLEABANE (*Erigeron modestus*)
Sunflower Family (Asteraceae)

Bloom Period: March–November

Description: Low, upright or trailing, hairy perennial 4–8 in. (1–2 dm) high; stems usually several, eventually much-branched, the branches occasionally trailing or spreading close to ground. **Flower** head about ¾ in. (2 cm) across; ray flowers 30–70, thread-like, white or occasionally pinkish or lavender; disk flowers numerous, yellow. Heads solitary, terminal on long, leafless stalks. **Leaves** to 3 in. (7.6 cm) long, narrow, crowded, entire or coarsely toothed to deeply lobed; stem leaves smaller, extremely narrow at base.

Habitat: Dry gravelly or rocky calcareous soils in open areas, on hillsides or slopes, in open brushland or cedar woodlands. In NC, PH, EP, FW.

Note: This plant exhibits three growth forms, depending on the season. In early spring the flowers occur on long, leafless stalks with lobed leaves all crowded at the base. Later the plant becomes much-branched, the lower leaves wither away, and the new leaves, which are unlobed, appear along upper branches. By fall, often the branches have fallen over, giving the plant a sprawling or trailing appearance, with the leaves small and very narrow.

PHILADELPHIA FLEABANE

LATE-FLOWERING BONESET   (Tveten)

PHILADELPHIA FLEABANE (*Erigeron philadelphicus*)
Sunflower Family (Asteraceae)

Bloom Period: March–May; fall

Description: Upright, slender, hairy short-lived perennial 8–28 in. (2–7 dm) high; stem usually solitary, grooved, branching in upper portion. **Flower** head to 1 in. (2.5 cm) across; ray flowers 150–400, white, threadlike; disk flowers many, yellow. Heads solitary, at ends of slender branches, forming large, loose terminal cluster. **Leaves** to 6 in. (15 cm) long, to 1⅛ in. (3 cm) wide; basal leaves long-stalked, toothed or lobed; upper leaves stalkless and clasping stem at base of blade, entire to shallowly toothed.

Habitat: Moist sandy, loamy or alluvial soils in fields, pastures, lowlands, woodland edges and openings. In all except PH, FW.

Note: Philadelphia fleabane is one of our largest-flowered fleabanes and is quite showy in early spring. The dried and crushed parts of the plant have traditionally been used in teas for sore throat and stomach ailments and as a poultice applied to swelling.

LATE-FLOWERING BONESET (*Eupatorium serotinum*)
Sunflower Family (Asteraceae)

Bloom Period: August–November

Description: Upright, densely hairy perennial 3–6 ft. (1–2 m) high; stems solitary, branched in upper portion, rising from slender roots (rhizomes) and spreading to form colonies. **Flower** head to ¼ in. (6 mm) long, whitish, slender; ray flowers absent, disk flowers 10–15. Several heads form small cluster with several clusters crowded in larger, broad-branching terminal mass. **Leaves** 2–4 in. (5–10 cm) long, opposite, stalked, grayish-green, broadest near base and usually only 3-veined, tapering at tip; margins coarsely toothed. Lower leaves long-stalked.

Habitat: Various soils of open areas, meadows, abandoned fields, edges of wooded lowlands and stream banks. In all except ST, FW.

Note: Late-flowering boneset closely resembles the very poisonous white snakeroot (*E. rugosum*). Their ranges overlap in some areas, but white snakeroot is lower-growing and has pure white flowers instead of the somewhat grayish or dirty-looking blooms of late-flowering boneset.

-WHITE

WOOLLY-WHITE (*Hymenopappus artemisiaefolius*)
Sunflower Family (Asteraceae)

Bloom Period: March–July

Description: Upright, rather stout biennial 1½–3 ft. (4.5–9 dm) high, with blue-green foliage; stem solitary, branched in upper portion. **Flower** head about ½ in. (13 mm) across, fragrant; ray flowers absent; disk flowers rose to dark wine; styles conspicuously exserted. Head surrounded by small, white, petallike bracts (phyllaries). Heads stalked, 30–60 per stem, the whole forming large, showy terminal cluster. **Leaves** 3¼–7¼ in. (8.3–18 cm) long, alternate, in basal rosette and along stem. Basal leaves long-stalked, usually cut or deeply lobed into broad segments. Stem leaves much smaller, usually stalkless.

Habitat: Sandy soils of old fields, prairies and open woodlands. In all except PH, EP, FW.

Note: Woolly-white, also commonly called *wild cauliflower*, is one of the more common wildflowers, with the plants growing singly and not crowded together, yet forming large colonies. It makes an excellent cut flower.

WHITE BARBARA'S-BUTTONS (*Marshallia caespitosa*)
Sunflower Family (Asteraceae)

Bloom Period: April–June

Description: Upright perennial herb to 18 in. (45 cm); stems solitary or several and forming clump, slender, unbranched. **Flower** head 1–1⅝ in. (2.5–4.1 cm) across, solitary, terminal on slender, usually leafless stalk; ray flowers absent; disk flowers numerous, white, cream-colored or occasionally purplish, sweetly fragrant, tubular, 5-lobed at rim. **Leaves** to 6 in. (15 cm) long, to ⅜ in. (10 mm) wide, alternate, stalkless or almost so, crowded near base of plant, the blade thick, gradually tapered in basal portion; margins entire.

Habitat: Sandy, clayey or chalky soils of prairies, ungrazed pastures, woodland edges and rocky hillsides. In all except PH, ST, FW.

Note: Another variety, *M. caespitosa* var. *signata*, is distinguished by leafy flowering stalks and is endemic to the midwestern and southern portions of the state, but is common there. Borders or specimen clumps of these plants are most delightful in the garden and also do well as cut flowers. Sow seeds in the fall, or transplant root divisions in fall or winter.

PLAINS BLACK-FOOT

(Worthington)

PLAINS BLACK-FOOT (*Melampodium leucanthum*)
Sunflower Family (Asteraceae)

Bloom Period: March–November
Description: Low, bushy, mounded perennial 8–12 in. (2–3 dm) high; stems solitary or few, much-branched. **Flower** head to 1 in. (25 mm) across, solitary, terminal on slender stalks; ray flowers 7–13, white, notched at tip, with each ray subtended by a small, foot-shaped bract which turns black upon maturity; disk flowers 25–50, yellow. Heads numerous, forming a mound of white and yellow. **Leaves** 1–2 in. (2.5–5 cm) long, opposite, narrow, entire or slightly lobed, both surfaces somewhat rough-hairy.
Habitat: Rocky, gravelly calcareous or sandy soils in prairies, pastures, deserts, dry plains and on hills and mountain slopes. In NC, PH, EP, FW.
Note: Plains black-foot is a showy, easily grown plant which should be used more in cultivation. It much resembles the white zinnia (*Zinnia acerosa*), and the two plants may occasionally be found growing together. This plant is also called *rock daisy* in reference to its preference for growing in rocky places.

CLIMBING HEMPWEED (*Mikania scandens*)
Sunflower Family (Asteraceae)

Bloom Period: June–November
Description: Sprawling, trailing or low-climbing herbaceous vine; stems slender, slightly 4-angled, branching, to 12 ft. (4 m) or longer. **Flower** head about ¼ in. (6 mm) across, dirty-white or pinkish, sweet-scented; ray flowers absent; disk flowers 4. Heads numerous, forming irregular terminal clusters on short branches rising from leaf axils. **Leaves** 1–4 in. (2.5–10 cm) long, to 3 in. (7.6 cm) wide, opposite, long-stalked; blade thin, broadly rounded and widely notched at base; margins wavy or shallowly lobed.
Habitat: Various moist or wet soils in lowlands, river bottoms, low woodlands, and along edges of streams, swamps and marshes. In all except NC, PH, FW.
Note: Climbing hempweed, also known as *climbing boneset*, forms large, dense mats of flowers and foliage, often completely covering its support of low shrubs, rocks or piles of debris. One of the most conspicuous flowering plants of low, moist areas in autumn, it is much used by late-season insects. It is the only climbing member of the sunflower family common to Texas.

FALSE RAGWEED

WHITE DANDELION (Young)

FALSE RAGWEED (*Parthenium hysterophorus*)
Sunflower Family (Asteraceae)

Bloom Period: August–December
Description: Upright, stout, coarse annual 12–40 in. (3–10 dm) high; stem solitary, ridged or grooved, branching in upper portion. **Flower** head about 3/16 in. (5 mm) across; ray flowers 5, white, broad but very short and hardly noticeable; disk flowers numerous, whitish. Heads numerous, forming large, wide-spreading terminal cluster. **Leaves** 4–8 in. (10–20 cm) long, alternate, the blade thin, soft, deeply lobed or divided into numerous segments. Early leaves form basal rosette.
Habitat: Various soils in almost all habitats. In all except FW.
Note: The flowers of false ragweed resemble tiny cauliflowers. They produce an abundance of pollen which is distributed by the wind, making this a major hay-fever plant.

WHITE DANDELION (*Pinaropappus roseus*)
Sunflower Family (Asteraceae)

Bloom Period: March–May
Description: Upright, smooth perennial 6–18 in. (15–45 cm) high; stem branched or unbranched, occasionally clumplike, mostly leafless. Plants contain milky sap. **Flower** heads 1–2 in. (2.5–5 cm) across, solitary, terminal, white to yellowish above, pink to dark rose-lavender beneath; ray flowers numerous, square at tips and finely toothed, at first rolled lengthwise and forming narrow tube, slowly expanding and becoming flattened; disk flowers absent. **Leaves** 2–4 in. (5–10 cm) long, narrow, alternate, often crowded near base; margins entire or segmented into shallow lobes. Stem leaves (if present) few, very narrow, entire or sparingly lobed.
Habitat: Dry gravelly or calcareous soils in open areas on hillsides, rock outcrops, gravel banks, edges of woodlands and thickets. In all except NE, SE, SC.
Note: White dandelion is quite similar in flower shape to yellow dandelion (*Taraxacum* spp.) and skeleton plant (*Lygodesmia texana*). Like the true dandelions, the flowers close quickly after being picked. Other common names include *pink dandelion* and *rock lettuce*.

PLUME-SEED (Wesby)

WHITE-FLOWERED ROSINWEED (Young)

PLUME-SEED (*Rafinesquia neomexicana*)
Sunflower Family (Asteraceae)

Bloom Period: March–May

Description: Upright to somewhat sprawling, smooth, grayish-green annual 6–20 in. (15–50 cm) high; stem usually solitary, weak, often zigzag, much branched near base. Plant has milky sap. **Flower** heads 1–1½ in. (2.5–3.8 cm) across, solitary at tips of branches; ray flowers few to numerous, white, often tinged with rose or purple on the outside; disk flowers absent. **Leaves** to 8 in. (20 cm) long, alternate, the blade deeply divided into narrow lobes; upper leaves very small, clasping stem at base.

Habitat: Sandy, rocky soils in deserts, flats, on hillsides and mountain slopes. In FW.

Note: Plume-seed gets its common name from the narrow, flattened fruit which bears long, feathery hairs the entire length except at the tip. The genus name commemorates Constantine Rafinesque, a brilliant but eccentric early-19th-century American botanist of ill repute. The plant is also commonly called *desert chicory*.

WHITE-FLOWERED ROSINWEED (*Silphium albiflorum*)
Sunflower Family (Asteraceae)

Bloom Period: May–July

Description: Upright, stocky, rough-hairy, rigid perennial herb to 40 in. (10 dm); stems solitary or few and bushy, very rough to the touch. **Flower** head to 3 in. (76 mm) across; ray flowers white, numerous, about 1 in. (25 mm) long; disk flowers white. Heads 2–8, almost stalkless, in upper portion of stem. **Leaves** to 12 in. (3 dm) long, about as wide, alternate, stalkless, rough, coarse, very stiff and rigid, the blade deeply lobed.

Habitat: Sandy, gravelly or limestone soils on prairies, hills or slopes. In NC, EP.

Note: This genus is called rosinweed because of the sticky secretions which cover the stems and leaves. An unusual characteristic of the genus is the fact that the ray flowers produce seed and the disk flowers do not. The opposite is true for most members of the sunflower family.

FROSTWEED (Wesby)

DWARF ZINNIA (Worthington)

FROSTWEED (*Verbesina virginica*)
Sunflower Family (Asteraceae)

Bloom Period: August–November

Description: Stiffly upright, coarse, soft-hairy perennial 3–7 ft. (1–2.8 m) high; stem solitary, branching only in flowering portion, conspicuously 4- or 5-winged in lower portion. Plants usually form dense colonies. **Flower** head to ½ in. (13 mm) across; ray flowers 3–4, white; disk flowers several, white. Heads few in cluster, with several clusters forming large, flat or rounded terminal cluster. **Leaves** 4–8 in. (1–2 dm) long, 1–3 in. (2.5–7.6 cm) wide, alternate, stalked, the stalks extending down stem as narrow wings; blade tapering in basal portion; margins coarsely toothed. Upper leaves usually smaller, stalkless.

Habitat: Various soils in usually semishaded areas under trees or along moist stream banks and slopes. In all except ST, PH, FW.

Note: With the first frost of autumn, the stems of these plants split and exude a sap which expands and freezes into a showy mass of frothy "ice." The leaves are said to have been dried and used as a tobacco substitute by both Indians and Mexicans, thus accounting for the common names *squaw-weed* and *Indian tobacco.* Also called *tickweed,* as it attracts seed ticks.

DWARF ZINNIA (*Zinnia acerosa*)
Sunflower Family (Asteraceae)

Bloom Period: June–October

Description: Low, hairy, almost shrublike perennial to 10 in. (25 cm); stems greenish, slender, usually several from base, much-branched and forming mound. **Flower** head to 1 in. (25 mm) across; ray flowers 4–6, white, green-nerved on lower surface, somewhat papery in texture; disk flowers 8–13, yellow, drying reddish. Heads solitary at ends of slender, leafy branches. **Leaves** to ¾ in. (2 cm) long, less than ⅛ in. (3 mm) wide or often needle-shaped, grayish, prominently 1-nerved in basal portion only.

Habitat: Arid, rocky, calcareous soils in deserts, desert grasslands or along slopes. In EP, FW.

Note: Dwarf zinnia is our only white-flowered native zinnia, the other two species having yellow flowers. The popular garden zinnia (*Z. elegans*) is derived from a native species of Mexico. Dwarf zinnia is often similar to plains black-foot (*Melampodium leucanthum*), but differs in having only 4–6 ray flowers, while plains black-foot has 7–13. This zinnia continues to bloom for several weeks, producing a wealth of flowers, and is excellent as a border or potted plant. Sow the seed in either fall or spring. Also called *spiny-leaf zinnia* because of its often sharp-pointed leaves.

MAYAPPLE

FRAGRANT HELIOTROPE (Darby)

MAYAPPLE (*Podophyllum peltatum*)
Barberry Family (Berberidaceae)

Bloom Period: March–April

Description: Upright, succulent, smooth perennial to 20 in. (5 dm); stem solitary. Plants usually numerous and forming large colonies from thick, creeping roots. **Flower** to 3 in. (7.6 cm) across, waxy white, sweetly fragrant, nodding, solitary at junction of leaf stalks; petals 6–9, cupped. **Leaves** to 12 in. (30 cm) across, round, long-stalked; leaf stalk attached near the center of blade and appearing umbrella-like; margins shallowly or deeply cut into 2–9 lobes. Two leaves present in flowering plants; 1 leaf in immature plants.

Habitat: Rich, loamy soils of woodlands, often on slopes and in damp, shady clearings. In NE, SE, SC.

Note: All parts of mayapple are poisonous if ingested to excess, except the pulp of the lemonlike fruit, which is edible when ripe. The plant contains podophyllin, a bitter resin which, if used properly, acts as a purgative, although an overdose may prove fatal. The roots were occasionally used medicinally by Indians and early settlers.

FRAGRANT HELIOTROPE (*Heliotropium convolvulaceum*)
Borage Family (Boraginaceae)

Bloom Period: June–October

Description: Upright or much-sprawling hairy annual 4–16 in. (1–4 dm) high or long; stems at first unbranched, later becoming much-branched and sprawling or lying on the ground. **Flower** to 1 in. (2.5 cm) across, white with yellow in center, shortly and broadly funnel-shaped, 5-lobed at rim, sweetly fragrant. Flowers solitary or few in short coils, terminal, from axils of leaves or along the stem between leaves. **Leaves** to 1⅝ in. (4.1 cm) long, to ⅝ in. (16 mm) wide, alternate, short-stalked, numerous, firm; margins sometimes rolled under toward lower surface.

Habitat: Loose, sandy soils of dunes, sandbars, beaches and other sand deposits. In SC, CT, PH, ST.

Note: This is an unusual heliotrope with flowers more like small morning glories (*Ipomoea* spp.) than the commonly small spikes of tightly coiled flowers of most heliotropes. The large, sweetly fragrant flowers distinguish this species from all other heliotropes in our area. The flowers open late in the afternoon and remain open the next morning until the heat causes them to wither.

SEASIDE HELIOTROPE

SPRING CRESS

SEASIDE HELIOTROPE (*Heliotropium curassavicum*)
Borage Family (Boraginaceae)

Bloom Period: March–November

Description: Low, usually sprawling or trailing, succulent, rubbery, smooth perennial; stems solitary to several, to 16 in. (4 dm) long, branched. Plants have whitish coating easily rubbed off. **Flower** to ⅛ in. (3 mm) across, white or bluish with yellow throat, funnel-shaped, 5-lobed at rim. Flowers numerous, along one side of usually paired, coiled spikes, the spikes uncoiling as flowers open. **Leaves** ⅜–2 in. (1–5 cm) long, ¾ in. (2 cm) wide, alternate, short-stalked, numerous, the blade thick, juicy, pale green.

Habitat: Sandy, usually alkaline or saline soils of beaches, mud flats, gravel banks and dried lake beds or edges. In all except NE, NC, EP.

Note: The coiled flower spikes of this plant are typical of the genus and make for easy identification. The Spanish name *cola de mico* means "monkey's tail," referring to the coiled spikes.

SPRING CRESS (*Cardamine bulbosa*)
Mustard Family (Brassicaceae)

Bloom Period: February–May

Description: Upright, smooth herb to 24 in. (6 dm) from short tuber; stems solitary or several and forming clump, branched or unbranched in upper portion. **Flower** to ½ in. (13 mm) across, white, the 4 petals arranged in a cross. Flowers usually several and forming a loose, elongating terminal cluster. **Leaves** to 1½ in. (38 mm) long, alternate; basal leaves long-stalked, the blade almost round; margins remotely and shallowly lobed or toothed; stem leaves becoming stalkless, narrower and reduced in size along stem, usually more sharply toothed.

Habitat: Rich loams in moist woodlands and along edges of meadows, marshes, creeks and ditches. In NE, SE, CT.

Note: The genus name is taken from the Greek word *kardia* meaning "belonging to the heart." The early botanist and physician Dioscorides applied the name *kardamine* to a species of cress, most probably to a plant used medicinally for heart ailments.

SPECTACLE-POD (Worthington)

WESTERN PEPPERGRASS (Mahler)

SPECTACLE-POD (*Dithyrea wislizenii*)
Mustard Family (Brassicaceae)

Bloom Period: February–May

Description: Upright, slender, hairy biennial or perennial herb to 24 in. (6 dm); stems solitary to several, branched or unbranched. Plant appears grayish from dense hairs. **Flower** about ¾ in. (20 mm) across; petals 4, white, broad and forming cross-shape. Flowers numerous, stalked, congested in elongating terminal spike. Fruit, flowers and buds all in spike at same time. **Leaves** to 5½ in. (14 cm) long, 1⅝ in. (4.1 cm) wide, alternate, thick; margins coarsely toothed or shallowly lobed; stem leaves smaller, less toothed or lobed.

Habitat: Loose, sandy soils in plants, rangelands, deserts and dunes. In PH, EP, FW.

Note: The common name for this plant is most appropriate, as the flat, two-lobed fruits very much resemble a pair of miniature "spectacles."

WESTERN PEPPERGRASS (*Lepidium montanum*)
Mustard Family (Brassicaceae)

Bloom Period: February–August

Description: Upright to sprawling biennial or perennial to 28 in. (7 dm); stems one to several, slender, unbranched or much-branched and forming large clump, somewhat woody at the base. **Flower** ¼ in. (6 mm) or more across; petals 4, white, flat and forming cross-shape. Flowers numerous, in elongating terminal spike; fruit forming in lower portion of spike while buds still opening in tip portion. **Leaves** to 6 in. (15 cm) long; lower leaves stalked, the blade divided or deeply lobed; stem leaves usually shorter, very narrow, stalkless, usually entire.

Habitat: Sandy, saline or calcareous soils in open areas, deserts, rangeland, brushland, and openings on cedar slopes. In PH, EP, FW.

Note: There are two varieties of this species in Texas, var. *angustifolium* and var. *alyssoides*, the latter species identifiable by the tiny roundish "bumps" or projections covering the entire plant. The small, flat fruits and young foliage of the *Lepidium*s have an aromatic-peppery flavor and can be used in salads and as flavorings. The dried seeds are an excellent pepper substitute.

MESA GREGGIA (Worthington)

CLAMMYWEED (Cheatham)

MESA GREGGIA (*Nerisyrenia camporum*)
Mustard Family (Brassicaceae)

Bloom Period: February–October

Description: Low, gray-hairy perennial herb 8–24 in. (2–6 dm) high; stems few to several, woody at base, branched in older plants. **Flower** about ¾ in. (2 cm) across, white or lavender-tinged; petals 4. Flowers few to numerous, in elongating terminal spikes (racemes). **Leaves** ½–2½ in. (1.3–6.3 cm) long, to ¾ in. (2 cm) wide, short-stalked, wider in tip portion, densely and velvety hairy on both surfaces; margins coarsely toothed to somewhat wavy.

Habitat: Dry sandy and gravelly soils on deserts, plains, arid grasslands, limestone hills and knolls and in outwashes. In EP, ST, FW.

Note: The spikes of large white flowers are most apparent in early spring, with the blooming season lasting into fall but with smaller spikes and fewer flowers. Another common name for this plant is *velvety nerisyrenia*. It does well in wildflower plantings where sandy soil and rather arid conditions are prevalent.

CLAMMYWEED (*Polanisia dodecandra*)
Caper Family (Capparidaceae)

Bloom Period: March–October

Description: Upright annual to 24 in. (6 dm) high, the stems and foliage bearing gland-tipped sticky or gummy hairs; stems branched or unbranched. **Flower** to ¾ in. (2 cm) long, white; petals 4, all spreading upward, tapered and narrow in basal portion, notched at tip; stamens dark purple, numerous, long-exserted, unequal in length, pointing outward. Flowers numerous, in elongating terminal spikes (racemes). **Leaves** alternate, stalkless, the blade divided into 3 leaflets, with each leaflet ½–1½ in. (13–38 mm) long; margins entire.

Habitat: Sandy soils of prairies, plains, deserts, flats, slopes, pastures, old fields and shrub thickets, and on beach shell. In all except NE, SE, ST, SC.

Note: Clammyweed is extremely variable in flower size. It is divided into three subspecies mostly according to flower size and geographic location in the state. The common name refers to the sticky or "clammy" residue left on the hands when the plant is handled.

SANDWORT (Myers)

BINDWEED

SANDWORT (*Arenaria drummondii*)
Pink Family (Caryophyllaceae)

Bloom Period: February–June

Description: Low, upright, clumped annual to 8 in. (2 dm), the stem slender, wiry, usually sparsely branched. **Flower** to 1⅛ in. (29 mm) across, appearing large for the plant; white or sometimes greenish at base; petals 5, somewhat cupped, deeply notched at tip. Flowers usually in pairs on opposite, slender stalks about 1 in. (25 mm) long. **Leaves** to 1¼ in. (32 mm) long, ¼ in. (6 mm) wide, opposite, stalkless, narrow, somewhat thickened. Upper leaves much smaller.

Habitat: Sandy soils of pastures, edges of fields, open savannahs, and along woodland edges. In SE, SC, EP, ST.

Note: Sandwort forms large colonies and is frequently found blooming with pointed phlox, Indian paintbrush, blue-eyed grass and wine-cups. The genus name comes from the Latin word *arena* meaning "sand" or "a sandy place," and describes the most common habitat of these small but showy plants.

BINDWEED (*Convolvulus arvensis*)
Morning-Glory Family (Convolvulaceae)

Bloom Period: April–October

Description: Trailing or twining vine with stems to 3 ft. (1 m) long or more, from deep perennial root; roots creeping and forming extensive colonies of plants. **Flower** to 2 in. (5 cm) across, white or pink, solitary, on stalks from leaf axils, broadly funnel-shaped, with 5 vertical veins leading to low lobes at rim. Flowers opening in morning, closing in afternoon. **Leaves** ⅜–2⅜ in. (1–7 cm) long, ¼–1½ in. (6–38 mm) wide, short-stalked; blade generally indented at base with spreading basal lobes, but widely varying in shape from somewhat triangular to longer than wide.

Habitat: Almost all soils along railroads, in abandoned areas, old fields, gardens and especially fields of cultivated crops. In all except NE, SE, ST.

Note: Introduced from Eurasia, bindweed has become established almost worldwide. Its deep, spreading roots make it extremely difficult to eradicate, a characteristic which accounts for another common name, *possession vine*.

TEXAS BINDWEED (Wesby)

DODDER (Darby)

TEXAS BINDWEED (*Convolvulus equitans*)
Morning-Glory Family (Convolvulaceae)

Bloom Period: April–October

Description: Trailing or twining, densely hairy perennial; stems solitary or few, to 6 ft. (2 m) long, mostly lying on ground, not rooting at the joints (nodes). **Flower** to 1⅛ in. (3 cm) long, to 1 in. (2.5 cm) across, white to pale pink with red center; petals 5, united into broadly flaring funnel-shape, 5-lobed at rim with the angles extending as slender points. Flowers solitary or few, stalked, from leaf axils. **Leaves** ⅜–2¾ in. (1–7 cm) long, to 1⅝ in. (4.1 cm) wide, alternate, stalked, with dense, silky-woolly hairs on both surfaces, variable in shape from entire to toothed or often with deep, narrow lobes near base.

Habitat: Sandy, loamy or rocky soils in almost all habitats. In all except NE, SE.

Note: Texas bindweed is a bane to farmers as the plant is most prolific and quickly becomes established in cultivated fields. The tightly twining habit of the plant strangles the stems of cultivated plants, and the abundant growth shuts out the sunlight, often causing crops to die.

DODDER (*Cuscuta cuspidata*)
Morning-Glory Family (Convolvulaceae)

Bloom Period: August–November

Description: Twining, smooth, herbaceous, parasitic vine; stems usually numerous and forming mats, threadlike, creamy yellow to orange. Plants at time of flowering rootless and leafless. **Flower** to ¼ in. (6 mm) across, white, few to many in small, dense, stalkless clusters; petals 5, united, tubular or narrowly funnel-shaped, deeply 5-lobed at rim. **Leaves** reduced to minute bracts or none.

Habitat: Parasitic on a variety of host plants, but frequently on sumpweed (*Iva annua*). In all except EP, FW.

Note: Plants of dodder start growth from seed, at first forming small roots in the soil but quickly attaching themselves to a host plant. Sinking minute disks into the tissue of the host, the true roots of dodder then shrivel and die, leaving it to obtain all its nutrients from the host. Many folktales have evolved around dodder, as might be guessed from its numerous descriptive common names, such as *love vine, angel's hair, tangle-gut, strangleweed* and *witches' shoelaces.* The plants yield a clear yellow dye color.

WILD POTATO

BEACH MORNING GLORY

WILD POTATO (*Ipomoea pandurata*)
Morning-Glory Family (Convolvulaceae)

Bloom Period: June–September

Description: Trailing or low-climbing herbaceous perennial vine from starchy, tuberous root; root large, often weighing 20 lbs. or more. Stems one to several, to 15 ft. (5 m) long, strong, usually purplish, branching in upper portion. **Flower** to 3¼ in. (8.3 cm) long, about as wide, white with wine-red throat, the 5 petals united into wide-spreading funnel-shape, somewhat 5-lobed at rim. Flowers 1–5 at tip of stalk from leaf axils, opening for only a few hours in early morning, generally closed by midday. **Leaves** 1¼–4 in. (3.2–10 cm) long, ¾–3⅜ in. (2–9 cm) wide, alternate, stalked, the blade broader at base and deeply notched, often with indented sides and appearing 3-lobed.

Habitat: Sandy soils of fencerows and along the edges of fields, thickets and woodlands. In NE, SE, NC, SC.

Note: Indians used the dried or roasted starchy root of this plant as a food source. The fresh root is said to be purgative. Due to the size of the root, the plant is descriptively known as *man-of-the-earth*.

BEACH MORNING GLORY (*Ipomoea stolonifera*)
Morning-Glory Family (Convolvulaceae)

Bloom Period: April–December

Description: Creeping or trailing but not twining, smooth, fleshy or somewhat succulent perennial vine from deep roots; stems to 18 ft. (6 m) long or more, rooting at the joints (nodes). **Flower** 1¾–2¾ in. (45–70 mm) long, white with yellow center, solitary on erect stalks from the leaf axils; petals 5, united into widely spreading funnel-shape, shallowly 5-lobed at rim. **Leaves** ¾–1½ in. (20–38 mm) long, ⅜–1½ in. (10–38 mm) wide, long-stalked, the blade thick, leathery, usually lobed at base; margins entire to variously lobed.

Habitat: Deep sands of the barrier islands, coastal beaches and dunes and in wettish depressions and flats. In CT.

Note: The large mats of vegetation and deeply anchored roots of beach morning glory make it a most important plant in helping to stabilize the coastal dunes. It is also called *fiddle-leaf morning glory* for its distinctively shaped leaves.

WHITE STYLISMA

BULL NETTLE

WHITE STYLISMA (*Stylisma humistrata*)
Morning-Glory Family (Convolvulaceae)

Bloom Period: June–August

Description: Sprawling or trailing, somewhat twining, delicate, soft-hairy, vinelike perennial; stems solitary, slender, unbranched or much-branched, the branches to 8 ft. (24 dm) long but usually much shorter. **Flower** to ¾ in. (2 cm) long, white, funnel-shaped, shallowly 5-lobed at rim. Flowers 2 or 3 in long-stalked cluster from leaf axils. **Leaves** ⅜–2⅜ in. (1–6 cm) long, to 1⅛ in. (3 cm) wide, alternate, short-stalked, usually somewhat notched at base; margins entire.

Habitat: Dry or moist sandy soils in stream bottoms, pinelands or edges of woodlands or thickets. In NE, SE.

Note: White stylisma is an eastern U.S. species, coming into Texas only along the eastern edge, but it is rather common there. The species name is from the Latin words *humus* meaning "the ground" and *stratus* meaning "spread out," or literally, "spread out on the ground."

BULL NETTLE (*Cnidoscolus texanus*)
Spurge Family (Euphorbiaceae)

Bloom Period: March–September

Description: Upright or sprawling branched perennial to 40 in. (10 dm), but usually much lower and wide-spreading in mature plants. Entire plant covered with stiff, stinging hairs. Plants often form widely scattered colonies. **Flower** about 1 in. (25 mm) across, white, fragrant, tubular, composed of 5 petallike sepals. Flowers few in terminal cluster with male and female flowers separate, but in same cluster. Female flowers central or terminal in cluster, with "petals" falling soon after fertilization. **Leaves** 3–6 in. (7.6–15 cm) long, alternate, dark-green, long-stalked; blade deeply 3–5 lobed with lobes running toward base. Lobes usually irregularly lobed or toothed again.

Habitat: Dry sandy soils in pastures, fields and openings in woodlands and lowlands. Throughout except western portion of PH.

Note: The hairs of this plant contain a caustic irritant which on contact produces a painful irritation and rash and can cause a severe reaction in some people. The three large, edible seeds are very tasty when ripe and were much used by various Indian tribes. Other common names are *tread-softly* and *mala mujer* (Spanish for "bad woman").

SNOW-ON-THE-PRAIRIE (Tveten)

SNOW-ON-THE-MOUNTAIN (Wesby)

SNOW-ON-THE-PRAIRIE (*Euphorbia bicolor*)
Spurge Family (Euphorbiaceae)

Bloom Period: July–November

Description: Upright, rather stout, hairy annual 1–3 ft. (3–9 dm) high; stem solitary, often reddish in lower portion, branched in upper portion with the branches in two's or three's. Plant contains sticky, milky sap. **Flower** minute; about 35 male and 1 female flower borne in a cup-shaped structure having 5 white, petallike glands around rim, the whole appearing as a 5-petaled flower. "Flowers" 2–5, in terminal cluster, with several clusters forming larger mass surrounded by leaflike bracts; bracts several, to 4 in. (10 cm) long, to ½ in. (13 mm) wide, conspicuously white-margined. **Leaves** 2–4 in. (5–10 cm) long, alternate, rather thin in texture; upper leaves usually in whorls of 3.

Habitat: Hard, clay soils of prairies, rangelands, openings and edges of elm or mesquite woodlands. In NE, SE, NC, SC.

Note: Snow-on-the-prairie usually forms extensive colonies and often covers many acres, truly appearing to blanket the summer prairies with snow. Many members of the spurge family are cultivated as ornamentals, one of our most familiar being the Christmas poinsettia (*E. pulcherrima*). Important commercial crops from this family include rubber, castor oil and tapioca.

SNOW-ON-THE-MOUNTAIN (*Euphorbia marginata*)
Spurge Family (Euphorbiaceae)

Bloom Period: August–October

Description: Stiffly upright, widely branching, hairy annual herb 12–40 in. (3–10 dm) high; stem solitary, much-branching in upper portion, the branches paired or in three's. Plant contains milky sap. **Flower** minute; 30–35 male and 1 female flower congested in small, cuplike structure, the cup with 5 white, petallike lobes and the whole appearing as a 5-petaled flower. "Flowers" few, in terminal cluster surrounded by several leaflike bracts in whorl; bracts narrower than leaves, with wide white borders or margins. **Leaves** 1⅛–3⅛ in. (3–8 cm) long, 2–4 times longer than broad, stalkless, green, thin; stem leaves alternate; upper leaves opposite.

Habitat: Clay, limestone or calcareous soils of rangelands, gravel flats, arroyos and floodplains. In NC, PH, EP, FW.

Note: A most attractive plant, snow-on-the-mountain is widely cultivated and is occasionally gathered and used by the floral trade in the making of bouquets. Many species from arid terrain in Africa are similar to cactus in growth habit and are grown as ornamentals in this country. The milky sap of the spurge family contains the poisonous substance euphorbium and may cause irritation or inflammation of the skin, eyes or mouth of some people.

PRAIRIE ACACIA

CANADA MILK-VETCH (Cheatham)

PRAIRIE ACACIA (*Acacia angustissima*)
Legume Family (Fabaceae)

Bloom Period: June–October

Description: Upright to somewhat sprawling smooth perennial to 30 in. (76 cm); stems one to several, sparingly or not branched, woody at base. Plants somewhat shrubby, often forming small colonies. **Flower** very small, creamy-white; petals 5; stamens numerous, long, protruding. Flowers numerous, congested in rounded terminal clusters on long stalks arising from upper leaf axils. **Leaves** alternate, the blade divided into usually 3–12 pairs of segments, these again divided into 6–20 pairs of tiny leaflets.

Habitat: Various soils in prairies, grasslands, brushlands, on rocky hillsides and along edges of woodlands. In all except SE, FW.

Note: Prairie acacia is high in protein and readily eaten by livestock. It decreases under heavy grazing and is a good indicator of range conditions. As with some other members of the legume family, the foliage of this native is sensitive and will fold when touched. Also known as *fern acacia* because of its fernlike foliage.

CANADA MILK-VETCH (*Astragalus canadensis*)
Legume Family (Fabaceae)

Bloom Period: May–July

Description: Upright, usually stout, hairy perennial to 2 ft. (6 dm) or more; stems leafy, few or several and forming clump, usually branched in upper portion. **Flower** ½–¾ in. (1.3–2 cm) long, creamy, greenish-white, yellowish or cream tinged with purple; petals 5, the uppermost petal or banner extending forward over side and lower petals. Flowers usually more than 20, somewhat drooping, forming dense terminal spikes (racemes), the spikes sometimes few and forming cluster. **Leaves** 2–14 in. (5–35 cm) long, alternate, stalked, the blade divided into 13–35 leaflets.

Habitat: Rocky or sandy soils in meadows, thickets, edges and openings in woodlands. In NE, SE, NC, CT.

Note: This is one of our showiest white-flowered milk-vetches. Although it contains toxic compounds, it does not seem to be seriously injurious to livestock. Perhaps this is because it is found mostly in the east and does not pick up the deadly poisonous element selenium, which occurs in western soils.

ILLINOIS BUNDLEFLOWER

WHITE SWEET CLOVER (Tveten)

ILLINOIS BUNDLEFLOWER (*Desmanthus illinoensis*)
Legume Family (Fabaceae)

Bloom Period: June–September

Description: Stiffly upright to spreading bushy perennial 12–40 in. (3–10 dm) high; stems striped, solitary or several from woody base. **Flower** minute, white, creamy or greenish; petals 5; stamens 5, conspicuously protruding. Flowers numerous and congested in ball-like cluster; clusters ½–1 in. (13–25 mm) across, on long stalks from leaf axils. **Leaves** 2–4 in. (5–10 cm) long, twice divided into 20–30 pairs of small leaflets; ultimate leaflets narrow, about ⅛ in. (3 mm) long.

Habitat: Clay or calcareous soils of prairies, plains, riverbanks and shell deposits. In all.except ST.

Note: The interesting fruit of Illinoiś bundleflower is a round, dense, rough cluster of curved pods, each pod about 1–1½ in. (25–38 mm) long. These clusters are much sought for use in dried arrangements. High in protein, this plant is considered one of our most important native legumes for livestock and wildlife. Readily eaten by them, it is an excellent range-condition indicator.

WHITE SWEET CLOVER (*Melilotus albus*)
Legume Family (Fabaceae)

Bloom Period: May–October

Description: Upright, smooth annual or biennial 3–8 ft. (9–24 dm) high; stem solitary, open and bushy-branched. **Flower** ⅛–¼ in. (3–6 mm) long, white; petals 5, the uppermost petal or banner erect. Flowers numerous and congested into slender, terminal, spikelike racemes 4–6 in. (10–15 cm) long from axils of the leaves. **Leaves** alternate, stalked, the blade divided into 3 narrow leaflets with each leaflet ½–1 in. (13–25 mm) long; margins finely toothed.

Habitat: Almost all soils in abandoned areas, prairies, plains, fields, open bottomlands or uplands. Throughout.

Note: White sweet clover is one of our more "weedy" species of wildflowers and was introduced from Europe. The entire plant is fragrant during warm, sunny weather or when cut and dried. Both white and yellow sweet clover (*M. officinalis*) are important pollen plants. The genus name is derived from the Greek word *meli* meaning "honey." Honey from bees foraging this plant is much desired for its light color and mild flavor.

WHITE PRAIRIE CLOVER

MULTIBLOOM TEPHROSIA

WHITE PRAIRIE CLOVER (*Petalostemum multiflorum*)
Legume Family (Fabaceae)

Bloom Period: June–August

Description: Upright or widely sprawling, smooth perennial 1–2 ft. (3–6 dm) high from woody base; stems several and commonly clumplike, grooved, much-branched, the branches short and with fewer and smaller leaves. Entire plant has small, dark, glandular dots. **Flower** minute, white, very fragrant; petals 5, separate and usually attached at different places; stamens 5, exserted. Flowers numerous, congested in dense, rounded, terminal, headlike cluster. **Leaves** ¾–1⁹⁄₁₆ in. (2–4 cm) long, numerous, the blade divided into 3–9 leaflets, each leaflet to ½ in. (13 mm) long, conspicuously dotted with glands on lower surface.

Habitat: Dry, sandy, clayey or chalky soils of prairies, hills, slopes or woodland edges. In all except NE, SE, FW.

Note: The genus *Petalostemum* comes from two Greek words for petal and stamen, alluding to the unusual structure of the flower parts, and an uncertainty as to whether the parts are actually petals or stamens—a moot point since "petals" are often only modified leaves, stamens or other organs. White prairie clover is an excellent plant for enriching the soil, and the white flowers and delicate foliage are very attractive in garden plantings.

MULTIBLOOM TEPHROSIA (*Tephrosia onobrychoides*)
Legume Family (Fabaceae)

Bloom Period: April–September

Description: Upright or sprawling, stout, hairy perennial herb 24–28 in. (6–7 dm) high; stems solitary or several, somewhat woody at base, very leafy. **Flower** to ¾ in. (2 cm) long, white becoming pink to dark rosy-red in age; petals 5, the banner or upper petal upright, widely spreading, with silky hairs on outer surface. Flowers several, loosely placed in elongated spike. **Leaves** alternate, stalked, the blade divided into usually 13–25 leaflets with each leaflet ¾–2⅛ in. (2–5.5 cm) long, to ⅝ in. (1.6 cm) wide.

Habitat: Sandy or gravelly soils in savannahs, woodland openings, edges of thickets, along fencerows and in coastal sands. In NE, SE, SC, CT.

Note: The snow-white flowers of this plant open in late evening and are closed by midmorning of the next day unless the weather is cloudy or misty. Shortly before closing, the blossoms turn a beautiful rosy-pink, and often both colors of open and closed flowers are on the same plant. These plants are easily grown from seed in sandy soils, and should be used more in home gardens.

WHITE CLOVER

LINDHEIMER BEEBALM

WHITE CLOVER (*Trifolium repens*)
Legume Family (Fabaceae)

Bloom Period. April–September

Description: Low, essentially smooth perennial often forming extensive mats from creeping stems or runners which root at the nodes. **Flower** less than ½ in. (13 mm) long, white or sometimes pinkish; petals 5, the upper petal or banner folded forward instead of upright. Flowers numerous, congested into long-stalked, terminal, roundish head or cluster to 1 in. (25 mm) across, from leaf axils. Flowers become brown and turn downward in age. **Leaves** alternate, long-stalked, the blade divided into usually 3 leaflets with each leaflet to ¾ in. (2 cm) long, conspicuously marked with a pale triangular line near the base. Leaflets may be rounded, pointed or notched at tip; margins sharply and finely toothed.

Habitat: Various soils in lawns, pastures, stream bottoms, edges and openings of fields and woodlands. In all except PH, FW.

Note: A native of Europe, white clover is now widely introduced throughout the country. The flowers are a rich, early source of pollen and nectar and are readily utilized by bees, their chief pollinators.

LINDHEIMER BEEBALM (*Monarda lindheimeri*)
Mint Family (Lamiaceae)

Bloom Period: April–August

Description: Upright, somewhat long-hairy, aromatic perennial herb 1–2 ft. (3–6 dm) high; stems usually several, forming clump, mostly unbranched but occasionally branched in upper portion. **Flower** to 1⅛ in. (3 cm) long, creamy-white, hairy with short, curling hairs, prominently 2-lipped; upper lip with small tuft of hairs at tip; lower lip spreading, 3-lobed. Flowers several, in whorl around stem; whorls 1 or 2, rarely more, each whorl subtended by leaflike bracts. **Leaves** to 2 in. (5 cm) long, usually ⅝–1 in. (16–25 mm) wide, short-stalked, smooth or finely downy, entire or toothed.

Habitat: Gravelly calcareous or sandy soils in meadows, on hills and slopes and along edges of thickets and woodlands. In NE, SE, NC, SC, CT.

Note: *Lindheimer beebalm* is an excellent plant for the herb or wildflower garden. The flowers do well in bouquets and the aromatic foliage is used in the making of teas, potpourris and sachets. Almost all of the *Monarda*s have many and varied medicinal uses.

COAST GERMANDER (Wesby)

WHITE DOG'S-TOOTH VIOLET

COAST GERMANDER (*Teucrium cubense*)
Mint Family (Lamiaceae)

Bloom Period: March–December

Description: Upright or sprawling, hairy annual or perennial herb to 2 ft. (6 dm), but often much lower; stems usually several, branched at base and often in upper portion, becoming bushy. **Flower** to ¾ in. (2 cm) long, white, sometimes with purple lines in throat, hairy, 2-lipped; upper lip very short and deeply notched into 2 small, toothlike segments; lower lip 3-lobed, the lower lobe broader and spreading, the side lobes much smaller. Flowers stalked, from upper leaf axils, numerous and appearing as if in terminal spike. **Leaves** ⅝–1½ in. (1.5–3.8 cm) long, opposite; basal leaves stalked, lobed to entire, soon withering; stem leaves lobed, becoming more lobed or cut in flowering portion of plant.

Habitat: Clay or hard sandy loam in grassy areas, plains, pastures, palm groves, woodlands or along streams or resacas. In NE, SE, NC, PH.

Note: Coast germander is very showy and deserves a place in wildflower plantings. The finely cut foliage appears almost fern-like, and the plants are especially attractive in borders or massed plantings. In its native range, the plant forms large colonies and is sometimes considered rather "weedy."

WHITE DOG'S-TOOTH VIOLET (*Erythronium albidum*)
Lily Family (Liliaceae)

Bloom Period: March–May

Description: Low, smooth perennial 4–6 in. (10–15 cm) high from deep bulb producing slender, underground shoots, with new plants rising from tips of shoots. **Flower** ¾–1½ in. (2–3.8 cm) long, white, often tinged with pink, blue or lavender on lower surface, solitary at tip of slender, leafless stem, nodding; petal-like segments 6, wide-spreading to sharply recurved. **Leaves** 3–8 in. (7.6–20 cm) long, tapering at both ends, 2 in flowering plants but only 1 in immature plants, the blade thick, smooth, mottled with brown or darker green on both surfaces.

Habitat: Rich, moist loams of lowland or upland woodlands, most commonly along slopes. In NE, SE, NC, SC.

Note: White dog's-tooth violet usually forms extensive colonies, often covering an entire woodland slope with white flowers in early spring. This plant is also called *trout lily* in reference to the spotted or mottled leaves resembling the speckling of a trout.

FALSE GARLIC

GREAT SOLOMON'S SEAL

FALSE GARLIC (*Nothoscordum bivalve*)
Lily Family (Liliaceae)

Bloom Period: Throughout year

Description: Upright, smooth perennial 6–22 in. (15–55 cm) high from small, fibrous-coated bulb. **Flower** about 1 in. (25 mm) across, whitish to creamy with narrow but prominent stripes of green, red or purple on outer surface, the 6 segments all pet-allike. Flowers 6–12, in small cluster at top of leafless stalk, closing during cold or cloudy weather. **Leaves** 4–16 in. (1–4 dm) long, less than ⅛ in. (3 mm) wide, basal, several, soft, flat or with lengthwise central groove on upper surface.

Habitat: Various soils in lawns, disturbed areas, pastures, prairies, bottomlands and open woodlands. Throughout.

Note: False garlic has the appearance of the wild onions but lacks the onion or garlic smell or taste typical of the *Allium*s. False garlic often forms large colonies of plants and is quite conspicuous in early spring and again in fall. It is also commonly called *crow poison*.

GREAT SOLOMON'S SEAL (*Polygonatum biflorum*)
Lily Family (Liliaceae)

Bloom Period: March–April

Description: Upright or usually arching, slender to stout, smooth perennial to 3 ft. (1 m); stem solitary. **Flower** to ⅝ in. (1.6 cm) long, greenish-white, the 6 petallike segments united into long, slender tube, 6-lobed at rim. Flowers usually in pairs, long-stalked, drooping from leaf axils along middle portion of stem. **Leaves** to 6 in. (15 cm) long, to 2¾ in. (7 cm) wide, alternate, stalkless and often clasping stem, prominently several-veined.

Habitat: Moist, rich soils on slopes and along edges of streams, thickets and woodlands. In NE, SE, NC.

Note: The thick, white root, or rhizome, of this plant appears "knotty" or "jointed." The "knots" form where the stem breaks off each year, leaving an enlarged scar. The new scar is said to resemble the official seal of King Solomon, hence the common name. The Cherokee reportedly used the young plants as pot-herbs. Dried roots were beaten and used as flour, and a root tea was used for general debility and stomach ailments.

GREEN LILY (Wesby)

DEATH CAMAS

GREEN LILY (*Schoenocaulon drummondii*)
Lily Family (Liliaceae)

Bloom Period: April–November

Description: Upright, smooth, slender, stemless perennial to 24 in. (6 dm), from bulb. Basal portion of plant covered with blackish scales and fibers. **Flower** about ⅛ in. (3 mm) long, the 6 petallike segments greenish to creamy; stamens 6, yellow. Flowers numerous, loosely congested in long spike at end of tall, leafless stalk. **Leaves** to ⁵⁄₁₆ in. (8 mm) wide, grasslike, curved, clustered at base of flowering stalk; margins rolled under toward lower surface.

Habitat: Sandy, clayey or gravelly soils of prairies, arroyos, grasslands, cedar brushlands, hillsides and slopes. In SC, CT, EP, ST, FW.

Note: The green lily most commonly blooms in the fall, but spikes of the greenish-colored flowers will occasionally be found in the spring or summer. Green lily is an interesting addition to the wildflower garden and is easily grown in dry soils by transplanting the bulb in late fall or early spring.

DEATH CAMAS (*Zigadenus nuttallii*)
Lily Family (Liliaceae)

Bloom Period: March–May

Description: Upright perennial 1–2½ ft. (30–75 cm) high from large, papery-coated bulb; stem solitary, stout, usually branched. **Flower** to ½ in. (13 mm) across, stalked, the 6 segments all petallike, yellowish-white or creamy, persisting after withering. Flowers numerous, in elongating, round-topped terminal cluster. **Leaves** 8–24 in. (20–60 cm) long, ⅜ in. (1 cm) wide, from bulb, numerous and forming clump, the blade slender and grasslike, folded lengthwise and curved downward. Leaves along stem much smaller or reduced to bracts.

Habitat: Calcareous soils of prairies, pastures, hillsides, and edges of open woodlands. In NE, NC, SC, EP.

Note: This plant, especially the bulb and seed, contains the toxic alkaloids zygadenine and zygacine, which can cause death to cattle and humans if eaten. The pollen and nectar do not appear to be poisonous to insects, since the flowers are regularly visited by numerous species, and larvae of certain insects feed on the inflorescence. The young leaves resemble leaves of the wild onion, but the death camas does not have the characteristic onion taste or smell. The plant was named in honor of the botanical collector Thomas Nuttall.

BLADDERPOD SIDA

(Young)

BLADDERPOD SIDA (*Sida physocalyx*)
Mallow Family (Malvaceae)

Bloom Period: March–December

Description: Reclining or trailing, hairy perennial; stems solitary or few, to 16 in. (4 dm) long. **Flower** to ⅞ in. (22 mm) across, whitish to yellowish or buff-colored, sometimes rose-pink, short-stalked, solitary from leaf axils; petals 5, wide-spreading or slightly cupped; stamens several, united at base into column. **Leaves** ⅜–2⅜ in. (1–6 cm) long, to 2 in. (5 cm) wide, alternate, long-stalked, soft, thick, roundish or blunt-tipped; margins coarsely toothed.

Habitat: Sandy, clayey-loam, gravelly or rocky soils of prairies, disturbed areas, chaparral, hillsides and slopes. In all except NE, SE, SC.

Note: Bladderpod sida can be easily distinguished from the other *Sidas* by the leaflike sepals surrounding the fruit. By maturity these sepals have become united to form an inflated or bladder-like, papery covering for the ring of flat seeds. Sepals of the other *Sidas* do not become united and inflated at maturity.

SWEET SAND-VERBENA (*Abronia fragrans*)
Four-o'clock Family (Nyctaginaceae)

Bloom Period: March–September

Description: Upright or widely sprawling, sticky-hairy perennial herb; stems few to numerous, 8–40 in. (2–10 dm) high or long, much-branched, often whitish in color. Plant covered with soft, glandular hairs and sticky to the touch. **Flower** ⅜–1⅛ in. (1–3 cm) long, usually white, sometimes tinged with green, lavender, pink or red, long funnel-shaped, deeply lobed around rim. Flowers numerous, in roundish cluster at ends of branches, opening in late afternoon, closing next morning. **Leaves** 2–4 in. (5–10 cm) long, opposite, the pair of unequal size, stalked, the blade thin, rounded at both ends.

Habitat: Deep sandy soils of prairies, plains, dunes, hillsides and slopes. In NC, PH, FW.

Note: Sweet sand-verbena, also commonly called *snowball* and *heart's-delight*, is one of our most beautiful native flowers. It does well in the wildflower garden where loose, sandy soils are available and is easily raised from fall-sown seed.

ANGEL TRUMPETS (Worthington)

VINE FOUR-O'CLOCK (Cheatham)

ANGEL TRUMPETS (*Acleisanthes longiflora*)
Four-o'clock Family (Nyctaginaceae)

Bloom Period: May–September

Description: Low, trailing or sprawling, hairy, vinelike perennial; stem branching at woody base, forking and spreading to form a loose clump 2–3 ft. (60–90 cm) across. **Flower** to 6½ in. (16.3 cm) long, white, sweetly fragrant, solitary from leaf axils, trumpet-shaped with tube very slender then abruptly expanded at rim and 1 in. (2.5 cm) across. **Leaves** 1–2 in. (2.5–5 cm) long, opposite, the blade thick, grayish or bluish-green, triangular or arrow-shaped; margins entire or wavy.

Habitat: Sandy, dry alkaline soils in granite, along talus slopes or open calcareous areas. In all except NE, SE, NC, SC.

Note: Flowers open during the cool of evening and night, closing soon after sunrise. Unopened flowers are held stiffly upright, blending with the foliage until they open. Night-flying moths feed on the nectar and, in the process, pollinate the flowers. Known in Spanish as *yerba-de-la-rabia*.

VINE FOUR-O'CLOCK (*Acleisanthes obtusa*)
Four-o'clock Family (Nyctaginaceae)

Bloom Period: April–December

Description: Trailing or climbing perennial herb or vine; stems slender, often reaching to tops of small trees, much-branched and forking. **Flower** to 2⅛ in. (54 mm) long, to ¾ in. (2 cm) across, white to pink tinged with purple, fragrant, trumpet-shaped, broadly flaring at rim. Flowers in clusters from leaf axils, opening in afternoon. **Leaves** to 2½ in. (63 mm) long, to 1¾ in. (45 mm) across, opposite, the pair unequal in size, stalked, the blade thin, bright-green.

Habitat: Sandy, clay or chalky soils in pastures, brushlands, fence-rows and edges of woodlands. In CT, ST.

Note: Vine four-o'clock is excellent for the wildflower garden, where with a little care it forms luxuriant growth and produces an abundance of sweetly fragrant flowers. The plants are easily propagated by root division and should be planted in late fall or early spring.

WHITE GAURA (Myers)

ENGELMANN EVENING PRIMROSE (Miller)

WHITE GAURA (*Gaura lindheimeri*)
Evening-Primrose Family (Onagraceae)

Bloom Period: April–November

Description: Upright to widely spreading, soft-hairy, slender perennial 20–60 in. (5–15 dm) high; stems solitary to several from base, much-branched in upper portion. **Flower** ½–⅞ in. (13–22 mm) long, white turning pink in age; petals 4, in one row on upward side; stamens 8, conspicuously long, red-tipped, upright to drooping downward opposite petals. Flowers few to several, in elongated terminal spikes and on axillary branches. **Leaves** ¼–3¼ in. (6–83 mm) long, to ½ in. (13 mm) wide, alternate, stalkless, entire or with scattered teeth; upper leaves much smaller.

Habitat: Rich clay or sandy soils of prairies, pinelands, moist edges of ponds, lakes and seepage areas. In NE, SE, SC.

Note: White gaura is one of our largest-flowered and showiest gauras. Often forming extensive colonies, the plants make a spectacular sight when they open in early morning. The flowers are visited by numerous species of insects, especially small bees and beelike flies.

ENGELMANN EVENING PRIMROSE (*Oenothera engelmannii*)
Evening-Primrose Family (Onagraceae)

Bloom Period: May–September

Description: Upright, slender, hairy annual herb to 32 in. (8 dm); stem usually solitary, with poorly developed branches. Plant densely covered with long, soft hairs throughout. **Flower** to 1⅛ in. (3 cm) or more across, white fading pink; stigma with 4 threadlike branches at tip; stamens 8, the anthers thickly covered with yellow pollen when first opening. Flowers few to several, stalked, from upper leaf axils; flower buds shaggy, nodding. **Leaves** ¾–2⅜ in. (2–6 cm) long, ⅜–¾ in. (1–2 cm) wide, alternate, stalkless; margins coarsely wavy-toothed.

Habitat: Deep sands of fields, dunes and open flats. In PH, EP, FW.

Note: Most of the evening primroses have yellow flowers, but the showy Engelmann evening primrose is one of the few white-flowered ones. The flowers open near sunset, remain open during the night, then close by noon the next day. They are pollinated by night-flying moths.

FALSE GAURA (Darby)

WHITE PRICKLY POPPY (Myers)

FALSE GAURA (*Stenosiphon linifolius*)
Evening-Primrose Family (Onagraceae)

Bloom Period: May–October

Description: Tall, stiffly upright, slender, straight, smooth perennial to 9 ft. (3 m) tall; stem solitary, brittle, unbranched or with few long branches. **Flower** about ½ in. (13 mm) across, white; petals 4. Flowers numerous, densely clustered in long, slender, wandlike terminal spike. **Leaves** ¾–2⅜ in. (2–6 cm) long, ⅛–⅝ in. (3–16 mm) wide, alternate, stalkless, numerous and crowded on stem; upper leaves becoming smaller near flowering portion of stem.

Habitat: Mostly limestone, sometimes sand or clay soils on rocky outcrops, banks, slopes and hillsides. In NC, PH, EP.

Note: An extremely spectacular plant, false gaura has flowering spikes to two feet long or more. The plants much resemble some species of gaura (*Gaura* spp.). This is an excellent honey plant and is much used by bees and other small insects. It is easily cultivated in soils with a lime content, and seed should be fall-sown where they are to grow. The genus name is from a combination of two Greek words, *steno* meaning "narrow or straight" and *sipho* meaning "tube." This refers to the narrow, whitish, threadlike flower tube.

WHITE PRICKLY POPPY (*Argemone albiflora* subsp. *texana*)
Poppy Family (Papaveraceae)

Bloom Period: April–October

Description: Upright, extremely prickly annual or biennial to 3 ft. (1 m); stem usually solitary, branching in upper portion. Plant contains a bright yellow juice. Widely distributed by seed, the plants usually form large colonies. **Flower** to 4 in. (10 cm) across, white, solitary or few in loose cluster; petals 6, fragile, crinkled; stamens numerous, yellowish or reddish. Flowers closely subtended by 1 or 2 leaflike, spiny bracts. **Leaves** 3–8 in. (7.6–20 cm) long, alternate, stalkless, bluish-green, covered with whitish coating easily rubbed off, sometimes mottled, usually parted or deeply lobed; margins wavy-edged and spiny.

Habitat: Sandy or gravelly soils in disturbed areas, along fencerows and railroads, on hills and slopes, but especially in old fields and overgrazed pastures. In all except PH, FW.

Note: This poppy, like all the poppies, is sought by the honeybee and other small insects for its abundant pollen—it yields little nectar. All parts of the plant are somewhat poisonous. The herbage is so prickly it is left untouched by cattle even through severe droughts when other herbs have been grazed to the ground.

PALE TRUMPETS (Cheatham)

WHITE MILKWORT (Cheatham)

PALE TRUMPETS (*Ipomopsis longiflora*)
Phlox Family (Polemoniaceae)

Bloom Period: March–October

Description: Upright or somewhat sprawling, smooth annual or biennial to 24 in. (6 dm); stem usually solitary, slender, firm, much-branched. **Flower** 1–1½ in. (25–38 mm) long, white or lavender, trumpet-shaped, the tube long, very slender, the rim 5-pointed, broadly flaring and appearing flat. Flowers solitary or in pairs at tip of slender stem rising from upper leaf axils. **Leaves** to 1½ in. (38 mm) long, alternate, widely spaced on stem. Leaves in basal portion of plant larger, deeply divided or lobed into narrow segments; upper leaves smaller and undivided.

Habitat: Dry sandy, rocky or calcareous soils on plains, mesas, in deserts, grasslands or on slopes. In PH, FW.

Note: This plant was once placed in the genus *Gilia* and is still commonly called *white-flower gilia* or *pale-flower gilia*. The plants are conspicuous and attractive and may be easily grown from fall-sown seed.

WHITE MILKWORT (*Polygala alba*)
Milkwort Family (Polygalaceae)

Bloom Period: March–October

Description: Upright or somewhat sprawling, smooth, perennial herb 8–16 in. (2–4 dm) high; stems slender, usually several from base, with clusters of short, leafy branches at base, few-branched in upper portion. **Flower** to ¼ in. (6 mm) across; petals 3, white, greenish at base, the lowest often purple-tinged, surrounded by 5 bracts; 2 bracts white, petallike, extending to side like wings. Flowers numerous, densely clustered in slender, terminal, spikelike raceme. **Leaves** ¼–1 in. (6–25 mm) long, very narrow, alternate except for lower few in 1 or 2 whorls at base of plant.

Habitat: Sandy, chalky or clay soils in mesquite plains, cedar thickets, arroyos, on rocky hills, rimrock, breaks and barrier islands. In all except NE.

Note: *Polygala* is taken from the Greek words *poly* meaning "much" and *gala* meaning "milk," and as Pliny, the early herbalist, reported: ". . . taken in drink, it increases the milk in nursing women." The dried, powdered root is sold in pharmacies as "senega" or "senegin" and is used for various respiratory ailments.

UCKWHEAT

EPAL WILD BUCKWHEAT

WILD BUCKWHEAT (*Eriogonum annuum*)
Knotweed Family (Polygonaceae)

Bloom Period: May–November

Description: Upright, slender, delicate annual herb 1–3 ft. (3–9 dm) high; stem solitary, branched in flowering portion. Plant has soft, silky, matted whitish or grayish hairs throughout. **Flower** about ¼ in. (6 mm) across, white or occasionally pink; petals absent; sepals 6, petallike, in 2 rows. Flowers numerous, forming flat-topped terminal cluster. **Leaves** 1–3 in. (2.5–7.6 cm) long, alternate, short-stalked, narrowed at base; margins entire.

Habitat: Dry sandy or gravelly soils in abandoned areas, old fields, pastures, plains, on hillsides and slopes. Throughout.

Note: Wild buckwheat usually forms extensive stands and is quite showy. Occasionally a pink-flowered form will be mixed in with the white-flowered plants. A few specimens in the wildflower garden will add a beautiful, lacy effect to a border planting. Rhubarb (*Rheum rhaponticum*) and the true buckwheat (*Fagopyrum esculentum*) are cultivated members of this family.

HEART-SEPAL WILD BUCKWHEAT (*Eriogonum multiflorum*)
Knotweed Family (Polygonaceae)

Bloom Period: September–December

Description: Upright, usually slender annual or biennial to 6½ ft. (20 dm), commonly about 2–3 ft. (6–9 dm) high; stem solitary, branching in upper portion. Plants have tufts of soft, woolly, whitish or brownish hair nearly throughout. **Flower** very small, to less than ⅛ in. (3 mm) long; sepals 6, petallike, white becoming tan with age, outer 3 sepals heart-shaped; petals absent. Flowers few in stalked cluster, the clusters numerous and forming large, rather compact, flat-topped terminal mass. **Leaves** to 1½ in. (38 mm) long, to ⅝ in. (15 mm) wide, alternate, stalkless or almost so, mostly in lower portion of plant; blade densely hairy on both surfaces; margins entire, wavy, often curled under.

Habitat: Sandy or gravelly soils in pastures, open areas and along edges and in openings of oak or pine woodlands. In all except FW.

Note: The word *Eriogonum* has its origin in the Greek words *erio*, meaning "wool," and *gony*, meaning "joint" or "knee," and this genus is so named in reference to the jointed, woolly stems.

SOUTHERN JOINTWEED (Myers)

SPRING BEAUTY

SOUTHERN JOINTWEED (*Polygonella americana*)
Knotweed Family (Polygonaceae)

Bloom Period: May–August

Description: Low, upright perennial to 32 in. (8 dm) from woody taproot; stems solitary or few and forming mound, profusely branched, the branches short, leafy. **Flower** very small, white, solitary, arising from papery sheath around stem; petallike sepals 5, with 2 outer ones soon reflexed and 3 inner ones distinctively increasing in size during maturity; petals absent. Flowers numerous along upper portion of branches, forming terminal mass. **Leaves** 3/16–1/2 in. (5–13 mm) long, hairlike in width, about as thick as wide, smooth, the blade entire.

Habitat: Loose, deep sands in pastures, along slopes and along edges and openings of woodlands. In NE, SE, NC, SC.

Note: Southern jointweed is an especially attractive plant in the wild, but does not grow well in most gardens. The deep sands required for growth are not normally encouraged and the plants are not tolerant of anything less. The jointweeds get their common name from the conspicuous, swollen "joints" (nodes) along the stem where the leaves are attached. The family is recognized by the thin, papery sheath surrounding the stem above the leaf.

SPRING BEAUTY (*Claytonia virginica*)
Purslane Family (Portulacaceae)

Bloom Period: January–April

Description: Upright or weakly sprawling, delicate, smooth perennial herb to 12 in. (3 dm) from small globelike bulb; stems 1 to several, unbranched or with few branches in upper portion. **Flower** 1/2–3/4 in. (1.3–2 cm) across, white or pinkish, prominently veined with rose or red; petals 5, flat and appearing starlike. Flowers usually several, in loose cluster at top of stem. **Leaves** 2–8 in. (5–20 cm) long, very narrow, dark green and succulent; often a solitary pair of smaller leaves occurs about halfway along stem.

Habitat: Rich, sandy soils in lawns, clearings, pastures and openings of thickets and woodlands. In all except ST, FW.

Note: Spring beauty is one of the first wildflowers to bloom in the spring, often forming extensive patches of snowy white on warm, sunny days. The bulblike corms are edible and were an important food source for many Indian tribes. Raw, they taste similar to a radish and when boiled have about the same taste and texture as boiled potatoes.

TEN-PETAL ANEMONE (Miller)

TEXAS VIRGIN'S BOWER (Young)

TEN-PETAL ANEMONE (*Anemone heterophylla*)
Crowfoot Family (Ranunculaceae)

Bloom Period: February–March

Description: Low, upright, unbranched hairy perennial 4–16 in. (1–4 dm) high when flowering or fruiting; stem solitary from small tuber, with no rhizomes or stolons present. **Flower** to 1¾ in. (45 mm) across, solitary at tip of long stalk rising from root; petals absent; sepals 10–20, petallike, white, pink, purplish or blue, the lower row usually reddish-wine on undersurface. Flowers open wide in full sun, close in evening or on cloudy days. **Leaves** mostly at base, stalked, usually purplish on lower surface; blade divided into 3 leaflets with each leaflet broad, toothed or shallowly cut. A whorl of 3 leaves occurs about half-way up the stem, with each leaf cut or divided into short, narrow segments.

Habitat: Sandy or calcareous clays or limestone soils in pastures, prairies, on hillsides and in openings and edges of woodlands. Almost throughout.

Note: The easiest way to distinguish the ten-petal anemone from Carolina anemone, which is also common, is by the very long— ¾–3 in. (20–76 mm)—fruiting head, which begins expanding even before the petals fall. The fruiting head of the Carolina anemone is much shorter.

TEXAS VIRGIN'S BOWER (*Clematis drummondii*)
Crowfoot Family (Ranunculaceae)

Bloom Period: April–September

Description: Low and sprawling or climbing, hairy, herbaceous perennial vine; stems woody at base, to 9 ft. (3 m) long, climbing by the twisting of some leaf-stalks. **Flower** to 1¼ in. (32 mm) across, creamy, greenish-yellow or almost white; petals absent; sepals 4, petallike, narrow, thin, silky beneath, with crinkled margins; male and female flowers on separate plants; stamens or pistils many. Flowers several, in loose clusters. **Leaves** opposite, the blade divided into 3–7 stalked leaflets; each leaflet ⅜–1⅛ in. (1–3 cm) long, variously lobed or toothed.

Habitat: Dry sandy, clayey or calcareous soils, climbing over rocks, bushes or fences. In all except NE, SE.

Note: The fruit of this vine is more conspicuous than the flowers. The seeds are in a small, tight cluster, each seed with a long feathery "tail" or "plume," the whole making an iridescent, silky, feathery ball. These feathery fruits give rise to many common names for the vine including *old man's beard, love-in-the-mist* and *barbas de chivato*, which in Spanish means "goat's beard."

PRAIRIE LARKSPUR (Wesby)

PURPLE MEADOW-RUE

PRAIRIE LARKSPUR (*Delphinium virescens*)
Crowfoot Family (Ranunculaceae)

Bloom Period: April–July

Description: Strictly upright, hairy perennial to 60 in. (15 dm), but more commonly 12–18 in. (30–45 cm) high, from deep roots; stem unbranched, very slender. **Flower** about 1 in. (25 mm) wide; whitish or faintly bluish, crinkled; sepals 5, petallike, upper sepal with backward-projecting spur. Petals 4, smaller, clustered in center of flower, the upper 2 of these also with short spurs extending into spur of upper sepal. Flowers several, arranged in narrow terminal spike borne well above foliage. **Leaves** about 3 in. (76 mm) long, about as wide, abundant, distributed along stem or clustered at base; blade repeatedly divided into narrow segments.

Habitat: Various soils in pastures, prairies, open woodlands and slopes. In all except NE, SE.

Note: All parts of these plants are poisonous, containing the alkaloids ajacine and delphinine; plants have been known to cause death among cattle feeding in overgrazed pastures. *Delphinium* is derived from the Greek word for "dolphin," due to some fancied resemblance. The word *virescens* means "becoming green." Also called *plains larkspur*.

PURPLE MEADOW-RUE (*Thalictrum dasycarpum*)
Crowfoot Family (Ranunculaceae)

Bloom Period: March–July

Description: Upright, stout perennial 2–6 ft. (6–18 dm) high; stems thick near base, often purplish, branching in upper portion. **Flower** creamy, greenish or yellowish; sepals 4 or 5, somewhat petallike, falling as they open; petals none. Flowers numerous, in loose, delicate, elongated terminal cluster, usually with male and female flowers on separate plants. Stamens numerous, threadlike, colored, soon drooping and becoming entangled. Pistils fewer, shorter, not so showy. **Leaves** alternate; blade 2 or 3 times divided into numerous leaflets, the leaflets firm, thick, entire to 3-lobed, to 2¼ in. (5.7 cm) long, to 1½ in. (3.8 cm) wide, lower surface prominently veined. Lower leaves long-stalked; upper leaves stalkless.

Habitat: Rich sandy or calcareous loams in meadows, swamps, along stream banks, edges of woodlands or along wooded slopes. In NE, SE, NC, SC, PH.

Note: The common name for this plant comes from its resemblance to a strongly scented European plant (*Ruta* spp.) known as "herb of grace." Purple meadow-rue is reportedly useful in the treatment of spasms or convulsions. The plants may be used in wildflower gardens and are especially lovely along woodland trails.

LIZARD'S-TAIL

GREEN FALSE NIGHTSHADE (Miller)

LIZARD'S-TAIL (*Saururus cernuus*)
Lizard's-tail Family (Saururaceae)

Bloom Period: April–August

Description: Upright, smooth, jointed-stemmed perennial to 36 in. (9 dm); stem usually branched in upper portion. Plants form large colonies by spreading from fleshy, underground roots. **Flower** to about ⅛ in. (4 mm) long, white, fragrant, consisting of 3–7 showy stamens and 1 short pistil; sepals and petals absent. Flowers numerous, congested along a slender, nodding, taillike spike to 12 in. (3 dm) long; spike drooping during flowering, becoming erect as seeds mature. **Leaves** 3–6 in. (7.6–15 cm) long, to 3½ in. (9 cm) wide, alternate, usually long-stalked, occurring mostly in upper portion of plant, dark green; blade deeply notched at base.

Habitat: Muddy soils, often in water, in ditches, marshes, floodplains, margins of streams and lakes. In NE, SE, SC, CT, EP.

Note: There is only one species of *Saururus* in North America. The common name is an English interpretation of the scientific name, which was taken from the Greek *saurus* meaning "lizard" and the Latin *cernuus* meaning "turned toward the earth." The name aptly describes the slender, drooping flower spike.

GREEN FALSE NIGHTSHADE (*Chamaesaracha coronopus*)
Nightshade Family (Solanaceae)

Bloom Period: Throughout year

Description: Low, sprawling or reclining, usually densely hairy perennial; stems solitary or few, much-branched from base, to 6 in. (15 cm) high or long, forming small colonies. Plants have glandular hairs throughout, making them sticky to the touch. **Flower** to ½ in. (13 mm) across, yellowish to greenish or white, usually darker in center; petals 5, united, flatly 5-lobed at rim. Flowers solitary or few in clusters from leaf axils. **Leaves** to 2⅜ in. (6 cm) long, alternate, stalkless or almost so, entire to shallowly toothed or lobed.

Habitat: Dry, sandy, rocky calcareous or clayey loams in openings, on plains and mesas. In all except NE, SE, NC, SC.

Note: This is a common but often overlooked wildflower, for usually the entire plant is covered with dust which adheres to the sticky leaves and makes it inconspicuous. The flowers are quite similar to those of the ground-cherries (*Physalis* spp.), but the fruit is almost white instead of yellow and also differs in having a tight covering instead of the inflated one of *Physalis*.

WOOLLY FALSE NIGHTSHADE (Cheatham)

FIDDLE-LEAF TOBACCO

WOOLLY FALSE NIGHTSHADE (*Chamaesaracha villosa*)
Nightshade Family (Solanaceae)

Bloom Period: Throughout year

Description: Low, upright, sprawling or reclining, densely hairy perennial; stems solitary or few, much-branched from base, to 20 in. (50 cm) or more long. Plant has glandular hairs throughout, making it sticky to the touch. **Flower** ³⁄₁₆–1⅛ in. (5–29 mm) across, greenish-white or yellowish or sometimes violet-purplish, usually darker in center, 5-lobed at rim. Flowers solitary or in pairs from leaf axils. **Leaves** to 2¾ in. (7 cm) long, to 1⅛ in. (29 mm) wide, alternate, short-stalked, entire to shallowly toothed or lobed.

Habitat: Dry, gravelly limestone in deserts or rangelands, on slopes or mesas. In FW.

Note: This is a common but not particularly conspicuous wildflower in the areas where it occurs. The entire plant is often obscured by dust adhering to the sticky leaves. The flowers are quite similar to flowers of the ground-cherries (*Physalis* spp.), but the fruit differs in having a tightly enveloping covering instead of the inflated one of *Physalis*.

FIDDLE-LEAF TOBACCO (*Nicotiana repanda*)
Nightshade Family (Solanaceae)

Bloom Period: Throughout year

Description: Upright, slender, smooth to somewhat hairy, aromatic annual to 52 in. (13 dm); stem usually solitary, loosely branched. **Flower** 1¾–3 in. (45–76 mm) long, white or sometimes tinged with rose, often brown-striped, tubular; the rim widely flaring, 5-lobed. Flowers few to several, widely spaced in spikelike racemes at top of slender branches, opening in late afternoon. **Leaves** to 8 in. (2 dm) long, to 4 in. (1 dm) wide, alternate, thin, with somewhat sticky glandular hairs, often contracted slightly below the middle and then expanded again; lower leaves narrowed into a winged stalk; upper leaves deeply notched and clasping stem; margins wavy.

Habitat: Usually moist sandy or clayey soils in depressions, pastures, on flats, among boulders, along thicket edges and wooded ravines. In CT, EP, ST.

Note: This wild tobacco's leaves have a fiddle shape, hence the common name. The species name *repanda* is from the Latin *repandus*, meaning "turned up," referring to the wavy leaf margins. As with other wild tobaccos, this plant has narcotic-poisonous and rather unpleasantly scented foliage, but was formerly used for smoking. Also called *tobacco cimarrón*.

DESERT TOBACCO

(Young)

CAROLINA HORSE-NETTLE

DESERT TOBACCO (*Nicotiana trigonophylla*)
Nightshade Family (Solanaceae)

Bloom Period: March–November

Description: Upright, sticky-hairy, strongly rank-smelling biennial or perennial herb to 3 ft. (1 m); stem solitary, with few branches. **Flower** ½–¾ in. (1.3–2 cm) long, to ⅜ in. (1 cm) across, greenish-white or yellowish, trumpet-shaped, abruptly flattened at rim, 5-lobed and wavy. Flowers few, in loosely branched terminal cluster, open throughout the day. **Leaves** 2–8¾ in. (5–22 cm) long, to 2⅜ in. (6 cm) wide; lower leaves broadly stalked; upper leaves stalkless, lobed at base and clasping stem.

Habitat: Sandy, gravelly or rocky soils on slopes, along arroyos, canyon walls, around ledges and boulders and along dry washes. In CT, EP, ST, FW.

Note: The wild tobaccos are plants with strongly and unpleasantly scented foliage, and their poisonous properties are well-known. The herbage was formerly dried and smoked by various Indian tribes during tribal meetings or ceremonies or used to make medicine. The genus is named for Jean Nicot, who introduced the use of tobacco into France during the 16th century.

CAROLINA HORSE-NETTLE (*Solanum carolinense*)
Nightshade Family (Solanaceae)

Bloom Period: April–October

Description: Upright, coarse, prickly perennial to 3½ ft. (10.5 dm) from creeping root, the plants usually forming small colonies; stems solitary or few, branched or unbranched, with straight, yellowish prickles. **Flower** to 1¼ in. (32 mm) across, white, the 5 petals united at base, spreading widely into 5-lobed star; stamens 5, in upright column. Flowers few, in one-sided terminal clusters, each cluster elongating as flowers open. **Leaves** to 4¾ in. (12 cm) long, alternate, stalked, with yellowish prickles on lower surface and along the midrib; margins lobed or shallowly toothed.

Habitat: Sandy or loamy soils in disturbed areas, old fields, pastures and open woodlands. In all except PH, ST, FW.

Note: The large clusters of small, tomatolike fruits become orange-yellow when ripe and are quite showy. Once established, Carolina horse-nettle is rather difficult to eradicate and sometimes is a problem in cultivated areas. Native to the Southern states, it has become introduced elsewhere.

WOODS CORN-SALAD

TEXAS FROG-FRUIT (Myers)

WOODS CORN-SALAD (*Valerianella woodsiana*)
Valerian Family (Valerianaceae)

Bloom Period: March–May

Description: Low, upright, rather delicate, almost smooth herbaceous annual 6–20 in. (1.5–5 dm) high; stems solitary, angled, with opposite, widely forking branches in upper portion. **Flower** minute, white, funnel-shaped, unequally 5-lobed at rim; stamens prominently exserted. Flowers numerous, in compact, squarish, flat-topped or rounded terminal clusters. **Leaves** 1½–2¼ in. (38–57 mm) long, narrow, opposite, somewhat succulent; the margins hairy. Lower leaves entire; upper leaves often toothed near base.

Habitat: Moist, low, sandy or clayey soils on prairies, in ditches, ravines, along stream banks and in open woodlands. In NE, SE, NC, SC.

Note: Woods corn-salad forms extensive masses of white in early summer and is quite showy. It is an excellent plant for the wildflower garden, the white, lacy bloom-clusters mixing well with other spring flowers. It is very difficult to distinguish the various species of corn-salad found in Texas, with the fruit-shape being the most definitive characteristic.

TEXAS FROG-FRUIT (*Phyla incisa*)
Vervain Family (Verbenaceae)

Bloom Period: March–November

Description: Low, creeping or trailing perennial; stems 4-angled, often purplish, numerous, branching, swollen and rooting at the joints (nodes), upright at tips. Plants form dense mats often several feet across or long. **Flower** to ¼ in. (6 mm) long, white or pale lavender with yellow center, trumpet-shaped, 4-lobed at rim. Flowers many, stalkless, congested in small, globelike, terminal spike. Spikes elongating and becoming cylindrical with age. **Leaves** to 2 in. (5 cm) long, to ⅝ in. (16 mm) wide, opposite, stalkless or almost so, thickish, wedge-shaped at base, sharp-pointed or rounded at tip; margins toothed from middle to tip of blade.

Habitat: Dry or moist soils in widely varying habitats. Throughout.

Note: With adequate moisture, frog-fruit makes an excellent flowering ground-cover plant. In problem areas it can be used to replace lawns. The larvae of the beautiful little phaon crescent butterfly use the leaves as their major food source.

PRIMROSE-LEAVED VIOLET

PRIMROSE-LEAVED VIOLET (*Viola primulifolia*)
Violet Family (Violaceae)

Bloom Period: March–May

Description: Low, hairy perennial reproducing from above-ground runners and forming large colonies of plants. **Flower** to ⅝ in. (1.6 cm) across, white with pale blue veins, solitary, terminal, long-stalked, from root; petals 5, upper 2 petals erect, the lowermost petal bearded, spurred at base. Unopening, seed-producing (cleistogamous) flowers nodding, on short, upright stalks late in season. **Leaves** 1½–2 times as long as broad, long-stalked, from root, broader near base with basal portion extending down onto stalk; margins with small, rounded teeth.

Habitat: Wet, sandy, somewhat acid soils in open meadows, savannahs, bogs, and along edges of marshes and streams. In NE, SE, SC.

Note: This is the largest-flowered violet of our native white-flowered species. The broad lower petals of almost all violets offer a convenient landing place for insects seeking nectar from the spur-reservoir.

YELLOW FLOWERS

COPPER LILY

YELLOW STAR-GRASS

COPPER LILY (*Habranthus texanus*)
Amaryllis Family (Amaryllidaceae)

Bloom Period: August–October

Description: Low, smooth perennial herb 6–12 in. (15–30 cm) high, from deep bulb. Flowering stem appears above ground before leaves. **Flower** to 1⅛ in. (3 cm) long, golden or orange-yellow, sometimes tinged brownish or reddish on outer surface, solitary, terminal on leafless stalk, the 6 segments all petal-like; each segment to ⅜ in. (1 cm) wide at tip. **Leaves** to 8 in. (20 cm) long, from bulb, very narrow, smooth, thick, firm, appearing after flowers have withered.

Habitat: Gravelly sand, calcareous or clay soils in lawns, prairies, mesquite flats, pastures and other grassy areas. In all except PH, FW.

Note: This plant flowers after the rains of late summer and fall. It is endemic to Texas, and the only species of *Habranthus* occurring here. Copper lily is a very showy and interesting plant for the wildflower garden or planted in groups in the lawn where the flowers make a mass of golden color after rains. Also called *stagger grass* and *Texas atamosco lily*.

YELLOW STAR-GRASS (*Hypoxis hirsuta*)
Amaryllis Family (Amaryllidaceae)

Bloom Period: March–May

Description: Small, low, often tufted, conspicuously hairy perennial 1½–14 in. (3.8–35 cm) high. **Flower** ½–¾ in. (13–20 mm) across, yellow, greenish on outer surface, the 6 segments all petallike, star-shaped. Flowers usually in loose clusters of 2 or 3 at tip of slender, leafless, upright or reclining stem; stems shorter than leaves. **Leaves** 4–12 in. (10–30 cm) long, ¼ in. (6 mm) wide, basal, longer than flowering stem during bloom period, narrow, grasslike.

Habitat: Various soils in prairies, pastures, meadows or open woodlands. In all except PH, ST, FW.

Note: This plant, with its narrow leaves, can easily be confused with grass unless the distinctive flowers are open. A rich, early source of both pollen and nectar, yellow star-grass is attractive to both small bees and butterflies. A species of small beetles ravenously devours the petals.

PRAIRIE PARSLEY

GOLDEN ALEXANDERS

PRAIRIE PARSLEY (*Polytaenia nuttallii*)
Parsley Family (Apiaceae)

Bloom Period: April–June

Description: Stiffly upright, smooth, stout biennial to 3 ft. (1 m) or more; stem solitary, branching in upper portion. **Flower** to ¼ in. (6 mm) across; petals 5, yellow. Flowers in small clusters with 10–20 clusters on stalks of unequal length, the clusters again forming larger clusters. **Leaves** to 7¼ in. (18 cm) long, 6 in. (15 cm) wide, divided to midrib into broad segments with scalloped, lobed or coarsely toothed margins. Upper leaves less divided.

Habitat: Sandy loam or clay in pastures, woodland openings, and especially blackland prairies. In NE, SE, SC.

Note: Prairie parsley, sometimes called *wild dill*, is very much like cultivated dill, and the foliage and seeds can be used in much the same way. Other well-known members of this family are parsley, chervil, caraway and celery. The genus name is from two Greek words—*polys*, meaning "many," and *tainia* meaning "thin strip" or "ribbon," in reference to the crowded oil tubes on the fruit. The species name honors Thomas Nuttall, an early botanist.

GOLDEN ALEXANDERS (*Zizia aurea*)
Parsley Family (Apiaceae)

Bloom Period: April–August

Description: Upright, smooth perennial 16–32 in. (4–8 dm) high; stem usually solitary, much-branched in upper portion. **Flower** very small, bright yellow; petals 5. Flowers several in small cluster; clusters several, long-stalked, forming axillary or terminal, rather flat-topped larger cluster. **Leaves** to 4 in. (1 dm) long, 4¾ in. (12 cm) wide, alternate, stalked, once or twice divided into leaflets; ultimate leaflets 1–2 in. (2.5–5 cm) long, sharply and finely toothed.

Habitat: Moist sandy or sandy-clay soils in floodplains, meadows, woodland edges and thickets. In NE, SE, SC.

Note: This genus is named for Johann Baptist Ziz, an early German botanist. The species name is from the Latin *aureolus* meaning "golden, splendid."

HUISACHE-DAISY (Wesby)

YERBA RATÓN (Worthington)

HUISACHE-DAISY (*Amblyolepis setigera*)
Sunflower Family (Asteraceae)

Bloom Period: February–June

Description: Upright or sprawling, usually soft-hairy, aromatic annual 4–20 in. (1–5 dm) high or long; stems solitary or several, sparingly branched, often lying on ground. **Flower** head to 1½ in. (38 mm) across, solitary, terminal on long, leafless stalk; ray flowers 8–10, yellow, deeply 3- or 4-toothed at tip; disk flowers numerous, yellow, the cluster (disk) becoming dome-shaped in age. **Leaves** to 2½ in. (63 mm) long, alternate, stalkless and clasping stem at base, bluish-green; margins with long, silky hairs.

Habitat: Sandy loam, limestone or chalky soils in prairies, plains, abandoned areas, on hillsides and slopes. In all except NE, SE, SC.

Note: Huisache-daisy is particularly fine for home plantings, with each plant usually bearing numerous flowers both striking in color and pleasantly fragrant. The plants are palatable to livestock and deer, and are often grazed from their natural range.

YERBA RATÓN (*Bahia absinthifolia*)
Sunflower Family (Asteraceae)

Bloom Period: April–October

Description: Upright, white-hairy perennial 4–16 in. (1–4 dm) high; stem solitary or branching from base. **Flower** head 1¼ in. (32 mm) or more across, to ⅝ in. (16 mm) high; ray flowers 10–13, yellow; disk flowers numerous, yellow. Flowers solitary or few, at ends of long stems and branches. **Leaves** ⅜–2 in. (1–5 cm) long, to ⅝ in. (16 mm) wide, highly variable in shape from entire to variously once or twice lobed or divided into narrow or broad segments; lower leaves opposite; upper leaves alternate.

Habitat: Dry, rocky, mostly calcareous soils of plains, arroyos, mesas and slopes. In EP, ST, FW.

Note: *Yerba ratón* is Spanish, meaning "mouse grass." The plants are also commonly known as *hairy-seed bahia* from the conspicuous tufts of hairs at the base of the seeds. This is one of the most common perennial herbs within its area of occurrence. The genus is named for botanist Juan Francisco Bahia.

DESERT MARIGOLD (Evans)

SOFT GREEN-EYES

DESERT MARIGOLD (*Baileya multiradiata*)
Sunflower Family (Asteraceae)

Bloom Period: Throughout year

Description: Upright or sprawling annual or weak perennial herb 8–12 in. (2–3 dm) high; stems usually many, forming clumps or mounds. Plant with long, whitish, woolly hairs throughout. **Flower** head 1½–2 in. (38–50 mm) across, solitary at tip of long, leafless stalks; ray flowers 25–50, bright yellow, 3-toothed at tip; disk flowers numerous, yellow. **Leaves** 1½–3 in. (38–76 mm) long, alternate, the blade divided into broad or narrow lobes, the lobes again divided or with rounded teeth.

Habitat: Sandy or rocky soils in deserts, plains and mesas. In EP, ST, FW.

Note: Desert marigold is one of our more common and colorful wildflowers, blooming throughout the year when weather conditions are favorable. It often forms golden borders for miles along roadsides. In the garden, a solitary plant will form a perfect and impressive mound of almost solid yellow. As the flowers fade, they remain on the plant and become papery, giving the species another of its common names, *paper-daisy*.

SOFT GREEN-EYES (*Berlandiera pumila*)
Sunflower Family (Asteraceae)

Bloom Period: April–September

Description: Upright or somewhat sprawling, soft-hairy perennial to 28 in. (7 dm); stems usually several from base, branching in upper portion, reddish. **Flower** head 2 in. (5 cm) or more across, solitary, on short, woolly stalks; ray flowers usually 8, yellow to orange-yellow, with green veins on lower surface; disk flowers red to maroon. Each head subtended by broad, leaflike bracts (phyllaries) spreading flat and appearing as green flowers after petals fall. Heads few, forming loose terminal clusters. **Leaves** 1–4 in. (2.5–10 cm) long, alternate, velvety, green above, whitish below; margins somewhat wavy, bluntly toothed.

Habitat: Loose, sandy soils in abandoned areas, pastures, woodland borders and openings. In NE, SE, SC.

Note: This genus was named in honor of Jean Louis Berlandier, a French-Swiss physician who collected plants in Texas and northern Mexico in the early 1800s. Soft green-eyes looks like a small sunflower and is an excellent plant for the garden. The flowers open continually throughout the growing season.

TICKSEED SUNFLOWER

SMOOTH BIDENS

TICKSEED SUNFLOWER (*Bidens aristosa*)
Sunflower Family (Asteraceae)

Bloom Period: July–November

Description: Upright, essentially smooth annual or biennial 1–5 ft. (3–15 dm) high; stem solitary, slender, often reddish, freely branching in upper portion. **Flower** head to 2 in. (5 cm) across, long-stalked, terminal or from leaf axils; ray flowers 6–10, to 1 in. (25 mm) long, yellow, with darker yellow basal spot; disk flowers yellow, in cluster very small in relation to length of ray flowers. **Leaves** 2–6 in. (5–15 cm) long, opposite, once or twice divided into segments, the segments coarsely and variously cut or lobed, fringed with hairs.

Habitat: Moist, sandy soils in prairies, meadows, abandoned fields, pinelands and especially along edges of marshes and streams, often standing in water. In NE, SE, CT.

Note: The ripe seeds of this plant are barbed with two spinelike awns which readily adhere to clothing and the fur of animals, and are most difficult to remove. Other common names include *sticktights* and *beggar-ticks*.

SMOOTH BIDENS (*Bidens laevis*)
Sunflower Family (Asteraceae)

Bloom Period: July–November

Description: Upright to somewhat sprawling, smooth perennial to 3 ft. (1 m); stems rooting at the joints (nodes) and forming dense, often extensive colonies. **Flower** head 1⅛–2¾ in. (3–7 cm) across; ray flowers 7 or 8, golden-yellow; disk flowers numerous, yellow. Heads few, from axils of upper leaves. **Leaves** 2–6 in. (5–15 cm) long, alternate, stalkless, dark-green, glossy; margins sharply toothed, sometimes fringed with hairs.

Habitat: Moist or wet areas along edges of marshes, pools, streams, lakes and in seepage areas. In all except CT, PH, ST.

Note: Extensive stands of smooth bidens are often seen in moist or wet areas. It often grows in water, with the stems and branches floating. The fruit of this plant is armed with backward-projecting barbs and, when mature, becomes easily attached to clothing or fur. Other common names include *wild-goldenglow* and *bur-marigold*.

SEA OXEYE (Tveten)

TOCALOTE (Myers)

SEA OXEYE (*Borrichia frutescens*)
Sunflower Family (Asteraceae)

Bloom Period: Throughout year

Description: Stiffly upright perennial 16–32 in. (4–8 dm) high; stems tough, brittle, branched, with branches upright. **Flower** head 1–1⅜ in. (25–35 mm) across, solitary; ray flowers 10–30, yellow or orangish, 3-toothed at tip; disk flowers numerous, yellowish or brownish. Heads stiff, hard, at tip of stem. **Leaves** 1⅛–2⅜ (3–6 cm) long, opposite, gray-green, thick, somewhat leathery.

Habitat: Moist, usually brackish or saline areas of poor drainage or with salt accumulation, bay beaches or saline marshes. In CT.

Note: Sea oxeye is one of the most common and abundant plants in the coastal portion of the state. It will almost always be found in large colonies, lining the edges of saline marshes or forming solid stands in moist depressions. The plants can be used most effectively as a border or hedge plant where moisture and saline conditions are adequate.

TOCALOTE (*Centaurea melitensis*)
Sunflower Family (Asteraceae)

Bloom Period: March–August

Description: Upright, densely woolly winter annual 1–2½ ft. (3–4.5 dm) high; stems several, from base, widely branching with branches upright. **Flower** head to ⅜ in. (1 cm) across, yellow, solitary at tips of branches; ray flowers absent; disk flowers numerous, subtended by 4 or 5 rows of spine-tipped bracts. **Leaves** 2–4 in. (5–10 cm) long, alternate, densely covered with cottony hairs; basal and lower leaves lobed; upper leaves narrow, unlobed, extending down stem as wings.

Habitat: Dry, calcareous soils in rangelands, woodland edges and openings, but especially in disturbed areas and along roadsides. In NC, EP, ST, FW.

Note: Tocalote, also called *Malta star-thistle*, is a native of Europe which has become naturalized in this country. It is spreading rapidly, and in some areas has become a serious problem, especially among cultivated crops, where it is difficult to eradicate.

YELLOW THISTLE

COREOPSIS

YELLOW THISTLE (*Cirsium horridulum*)
Sunflower Family (Asteraceae)

Bloom Period: March–June

Description: Upright, extremely prickly biennial or winter annual 1–5½ ft. (3–16.5 dm) high; stem very thick, unbranched at first, usually branched later in extreme tip portion. **Flower** head 1⅝–3⅛ in. (4.1–8 cm) across, about as high, solitary or few at tip of stem; ray flowers absent; disk flowers creamy to dark yellow or pink to dark purple, numerous, held in deep cup of weakly spiny bracts (phyllaries), the cup subtended by a whorl of larger, lobed and bristly tipped bracts. **Leaves** 8–24 in. (2–6 dm) long, alternate; basal leaves stalked, forming large winter rosette; blade irregularly lobed and toothed, the lobes and teeth ending in long, rigid spines.

Habitat: Sandy, gravelly or loamy soils in open places in almost all areas. In NE, SE, SC.

Note: This plant can become a pest in pastures. It spreads rapidly from seed and forms a deep root which is very difficult to eradicate. Thistle roots were formerly boiled and eaten but the foliage is so prickly the early herbalist Pliny wrote that ". . . no four-footed animal save the ass will eat it." In the Old World, thistles were associated with magic and were also held sacred to Thor, the god of thunder.

COREOPSIS (*Coreopsis basalis*)
Sunflower Family (Asteraceae)

Bloom Period: April–July

Description: Upright, rather delicate annual 8–16 in. (2–4 dm) high; stem usually much-branched from near base, with the stem and branches noticeably grooved. **Flower** head 1⅜–2 in. (3.5–5 cm) across, solitary, terminal on slender, leafless stalk; ray flowers usually 8, yellow, sometimes reddish-brown at base, wide-spreading, lobed or toothed at tip; disk flowers numerous, reddish-brown. **Leaves** to 2¾ in. (7 cm) long, opposite, long-stalked, the blade divided into narrow segments.

Habitat: Deep sandy or limestone soils of prairies, edges of old fields and woodland openings. In all except NE, SE, PH, FW.

Note: *Coreopsis* is from a combination of Greek and Latin words meaning "the appearance of, or looking like, a bug." This refers to the fruit, which is flattened and has two short, forward-projecting awns at the end, resembling in some respects a small beetle. The shape of these fruits gives the plant another common name, *tickseed*. There are two varieties of this coreopsis, var. *basalis*, found on sandy soils, and var. *wrightii*, found on limestone soils.

PLAINS COREOPSIS

CLASPING-LEAVED CONEFLOWER

PLAINS COREOPSIS (*Coreopsis tinctoria*)
Sunflower Family (Asteraceae)

Bloom Period: February–December

Description: Upright to sprawling, smooth, slender, rather delicate annual to 4 ft. (12 dm), but usually 1–2 ft (3–6 dm) high; stem solitary, leafy, much-branched. **Flower** head to 1⅛ in. (3 cm) across, solitary, terminal on slender branches; ray flowers 5–7, yellow, generally with red-brown spot at base but occasionally all yellow or all brown, 3-toothed at tip; disk flowers reddish-brown. **Leaves** 2–4 in. (5–10 cm) long, opposite, stalkless or nearly so, occurring mostly in lower portion of plant, once or twice divided into numerous narrow segments. Upper leaves often undivided.

Habitat: Various soils, usually moist areas in prairies, pastures, swales and fields. Throughout.

Note: Plains coreopsis often forms large patches in ungrazed areas, or long, showy borders along roadsides, especially in the more moist soils of eastern Texas. It is a most attractive wildflower and is much used in garden plantings. Weavers can extract a red dye from this plant for dyeing woolen yarn.

CLASPING-LEAVED CONEFLOWER (*Dracopis amplexicaulis*)
Sunflower Family (Asteraceae)

Bloom Period: May–June

Description: Upright, smooth annual 12–28 in. (3–7 dm) high; stem solitary, branching in upper portion. Plant covered with thin, whitish coating which comes off when rubbed. **Flower** head to 2 in. (5 cm) across, solitary, terminal at ends of long, slender branches; ray flowers 5–9, solid yellow or more commonly reddish-brown in basal portion, wide-spreading or drooping; disk flowers brownish, forming an elongated cone ½–1¼ in. (1.3–3.2 cm) high. **Leaves** 1⅝–4 in. (4.1–10 cm) long, alternate, stalkless and clasping stem at base of blade, the blade thick, conspicuously 1-ribbed, entire.

Habitat: Low, moist, often clay soils, most commonly in prairies and floodplains. In all except FW.

Note: Clasping-leaved coneflower is quite showy when in bloom, and the plants form extensive colonies, often shading out all other vegetation. The species name is from the Latin words *amplexus*, meaning "encircling" or "embracing," and *caulis*, for "stem," referring to the distinctively shaped leaves.

PARRALENA (Tveten)

PARRALENA (*Dyssodia pentachaeta*)
Sunflower Family (Asteraceae)

Bloom Period: March–December

Description: Low, strong-scented annual or short-lived perennial herb 4–8 in. (1–2 dm) high; stems solitary or few and forming clump, branched from near base. **Flower** head to ⅝ in. (1.6 cm) across, solitary, terminal on long stalk; ray flowers mostly 8–13, yellow to yellow-orange; disk flowers 16–70, dull yellow. Usually several heads open at once on plant. **Leaves** opposite, the blade divided into 5–11 very narrow lobes or segments, the segments about ½ in. (1.3 cm) long, rather stiff to the touch.

Habitat: Dry calcareous or chalky soils in plains, rangelands, chaparral, along ravines and bluffs. In NC, PH, EP, ST, FW.

Note: Like most other *Dyssodias*, parralena is a beautiful plant to use in wildflower gardens, especially as a border. The foliage is rather unpleasantly scented if plants are handled. Also known as *common dogweed*, the species has a wide distribution, with several varieties.

BRISTLE-LEAF DYSSODIA (*Dyssodia tenuiloba*)
Sunflower Family (Asteraceae)

Bloom Period: March–December

Description: Upright to sprawling, moundlike, somewhat rough-hairy annual or short-lived perennial 4–12 in. (1–3 dm) high; stems usually solitary but much-branched in upper portion. Plant strongly scented. **Flower** head to 1⅛ in. (3 cm) across, solitary, terminal; ray flowers about 13, golden-yellow; disk flowers numerous, yellow. Heads few to numerous. **Leaves** to 1¼ in. (32 mm) long, alternate, stalkless, the blade dotted with translucent orange or dark brown oil glands, entire or deeply cut into 7–15 threadlike segments or lobes.

Habitat: Sandy or loamy soils in prairies, openings or on hillsides and slopes. In all except NE, NC, FW.

Note: Bristle-leaf dyssodia is a most attractive plant for the wildflower garden, forming low mounds of almost solid golden-orange. Seed should be sown in the fall. Also called *tiny Tim*.

ENGELMANN DAISY

SLENDER-HEADED EUTHAMIA (Cheatha)

ENGELMANN DAISY (*Engelmannia pinnatifida*)
Sunflower Family (Asteraceae)

Bloom Period: February–November

Description: Upright to spreading, stout-stemmed, densely coarse-hairy perennial herb to 3 ft. (1 m); stems one to several from stout, woody taproot, branched in upper portion to form rounded crown. **Flower** heads 1–2 in. (2.5–5 cm) across, long-stalked; ray flowers usually 8, yellow, expanding in late afternoon, then folding under or downward in intense heat and sunlight the next day; disk flowers yellow. Heads few to several in terminal clusters. **Leaves** mostly basal, 8–12 in. (2–3 dm) long, forming large clump or winter rosette, alternate, long-stalked, the blade deeply cut or lobed, the lobes themselves lobed or toothed. Upper leaves smaller, stalkless, entire or coarsely toothed.

Habitat: Calcareous loam and clays in grasslands, savannahs and prairies. In all except NE, SE.

Note: Engelmann daisy is readily eaten by livestock and has been grazed from much of its former range. It is primarily a species of native grasslands and ungrazed areas. The genus honors George Engelmann (1809–1884), a German-American botanist based in St. Louis, who classified many new Western species.

SLENDER-HEADED EUTHAMIA (*Euthamia leptocephala*)
Sunflower Family (Asteraceae)

Bloom Period: September–November

Description: Rather stiffly upright, smooth perennial 16–32 in. (4–8 dm) high; stems usually several and forming clump, thick near base, freely branching in upper portion with branches stiffly upright and the plant appearing broad and flat on top. **Flower** head to ¼ in. (6 mm) high, often sticky to the touch; ray flowers few, minute, yellow; disk flowers 10–15 per head, yellow. Heads solitary or in clusters of 2–4 at tips of slender branches, the whole forming flat-topped mass. **Leaves** 1⅝–2⅜ in. (41–60 mm) long, ⅛–³⁄₁₆ in. (3–5 mm) broad at midstem, alternate, stalkless, upright, dark-green, dotted with minute glands.

Habitat: Sandy soils along edges of pastures, creeks, woodlands and open coastal areas. In NE, SE, SC, CT.

Note: The *Euthamia*s in Texas are very similar to some of our species of goldenrod (*Solidago* spp.) and may easily be confused with them. *Euthamia* differs in having gland-dotted leaves. The genus name *Euthamia* is from the Greek word *euthemon*, meaning "neat, pretty"; the species name is derived from a combination of words meaning "slender-headed."

FRAGRANT GAILLARDIA (Wesby)

BITTERWEED (Miller)

FRAGRANT GAILLARDIA (*Gaillardia suavis*)
Sunflower Family (Asteraceae)

Bloom Period: March–May

Description: Upright, slender, clumped perennial herb to 24 in. (6 dm); stems few to several, grooved, unbranched. Plants often form dense stands. **Flower** head ¾–1¾ in. (2–4.5 cm) across, very fragrant, solitary, terminal on slender, leafless stalks; ray flowers few, yellow to orange or red, very short, deeply 3-lobed, often absent, or if present soon falling off; disk flowers numerous, reddish-brown. **Leaves** to 6 in. (15 cm) long, alternate, all basal, thick, widest near tip, the blade entire to deeply lobed.

Habitat: Heavy loams, clay, calcareous or sandy-calcareous soils of prairies, openings, old fields and pastures. In all except NE, SE, SC.

Note: Fragrant gaillardia is not quite as showy as the Indian blanket (*G. pulchella*), but what it lacks in color is made up for by its heavy but pleasing fragrance somewhat suggestive of gardenias. It is easily grown from seed and, with adequate moisture and removal of maturing flower heads, will continue blooming until fall.

BITTERWEED (*Helenium amarum*)
Sunflower Family (Asteraceae)

Bloom Period: April–December

Descripton: Upright, moundlike annual herb 4–20 in. (1–5 dm) high; stem conspicuously grooved or ribbed, solitary or few, slender at base, usually much-branched in upper portion. Entire plant bitterly aromatic. **Flower** head to 1 in. (25 mm) or more across, solitary on slender stalks 2–6 in. (5–15 cm) long; ray flowers usually 8, yellow, toothed at tip, somewhat drooping; disk flowers several. Heads numerous, forming loose, open, terminal cluster. **Leaves** 1½–3 in. (38–76 mm) long, very narrow or threadlike, alternate, stalkless, numerous. Leaves in lower portion of plant usually dying or withered away by flowering time.

Habitat: Sandy or loamy soils in disturbed areas, pastures, fields, prairies, woodland openings and edges. In all except FW.

Note: Bitterweed is usually not eaten by cattle and increases greatly in heavily grazed areas. Milk of cows that do feed on the herbage is extremely distasteful, and honey from the pollen is reportedly very bitter and unpalatable.

PURPLE-HEAD SNEEZEWEED

SWAMP SUNFLOWER

PURPLE-HEAD SNEEZEWEED (*Helenium flexuosum*)
Sunflower Family (Asteraceae)

Bloom Period: May–June

Description: Upright perennial 16–40 in. (4–10 dm) high; stems solitary or few, branching in upper portion, conspicuously winged in lower portion. **Flower** about 1¼ in. (3.2 cm) high; ray flowers yellow, orange or reddish-brown, often drooping, sometimes absent; disk flowers numerous, red-brown to red-purple. Heads solitary at ends of long stalks, several in loose, open terminal cluster. **Leaves** 1½–3 in. (3.8–7.6 cm) long, to ½ in. (1.3 cm) wide, alternate, stalkless, basally extending down stem as wings; margins entire or sparsely toothed. Lower leaves much larger, usually withered at flowering time.

Habitat: Moist or wet sandy or alluvial soils in lowland pastures, floodplains, meadows, swales and ditches, and along stream banks. In NE, SE, SC.

Note: Plants of purple-head sneezeweed can be found with the ray flowers present or absent; in some instances, the rays are very short and hardly noticeable. The dried, powdered leaves and flower heads will cause violent sneezing when sniffed, and were formerly used in the treatment of colds and congestion. An infusion of the leaves was reportedly used by some Indians as a laxative. The plants are toxic to cattle and may cause severe sickness or even death.

SWAMP SUNFLOWER (*Helianthus angustifolius*)
Sunflower Family (Asteraceae)

Bloom Period: August–November

Description: Upright, slender, rough-hairy perennial 3–6 ft. (1–2 m) high; stem solitary, much-branched in upper portion. Plants form colonies. **Flower** head to 2½ in. (63 mm) across, solitary at tip of slender stem; ray flowers 10–15, yellow; disk flowers numerous, purplish-red. **Leaves** 4–8 in. (1–2 dm) long, to ⅝ in. (16 mm) wide, alternate, stalkless, firm, rough-hairy; margins often rolled toward underside.

Habitat: Rich, moist soils in open depressions, edges of streams, lakes and marshes. In NE, SE, SC.

Note: Swamp sunflower is one of the most spectacular plants of fall. Often growing in extensive colonies, it forms patches of brilliant yellow against the greens of pine and hardwood forest throughout the eastern portion of the state. Easily grown in moist soils, it makes an excellent background plant for the garden. The species name is from the Latin word *angustus*, meaning "narrow," which refers to the narrow leaves.

COMMON SUNFLOWER

MAXIMILIAN SUNFLOWER

COMMON SUNFLOWER (*Helianthus annuus*)
Sunflower Family (Asteraceae)

Bloom Period: March–December

Description: Upright, stout, very rough and hairy annual to 6 ft. (2 m) or more; stem solitary, much-branched, often mottled, sticky to the touch. **Flower** heads 2⅜–5 in. (6–12.5 cm) across, solitary, terminal on long, rough stalks; ray flowers 20–25, yellow; disk flowers numerous, red or purple. **Leaves** to 12 in. (30 cm) long, almost all alternate, long-stalked, rough; blade conspicuously 3-veined at base; margins toothed. Upper leaves smaller.

Habitat: Clay or heavy sands in abandoned areas, fields, pastures, open stream banks and along railroad tracks. Throughout.

Note: This is the most abundant sunflower in the state and is found, in one of its three subspecies forms, throughout. It often follows fencerows for miles or covers many acres of old fields or disturbed open bottomlands. It is a most useful plant, formerly being of great value to Indians for medicines, as a source for fiber and cordage, and as a highly nutritious food. The seeds are readily sought by several species of wild birds, and a cultivated form provides many modern food products.

MAXIMILIAN SUNFLOWER (*Helianthus maximiliani*)
Sunflower Family (Asteraceae)

Bloom Period: July–October

Description: Upright, tall, leafy, rough-hairy perennial 3–10 ft. (1–3.3 m) high; stems usually several from base, mostly unbranched. Plants form large colonies. **Flower** head to 3 in. (76 mm) across, short-stalked, terminal, from leaf axils; ray flowers bright yellow; disk flowers yellow. Heads several, forming slender spike in upper third or half of stem. **Leaves** 4–12 in. (1–3 dm) long, ¾–2⅛ in. (20–55 mm) wide, alternate, stalkless, tapered at both ends, grayish-green, stiff, rough to the touch, often folded lengthwise and curving downward in tip portion.

Habitat: Seasonally moist, fertile calcareous or clay soils in prairies, ditches, swales or depressions. In all except ST, FW.

Note: A naturally dominant plant of prairies, Maximilian sunflower is readily grazed by livestock, which has eliminated it from much of its natural range. It is important in wildlife plantings because of its palatability to deer and numerous species of birds, which eat the seed. The tubers were an important food source for Western tribes of Indians. The plant was named for Prince Maximilian of Wied Neuweid, a naturalist who traveled in the American West during the 1830s.

GRAY GOLDEN-ASTER (Mahler)

GOLDEN-ASTER (Miller)

GRAY GOLDEN-ASTER (*Heterotheca canescens*)
Sunflower Family (Asteraceae)

Bloom Period: June–November

Description: Upright or sprawling, densely gray-hairy, aromatic perennial to 24 in. (6 dm); stems usually many, curved, finely branched in upper portion. Plants usually form small colonies from short, underground stems. **Flower** head to 1 in. (2.5 cm) across; ray flowers 14–20, yellow, curling under at night or in age; disk flowers yellow. Heads solitary or few in cluster at tips of short branches. **Leaves** 1–1⅝ in. (2.5–4.1 cm) long, mostly more than 5 times longer than broad, alternate, numerous and crowded on stem, gray with covering of fine, dense, silky hairs; margins fringed with few shaggy hairs. Lower leaves stalked, soon withering and falling.

Habitat: Dry, shallow, sandy or rocky soils in prairies, openings, rock outcrops, along hillsides and slopes. In all except NE, SE, SC.

Note: Gray golden-aster is a conspicuous component of the late summer and fall flora, with the silvery foliage making a lovely backdrop for the golden-colored flowers. The colonies of plants often form large, showy displays against hillsides, among rocks and boulders or along roadsides. As with the other *Heterothecas*, the foliage is pleasantly aromatic.

GOLDEN-ASTER (*Heterotheca latifolia*)
Sunflower Family (Asteraceae)

Bloom Period: August–November

Description: Upright to widely sprawling, densely hairy, aromatic annual to 6 ft. (2 m), but more often only 1–3 ft. (3–9 dm) high; stem solitary, usually much branched, the branches slender, few-leaved. Plants have gland-tipped hairs, making the herbage sticky to the touch. **Flower** head ⅝–1 in. (1.6–2.5 cm) across; ray flowers 15–35, yellow; disk flowers 35–40, yellow. Heads numerous, stalked, forming large, widely branched terminal mass. **Leaves** to 1 in. (2.5 cm) long, to ¾ in. (2 cm) wide, alternate; blade coarse, rough, the margins coarsely toothed. Lower leaves stalked, soon falling and usually absent at flowering time; upper leaves stalkless, basally clasping stem.

Habitat: Mostly sandy soils in prairies, rangelands, disturbed areas, edges and openings of woodlands. Throughout.

Note: Golden-aster, also called *camphor daisy*, is easily recognized by the foliage, which emits a strong camphor scent when crushed or disturbed. The plants usually form extensive stands and, since they are not grazed by livestock, are considered a nuisance or "pest" by the farmer or rancher. They are of interest in the wildflower garden, especially if cut low in late summer, for then they will bloom profusely until frost or after, forming low mounds of golden yellow.

SOFT GOLDEN-ASTER

FINE-LEAF WOOLLY-WHITE

(Wesby)

SOFT GOLDEN-ASTER (*Heterotheca pilosa*)
Sunflower Family (Asteraceae)

Bloom Period: May–November

Description: Upright, soft-hairy, aromatic annual 12–24 in. (3–6 dm) high; stem solitary, usually branched only above the middle. Plants often have some glandular hairs, making them sticky to the touch. **Flower** head to 1⅛ in. (3 cm) across; ray flowers yellow, remaining straight and becoming erect at night; disk flowers numerous, yellow. Heads solitary, terminal on short branches, the branches several and forming terminal mass. **Leaves** to 2¾ in. (7 cm) long, alternate, stalkless or almost so, numerous and crowded on stem, the blade distinctly green, soft, flexible; margins usually toothed; upper leaves smaller, entire.

Habitat: Dry, sandy soils of prairies, pastures, old fields, rangelands, hillsides, woodland openings and edges, beaches and barrier islands. In NE, SE, NC, SC, CT.

Note: The dark green herbage of soft golden-aster distinguishes it from other *Heterotheca*s growing in the same area. It is an attractive plant while flowering but tends to become rather tall and rank under garden conditions. The foliage is not as aromatic as that of some of the other species.

FINE-LEAF WOOLLY-WHITE (*Hymenopappus filifolius* var. *cinereus*)
Sunflower Family (Asteraceae)

Bloom Period: May–September

Description: Upright, hairy perennial 6–16 in. (15–40 cm) high; stems solitary or few, branched in upper portion. Plant is variable, both in size and hairiness. **Flower** head less than ½ in. (13 mm) across; ray flowers absent; disk flowers 25–40, yellow, rarely white, forming cluster, surrounded by small, yellow, petallike bracts; clusters stalked, 1–6 per stem, the whole forming terminal cluster. **Leaves** 2–5½ in. (5–14 cm) long, alternate, mostly in basal rosette, the blade divided into hairlike segments. Stem leaves none or few and smaller.

Habitat: Sandy or rocky soils on plains, open areas, hills and slopes. In PH.

Note: Fine-leaf woolly-white is a wide-ranging species, growing well in various soils and making an attractive garden plant. The ferny foliage and yellow flowers blend with coarser plants for a lacy effect in borders or background plantings.

PLAINS YELLOW DAISY (Wesby)

JIMMYWEED (Wesby)

PLAINS YELLOW DAISY (*Hymenoxys scaposa*)
Sunflower Family (Asteraceae)

Bloom Period: February–October
Description: Low, upright, silvery-hairy perennial to 16 in. (4 dm),
from woody base; stem usually solitary, much-branched at base
and forming clump. **Flower** head to 2 in. (5 cm) across; ray
flowers 12–31, bright yellow, 3-toothed at tip, 4-veined with the
veins purplish-brown and conspicuous on both surfaces; disk
flowers yellow. Heads solitary, terminal on long, leafless stalks,
the stalks densely silky-hairy especially near top. **Leaves** 3–5 in.
(76–125 mm) long, stalkless or almost so, crowded and mostly
toward base; margins entire to few-lobed.
Habitat: Dry sandy, chalky but mostly limestone soils on prairies,
plains and rocky hillsides. In PH, EP, ST, FW.
Note: Herbage of the plains yellow daisy is dotted with thin gran-
ules of a resinlike substance which makes the plant bitter to the
taste and emits a disagreeable odor when crushed. (Collectively, the plants of this genus are commonly known as *bitterweed*.) The petals become reflexed in age and remain on the
plant for some time.

JIMMYWEED (*Isocoma wrightii*)
Sunflower Family (Asteraceae)

Bloom Period: June–October
Description: Upright or partially sprawling, smooth but sticky perennial 8–32 in. (2–8 dm) high; stems usually several, forming
clump, much-branched at base and again in flowering portion.
Flower head ⁵⁄₁₆–½ in. (8–13 mm) high; ray flowers absent; disk
flowers 10–40, yellow. Heads solitary or in small clusters of 2 to
6, the clusters several and forming a large terminal mass. **Leaves**
alternate, very narrow, entire.
Habitat: Mostly alkaline soils in open areas, disturbed sites,
plains, rangelands and brushlands. In PH, FW.
Note: Jimmyweed, also commonly known as *rayless goldenrod*,
often occurs in overgrazed rangeland and is a common "weed"
in irrigated areas. The plants contain the toxic alcohol tremetol
and, if eaten in quantity by cattle, will cause the disease known
as "milk sickness" or "trembles." This disease is transmissible
through the milk to humans. The plants exude a gooey substance which makes them sticky to the touch, but in the wildflower garden, a few clumps are most attractive.

DWARF DANDELION

(Tveten)

TEXAS YELLOW STAR

DWARF DANDELION (*Krigia oppositifolia*)
Sunflower Family (Asteraceae)

Bloom Period: March–June

Description: Low, upright or widely sprawling, usually smooth annual 1⅝–6½ in. (4.1–16.3 mm) high; stems solitary to several, freely branching. Plant has milky sap. Herbage pale bluish-green. **Flower** head to ⅜ in. (1 cm) across; ray flowers several, orange-yellow, finely 5-toothed across square tips; disk flowers yellow. Heads terminal on slender stalks from upper leaf axils. **Leaves** to 2⅛ in. (54 mm) long, opposite or almost so; upper leaves smaller, more opposite; margins entire to irregularly and shallowly lobed.

Habitat: Dry sandy or rocky soils in disturbed areas, pastures, edges of fields, stream banks, ditches, woodland edges and openings. In all except PH, FW.

Note: The individual flowers of dwarf dandelion are not very showy, but several are usually open on each plant at once, and the plants form large colonies, so the sight is usually quite spectacular. The flowers are open only in the morning during warm, sunny weather. They provide an early source of pollen and nectar relished by numerous small insects.

TEXAS YELLOW STAR (*Lindheimera texana*)
Sunflower Family (Asteraceae)

Bloom Period: March–May

Description: Upright, somewhat rough-hairy annual to 20 in. (5 dm) from slender taproot; stem leafy, usually solitary, un-branched or branched in upper portion. Plant sometimes begins flowering when not over 2 in. tall, continues blooming while growing taller. **Flower** heads ¾–1⅛ in. (2–3 cm) across, solitary or few together at tip of stem; ray flowers 4 or 5, yellow, notched at tip; disk flowers yellow. **Leaves** 1⅛–3⅛ in. (3–8 cm) long, alternate, crowded along stem, bright green, tapered at both ends, toothed in tip portion.

Habitat: Clay or calcareous soils, occasionally on plains but more commonly on prairies. In all except SE, ST, FW.

Note: This genus is named for Ferdinand Lindheimer (1801–1879), a German-born botanist who settled in New Braunfels. Texas yellow star is easily cultivated and does quite well in garden plantings. Also called *star daisy* and *Lindheimer daisy*.

YELLOW SPINY DAISY (Mahler)

CAMPHOR DAISY (Tveten)

YELLOW SPINY DAISY (*Machaeranthera australis*)
Sunflower Family (Asteraceae)

Bloom Period: May–October

Description: Upright to weakly sprawling, usually hairy perennial herb 4–8 in. (1–2 dm) or more high; stems few to several, from woody base, freely branching and forming loose clump. **Flower** head about 1 in. (25 mm) across; ray flowers several, narrow; disk flowers yellow. Heads solitary, at ends of branches, not crowded on plant. **Leaves** ⅛–¾ in. (3–20 mm) long, narrow, alternate, stalkless, pale-green, usually rather densely covered with whitish hairs; blade in lower portion of plant twice lobed into narrow segments; blade in upper portion once lobed; lobes ending in spiny bristle.

Habitat: Dry sandy or rocky soils of arid plains, deserts, slopes, hillsides and evergreen brushlands. In all except NE, SE, SC.

Note: Yellow spiny daisy is a conspicuous component of the summer and fall flora in the western portion of the state. Formerly, this genus was placed by some authorities in the genera *Haplopappus* and *Aster*, showing its close relationship to these groups.

CAMPHOR DAISY (*Machaeranthera phyllocephala*)
Sunflower Family (Asteraceae)

Bloom Period: March–December

Description: Upright or low-sprawling, aromatic, hairy annual to 2 ft. (6 dm); stem usually solitary but freely branching near base. Plants usually exude a gooey substance and are very sticky to the touch. **Flower** head 1⅝ in. (25–41 mm) across; ray and disk flowers yellow. Heads solitary or few together, usually closely clasped by leaves. **Leaves** ¾–1⅜ in. (20–35 mm) long, alternate, stalkless, upright, crowded even in flowering portion of plant, thick, firm, the margins sharply toothed.

Habitat: Sandy, saline or brackish soils of salt flats, shell beaches and offshore islands. In CT.

Note: Camphor daisy, also called *golden beach daisy*, is a common and abundant wildflower of the coastal area. The sawlike teeth of the leaf margins and the leaves' presence around the flower head make field identification of this plant easy. It often lives over winter, producing flowers the entire year.

SCENTED PECTIS (Miller)

LEMON-SCENTED PECTIS (*Pectis angustifolia*)
Sunflower Family (Asteraceae)

Bloom Period: June–October

Description: Upright or sprawling, smooth, aromatic annual 4–8 in. (1–2 dm) high; stems forking, much-branched from base or in upper portion of plant. **Flower** head about ½ in. (13 mm) across, in clusters at end of slender stem; ray flowers 8–10, yellow, upright; disk flowers 10–15, yellow. Each head surrounded by 8–10 leaflike bracts, the bracts with a conspicuous oil gland at tip. **Leaves** ⅜—1½ in. (10–38 mm) long, very narrow, opposite, dotted with reddish oil glands, and having bristle-tipped lobes near base.

Habitat: Dry sandy or calcareous soils of open areas, plains, deserts, hills and slopes. In PH, EP, FW.

Note: These plants flower throughout the summer, often growing in solid stands that are very showy. The foliage is so fragrant with a strong lemon odor that often the plants can be smelled before they are seen. Easily cultivated, lemon-scented pectis is much used in flower gardens in the western part of the state, especially as a border or massed planting.

SAW-LEAF DAISY (*Prionopsis ciliata*)
Sunflower Family (Asteraceae)

Bloom Period: August–October

Description: Stiffly upright, stout, smooth, annual herb 20–60 in. (5–15 dm) high; stem solitary, branching only in flowering portion. Plants usually sticky to the touch. **Flower** head about 1¾ in. (4.5 cm) across; ray flowers numerous, yellow; disk flowers yellow. Heads few to numerous, short-stalked, congested near top of stalk. **Leaves** to 3 in. (7.6 cm) long, alternate, stalkless, basally clasping stem, thick, stiff, the margins coarsely toothed. Upper leaves not much reduced in size.

Habitat: Mostly clay soils in prairies, plains, rangelands and open ground. All except SE, ST.

Note: Saw-leaf daisy is a showy annual that serves well as a background plant in the landscape. In the field, it is not grazed by livestock and usually forms large, conspicuous stands. Saw-leaf daisy closely resembles species of *Grindelia* and probably should be included in that classification.

WOOLLY PAPER-FLOWER (Worthington)

PLAINS PAPER-FLOWER

WOOLLY PAPER-FLOWER (*Psilostrophe tagetina*)
Sunflower Family (Asteraceae)

Bloom Period: February–October

Description: Low, densely white-hairy perennial herb 4–20 in. (1–5 dm) high; stems several from base, much-branched and forming clump. **Flower** head to 1¼ in. (32 mm) across; ray flowers 3–5, yellow; disk flowers 6–12, yellow. Heads generally numerous, in dense or loose clusters on leafless stems. **Leaves** to 4 in. (1 dm) long in basal portion of plant, stalked, sometimes lobed, densely to slightly white-hairy or woolly; upper leaves smaller, stalkless, greener.

Habitat: Various soils in plains, rangelands, along hillsides and slopes. In PH, EP, ST, FW.

Note: This is the largest-flowered paper-flower in the state. The blooms remain on the plant for months, eventually turning brownish or whitish and papery, and are much used in winter bouquets. Woolly paper-flower makes an excellent border or specimen plant. It is poisonous to livestock, but is usually not eaten unless all other forage is exhausted.

PLAINS PAPER-FLOWER (*Psilostrophe villosa*)
Sunflower Family (Asteraceae)

Bloom Period: March–October

Description: Low, upright or somewhat sprawling, densely hairy perennial herb 4–24 in. (1–6 dm) high; stems usually several, forming clumps, branched in upper portion. **Flower** head about ⁵⁄₁₆–½ in. (8–13 mm) across; ray flowers 3–4, about as broad as long, yellow, 3-lobed at tip; disk flowers usually 6–8, yellow. Heads several, closely congested in small terminal clusters. **Leaves** 2–4 in. (5–10 cm) long, alternate, short-stalked, entire or 3- to 5-lobed; upper leaves smaller, stalkless, rarely lobed.

Habitat: Usually in gyp soils, most commonly on plains, but occasionally in pastures, on hillsides, slopes and brushlands. In all except NE, SE, NC, SC.

Note: The dense, woolly coating of soft hairs covering the herbage enables this plant to survive during extremely dry conditions by reducing moisture loss due to evaporation. As with the woolly paper-flower, the ray flowers of this species remain for a long period, becoming papery and somewhat folded downward in age. The plants are reportedly quite toxic to livestock.

ANDELION

TEXAS DANDELION (*Pyrrhopappus multicaulis*)
Sunflower Family (Asteraceae)

Bloom Period: February–June

Description: Upright, smooth annual 8–20 in. (2–5 dm) high; stems solitary or several from base, widely and erratically branching. Plant contains milky sap. **Flower** heads 1⅝–2 in. (41–50 mm) across, terminal, solitary or few on short stalks; ray flowers many, in 2 or 3 rows, lemon-yellow; disk flowers absent. Flowers open in morning and close about noon. **Leaves** 2–6 in. (5–15 cm) long, alternate, stalked, mostly in basal rosette, the blade usually deeply lobed, occasionally merely toothed. Upper leaves few, much smaller, with 2 or 3 lobes on each side, or sometimes narrow and entire.

Habitat: Dry clay or sandy loams of abandoned areas, lawns, pastures, cultivated fields and, especially, prairies. In all except NE, SE, FW.

Note: The numerous narrow fruits of Texas dandelion are tipped with a spreading tuft of feathery bristles which acts as a parachute in the wind, scattering the seeds far and wide. The young leaves are sometimes used as a potherb, but often must be parboiled in order to eliminate their bitter taste. Very young leaves can be mixed with other salad greens. Also called *false dandelion* and *pata de Leon*.

MEXICAN HAT (*Ratibida columnaris*)
Sunflower Family (Asteraceae)

Bloom Period: March–November

Description: Upright or somewhat sprawling perennial to 2½ ft. (7.5 dm), from woody root; stems solitary or several from base, grooved, usually much-branched in upper portion. **Flower** head solitary, terminal on long, slender branches; ray flowers 4–10, solid yellow, solid reddish-brown, or more commonly velvety reddish-brown in basal portion and yellow in tip portion, drooping; disk flowers green or brown, congested in conspicuously elongated cone. **Leaves** 2–4 in. (5–10 cm) long, 1–2 in. (2.5–5 cm) wide, alternate, the blade deeply divided into 5–13 narrow segments, the segments entire or again lobed or divided.

Habitat: Almost all soils and habitats. Throughout.

Note: Mexican hat is one of our most common wildflowers and will often be seen in large masses extending for many miles along roadways, or covering large areas in ungrazed fields or prairies. A few plants are most attractive in garden plantings, and the flowers last for several days when cut.

BROWN-EYED SUSAN

BROWN-EYED SUSAN (*Rudbeckia hirta* var. *angustifolia*)
Sunflower Family (Asteraceae)

Bloom Period: May–November

Description: Stiffly upright to somewhat sprawling, coarse, bristly-hairy annual or short-lived perennial 1–3 ft. (3–9 dm) high; stems solitary or several, usually branched at or near the middle, forming a clump or mound. **Flower** head 2–3 in. (50–76 mm) across, solitary, terminal on long, slender stem; ray flowers 8–20, solid yellow or brown in basal portion and yellow in tip portion, usually wide-spreading; disk flowers velvety chocolate-brown, numerous, forming small, flattish cone. **Leaves** 2–7¼ in. (5–18 cm) long, ⅜–3¼ in. (1–8.3 cm) wide, alternate, short-stalked or stalkless, occurring mostly in lower portion of plant, the blade entire or occasionally somewhat toothed.

Habitat: Various soils, especially sandy ones, in prairies, fields, pastures, open woodlands and borders. In all except FW.

Note: This easily grown, very attractive wildflower should be used more in cultivation. The flowers last for several days when cut. The Cherokee used juice from the roots for earache. A tea from the dried leaves and flowers makes a pleasant drink and tonic. The plant may be used for dyeing, producing greenish and yellowish colors.

TEXAS SQUAW-WEED (*Senecio ampullaceus*)
Sunflower Family (Asteraceae)

Bloom Period: February–April

Description: Upright, slender annual 1–3 ft. (3–9 dm) high; stem solitary, branching in upper portion, woolly with soft, whitish hairs when young, becoming smooth and shiny in age. **Flower** heads to 1¼ in. (32 mm) across; ray flowers usually 8, bright yellow; disk flowers yellow. Heads few in clusters, each cluster at end of stem with all stems about same height and forming a rather flat-topped mass sometimes 1 ft. (3 dm) across. **Leaves** to 4 in. (1 dm) long in lower portion of plant, becoming progressively smaller toward upper portion, alternate, the blade clasping stem at base, entire or coarsely toothed along margins but never divided.

Habitat: Deep, sandy soils in abandoned areas, old fields and heavily grazed pastures. In all except PH, FW.

Note: Texas squaw-weed is an endemic, but where found is one of the most abundant plants of sandy soils and may form almost solid stands for miles in pastures or old fields. It is a most attractive and showy plant. This *Senecio* differs from all the others in having entire leaves. Other common names include *ragwort, clasping-leaf groundsel* and *Texas groundsel*.

BUTTERWEED

SIMPSON ROSINWEED

BUTTERWEED (*Senecio glabellus*)
Sunflower Family (Asteraceae)

Bloom Period: March–May

Description: Upright, smooth, succulent annual 18–20 in. (45–50 cm) high; stems solitary or occasionally few, hollow, rather stout, unbranched or branched in upper portion. **Flower** head about ¾ in. (2 cm) across; ray flowers 10–14, yellow; disk flowers numerous, yellow. Heads solitary on short stalks, numerous and forming large terminal cluster. **Leaves** to 4 in. (10 cm) long, ¾–2¾ in. (2–7 cm) wide, alternate, stalked, the blade deeply divided into numerous, somewhat rounded segments or lobes with the end or tip segment of lower leaves much larger than others and often wider than long. Leaves gradually become smaller toward upper portion of plant.

Habitat: Clay or heavy loams in disturbed areas, prairies and especially stream bottoms and open floodplains. In NE, SE, NC, SC, PH.

Note: Butterweed usually forms large colonies and will often cover several acres with an almost solid mass of gold in early spring. These plants are easily cultivated and under normal growing conditions will make robust specimens with large showy flower clusters lasting for several weeks. A pale yellow dye may be obtained from the flowers.

SIMPSON ROSINWEED (*Silphium simpsonii* var. *wrightii*)
Sunflower Family (Asteraceae)

Bloom Period: June–July

Description: Upright, stout, coarse, rough-hairy perennial to 4 ft. (12 dm); stems solitary or few from tough base, usually sparingly branched in upper portion. **Flower** head to 3 in. (76 mm) across; ray flowers 16–20, yellow; disk flowers numerous, yellow. Heads solitary, few, terminal at ends of leafless branches of irregular lengths and in no particular pattern. **Leaves** to 6 in. (15 cm) long, coarse-textured and rough to the touch; lower leaves opposite, usually coarsely toothed; upper leaves becoming alternate, fewer, smaller, entire.

Habitat: Sandy, gravelly or clayey soils of prairies and openings and edges of woodlands. In NE, SE, SC.

Note: The common name of this plant derives from the sticky sap secreted along the stems and leaves. This resinous material was formerly used medicinally by Indians. Both Indians and the children of early settlers used the resin as a chewing gum.

TALL GOLDENROD (Myers)

SQUARE-BUD DAISY (*Tetragonotheca texana*)
Sunflower Family (Asteraceae)

Bloom Period: May–September

Description: Upright to sprawling perennial herb 12–24 in. (3–6 dm) high from enlarged, soft-woody taproot; stems solitary or few, leafy. **Flower** head 2 in. (5 cm) or more across; ray flowers about 10, yellow, narrow, with 5 lines on lower surface; disk flowers numerous, yellow or brown. Heads solitary and terminal on long, slender, leafless stalks. Buds surrounded by 4 large, broad, leaflike bracts which form a conspicuous square, and which later spread flat and surround head. **Leaves** 1⅛–4 in. (3–10 cm) long, opposite, stalkless; upper leaves deeply cut, wavy or coarsely and bluntly toothed; each pair basally united around stem.

Habitat: Sandy or rocky calcareous soils in plains, brushlands, chaparral, along rocky hillsides, slopes and cuestas. In NC, EP, FW.

Note: The square buds of this genus make it easy to identify in the field. *Tetragonotheca* means "four-cornered case" and refers to the bracts covering the bud. These hardy plants do well in cultivation and should be started from root divisions. Other common names include *ragged-daisy* and *nerve-ray*, the latter from the distinct lines on the undersides of the ray flowers.

BURRIDGE GREEN-THREAD (*Thelesperma burridgeanum*)
Sunflower Family (Asteraceae)

Bloom Period: April–June

Description: Upright or sprawling, smooth annual 12–28 in. (3–7 dm) high; stems solitary or several from base, branching in upper portion. **Flower** head to 1½ in. (3.8 cm) across; ray flowers several, purple-brown, with narrow yellow-orange band at tip; disk flowers several, purple-brown. Heads solitary on long stalks, usually with several on plant flowering at one time. **Leaves** 2–6 in. (5–15 cm) long, opposite, the blade deeply and finely divided into threadlike segments. Leaves mostly crowded in basal portion of plant but never forming basal rosette.

Habitat: Sandy soils in rangelands, chaparral, open areas, and edges and openings in woodlands. In ST.

Note: This is a rather tall, coreopsis-like plant, well-suited to use in wildflower plantings. It is sold in nursery catalogues under the name *Cosmidium burridgeanum*. The flowers yield a greenish or yellowish dye.

THELESPERMA (Wesby)

THELESPERMA (*Thelesperma filifolium*)
Sunflower Family (Asteraceae)

Bloom Period: February–December

Description: Upright, smooth, slender annual or short-lived perennial 8–30 in. (20–76 cm) high; stem solitary, usually branched at base, then branching again in upper portion. **Flower** head about 1½ in. (38 mm) across, terminal on slender, delicate, leafless stalks; ray flowers usually 8, yellow or sometimes with red-brown at base, 3-lobed at tip; disk flowers numerous, yellow, purplish or brown. Heads nodding in bud. **Leaves** 1½–4 in. (3.8–10 cm) long, opposite, the blade 1–3 times divided into very narrow or threadlike segments.

Habitat: Dry, sandy, clay or calcareous soils in prairies, plains, on hills and slopes, and on shell or sand beaches. In all except NE, SE, ST.

Note: In moist years, thelesperma thickly covers extensive areas with golden-yellow. The bloom period is often short in some areas, due to an insect larva which consumes the buds. Other common names are *green-thread*, in reference to the finely cut leaves, and *black-eyed Susans*, a name more commonly applied to *Rudbeckia hirta*. Thelesperma performs well in the wildflower garden, but does not make a good cut flower, as the ray flowers drop quickly.

RAYLESS GREEN-THREAD (*Thelesperma megapotamicum*)
Sunflower Family (Asteraceae)

Bloom Period: April–October

Description: Upright, smooth perennial herb to 3 ft. (1 m); stems several from base, slender, branched. **Flower** head to ⁵⁄₁₆ in. (8 mm) high; ray flowers absent; disk flowers numerous, yellowish to yellowish-brown, turning darker with age. Heads solitary at ends of branches, the branches leafless for some distance below head. **Leaves** 1–3 in. (25–76 mm) long, opposite, mostly confined to lower portion of plant, commonly twice divided into threadlike segments; upper leaves generally undivided.

Habitat: Dry calcareous or alkaline soils in lowlands, on plains, mesas, hillsides and mountain slopes. In all except NE, SE, SC, ST.

Note: The Hopi Indians of Arizona made a tea from the dried, young leaves of this plant and also made a reddish-brown dye which was used for baskets and cloth. Most likely the plant was formerly used in a similar manner by Indian tribes of western Texas. Reportedly, a strong decoction can be taken to reduce fever, and irritated or chafed skin may be bathed with a weak solution for soothing relief.

GOATSBEARD (Wesby)

GOLDEN CROWNBEARD

GOATSBEARD (*Tragopogon dubius*)
Sunflower Family (Asteraceae)

Bloom Period: May–July

Description: Low, coarse, widely spreading biennial herb 12–32 in. (3–8 dm) high from deep roots; stems hollow, usually several from near base, forming bushy clump, sparingly branched in upper portion, the branches upright. Plant contains milky sap. **Flower** head 1½–2 in. (38–50 mm) across; ray flowers 100–200 per head, lemon-yellow; disk flowers absent. Heads solitary, terminal at end of almost leafless stalk, subtended by about 13 very narrow bracts longer than flowers. **Leaves** 5–6 in. (12.5–15 cm) long, alternate, bluish-green, clasping stem at base.

Habitat: Almost all soils in disturbed sites, abandoned areas, edges of fields and cultivated areas. In PH, EP, FW.

Note: An introduced species from Europe, goatsbeard is now widely established and has become a common "weed" in many areas. Perhaps more familiar than the flower is the fruit, which is a round, feathery ball of silvery-bristled seeds, when fully mature. The stems of this plant are tough and very difficult to break.

GOLDEN CROWNBEARD (*Verbesina encelioides*)
Sunflower Family (Asteraceae)

Bloom Period: February–December

Description: Upright to sprawling annual to 3 ft. (1 m), with blue-green foliage; stem solitary or branching from base, branching in upper portion. **Flower** head to 2 in. (5 cm) across, solitary, terminal on long, slender stalks; ray flowers usually 12, yellow, deeply 3-toothed at tip; disk flowers numerous, yellow. **Leaves** 2⅜–4 in. (6–10 cm) long, the lower leaves mostly opposite; upper leaves alternate; blade thick, prominently veined underneath, the basal portion with large, toothed appendages or lobes on each side; margins coarsely toothed.

Habitat: Sandy soils in prairies, abandoned fields, openings and especially disturbed areas and barnyards. In all except eastern portion of PH.

Note: The entire plant has an unpleasant odor when crushed or even touched. Reportedly, Indians and early settlers used some portions of the plant in treating boils, skin diseases, and spider bites. Another common name is *cow-pen daisy*.

DWARF CROWNBEARD

(Young)

DWARF CROWNBEARD (*Verbesina nana*)
Sunflower Family (Asteraceae)

Bloom Period: June–October

Description: Low, upright or sprawling hairy perennial 4–8 in. (1–2 dm) high; stems solitary or few, much-branched with the branches often lying on ground. Plants spread from underground roots. **Flower** head to 1¾ in. (45 mm) across, solitary at ends of branches; ray flowers orangish, usually less than ⅜ in. (1 cm) long, deeply 3-lobed at tip; disk flowers dark orangish or brownish. **Leaves** usually 1⅛–2 in. (3–5 cm) long, almost half as broad, mostly opposite, soft-hairy, narrowed at base; margins toothed near base.

Habitat: Sandy, gravelly or primarily calcareous soils in fields, deserts or plains. In PH, FW.

Note: The species name comes from the Latin word *nanus*, meaning "dwarf," and the plants are so called because of their low growth habit. Dwarf crownbeard is grazed by cattle and not often seen on rangeland.

GOLDEN-EYE (*Viguiera dentata*)
Sunflower Family (Asteraceae)

Bloom Period: October–November

Description: Upright, stout perennial herb 3–6 ft. (1–2 m) high; stem much-branched, the branches slender, widely spreading. **Flower** head ⅞–1½ in. (22–38 mm) across; ray flowers 10–12, yellow, toothed at tip; disk flowers numerous, yellow. Heads solitary, terminal on long, slender, leafless stalks. **Leaves** 1⅜–5 in. (35–125 mm) long, to 3 in. (76 mm) wide, opposite in lower portion of plant, alternate in upper portion, stalked, the blade tapering at base, pointed in tip portion; margins finely or sharply and coarsely toothed.

Habitat: Dry, calcareous soils in fields, canyons, edges and openings of woodlands, and on hillsides and slopes. In NC, EP, FW.

Note: Golden-eye is a sunflower-like plant with a somewhat musky odor. It is a very attractive plant and does well in wildflower gardens when used toward the back of a border or in accent clumps. Sow seed in either fall or early spring.

HAIRY WEDELIA (Miller)

SLEEPY-DAISY (Miller)

HAIRY WEDELIA (*Wedelia hispida*)
Sunflower Family (Asteraceae)

Bloom Period: March–November

Description: Upright or spreading, rough-hairy perennial 20–40 in. (5–10 dm) high; stems usually solitary, rather stiff, woody at base, much-branched. Plants somewhat shrublike. **Flower** head to 1⅛ in. (3 cm) across, solitary, terminal on long, slender, almost leafless stalk; ray flowers 7–15, yellowish-orange, broad, spreading flat; disk flowers several, yellow or orange. **Leaves** 2–3 in. (5–7.6 cm) long, mostly opposite, stalkless or nearly so, rough with bristly hairs; margins coarsely toothed.

Habitat: Dry gravelly, rocky and especially calcareous soils, often shaded, of pastures, hillsides and slopes, brushlands or open woodlands. In CT, EP, ST.

Note: Hairy wedelia is one of the most common wildflowers in its area. Its flowers are very "orangy" in color, hence its other common name, *orange daisy*. Easily cultivated, it grows equally well in extremely dry or moist situations, and is a desirable addition to the garden. In its native range it is browsed by deer, sheep and goats.

SLEEPY-DAISY (*Xanthisma texanum*)
Sunflower Family (Asteraceae)

Bloom Period: April–November

Description: Rather stiffly upright, smooth annual herb 8–40 in. (2–10 dm) high; stem solitary, branching in upper portion with branches stiff and upright. **Flower** head to 1½ in. (3.8 cm) across, solitary at tips of slender stalks; ray flowers 18–22, lemon-yellow; disk flowers numerous, yellow. **Leaves** to 2½ in. (6.3 cm) long, narrow, alternate, stalkless, glossy-green; lower leaves toothed to deeply lobed; upper leaves smaller, not toothed.

Habitat: Dry, sandy soils in prairies, old fields, pastures, open rangelands and open woodlands. In NC, SC, CT, PH, EP.

Note: The common name is derived from the ray flowers' not opening until midmorning and then closing again by late afternoon. When the flowers are fully expanded they are very attractive, and this plant is widely used in cultivation. Seed should be sown in November or December in well-prepared soil.

COMMON BROOMWEED (Wenk)

SNAKEWEED (Cheatham)

COMMON BROOMWEED (*Xanthocephalum dracunculoides*)
Sunflower Family (Asteraceae)

Bloom Period: September–December

Description: Upright, smooth annual 4–48 in. (1–12 dm) high; stem solitary, much-branched in upper two-thirds; plant mound-like. **Flower** head ⅜–⅝ in. (1–1.6 cm) across; ray flowers 7–15, yellow; disk flowers 10–35, yellow. Heads solitary at ends of short branches, often a little crowded on plant. **Leaves** ¾–2 in. (2–5 cm) long, very narrow, alternate, dotted with small glands; upper leaves few and very short; younger leaves wider and longer.

Habitat: Sandy, clayey, gravelly or rocky soils in almost all habitats. In all except SE, EP, ST.

Note: Common broomweed is one of the predominant flowers of fall, often being quite conspicuous as it covers acres of overgrazed pasture or rangeland. At time of blooming almost all leaves have dropped from the plant, leaving the stalk and branches bare except for the flowers. The plants are toxic to livestock and may cause an inflammation of the eyes in both man and livestock. Early settlers gathered these plants, tied them to sticks and used them as brooms, hence the common name.

SNAKEWEED (*Xanthocephalum sarothrae*)
Sunflower Family (Asteraceae)

Bloom Period: August–November

Description: Upright, smooth, short-lived perennial 6–36 in. (15–90 cm) high from woody base; stem solitary, densely branched at base and in upper portion, the branches slender, brittle. Plant covered with resin-producing glands and somewhat sticky to the touch. **Flower** head ⅛–⅜ in. (3–10 mm) long; ray flowers 3–7, orange-yellow; disk flowers 2–6, very small, orange-yellow. Heads solitary or in small clusters at tips of branches, the whole forming large, rounded, terminal mass. **Leaves** ¼–2½ in. (6–63 mm) long, less than ⅛ in. (3 mm) wide, alternate, entire.

Habitat: Dry sand, clay or chalky soils in prairies, plains, deserts and cedar brushlands. In all except NE, SC, ST.

Note: Snakeweed is one of the most conspicuous fall-flowering plants, especially in rangelands, where it is a prevalent indicator of overgrazing. Other common names for this plant are *matchweed, matchbrush* and *kindling weed*, all referring to the highly flammable quality of the dried stalks, which were formerly much used in the starting of fires. This plant is also known as *yerba de vibora*, a Spanish common name meaning *viper's weed*.

PLAINS ZINNIA (Miller)

FRINGED PUCCOON

PLAINS ZINNIA (*Zinnia grandiflora*)
Sunflower Family (Asteraceae)

Bloom Period: June–October

Description: Low, upright, almost shrublike rough-hairy perennial 3⅛–8⅝ in. (8–22 cm) high; stems usually several from woody base, much-branched and forming rounded clump or mound. **Flower** head 1–1½ in. (25–38 mm) wide; ray flowers 3–6, broad, roundish, yellow; disk flowers 18–24, red or green, to ⅜ in. (1 cm) high. Flowers solitary, terminal on the stems and branches, not much extended above the foliage. **Leaves** to 1 in. (25 mm) long, very narrow, opposite, stalkless, 3-nerved from base for half of length or more.

Habitat: Dry, calcareous soils on plains, deserts, mesas and slopes. In PH, EP, FW.

Note: Plains zinnia is one of the showiest and most common wildflowers within its range. The flowering period is long, and these plants are excellent when used in rock gardens or as borders or massed plantings. The genus is named for Johann Zinn (1727–1759), a German professor of medicine who was known for his botanical work in Mexico.

FRINGED PUCCOON (*Lithospermum incisum*)
Borage Family (Boraginaceae)

Bloom Period: November–June

Description: Upright, hairy perennial to 12 in. (3 dm); stems 1 to several, rising from cluster of leaves at base, becoming branched in upper portion. **Flower** to 1½ in. (38 mm) long, yellow, tubular, 5-lobed at rim; lobes conspicuously fringed. Flowers numerous, in curled or coiled terminal spike which elongates and uncurls as flowers open. Fertile, unopening (cleistogamous) flowers are produced in late spring and early summer. **Leaves** to 4 in. (10 cm) long, less than ½ in. (13 mm) wide, in rosette at base of plant, usually dried and withered away by flowering time; stem leaves becoming reduced in size upward along stem.

Habitat: Generally sandy soils of pastures, prairies, openings and edges of wooded uplands. Throughout.

Note: The roots of the *Lithospermum*s yield a red dye that was much used by Indians and early settlers. It is used to some extent today in dying wool for weaving. Roots were used medicinally in various forms by both Eastern and Western Indians, and Western tribes supposedly ate the roots after cooking. Recent interest has been shown in this plant as a possible source for modern drugs.

USTARD

INDIA MUSTARD (*Brassica juncea*)
Mustard Family (Brassicaceae)

Bloom Period: April–June

Description: Upright, smooth annual herb to 3 ft. (1 m); stem usually solitary, widely branched in upper portion. Plant covered with whitish coating which comes off when rubbed. **Flowers** to 1 in. (25 mm) across; petals 4, yellow. Flowers numerous, in short, dense terminal spikes, opening from bottom upward. **Leaves** 1⅛–8 in. (3–20 cm) long, long-stalked, the blade deeply divided into irregular lobes with large terminal lobe; upper leaves smaller, entire to somewhat lobed.

Habitat: Almost all soils in abandoned areas, disturbed sites, edges of pastures, fields and cultivated croplands. In NC, SC, CT, EP.

Note: India mustard is a native of Eurasia that has escaped and now grows wild in North America. Sporadic but common, the plant often becomes a pest in cultivated areas and is usually considered a "weedy" species. Entire fields of many acres often become an almost solid sheet of yellow in early spring when the plants are in full flower. Also called *Chinese mustard* and *brown* or *leaf mustard*.

CHARLOCK (*Brassica kaber*)
Mustard Family (Brassicaceae)

Bloom Period: March–May

Description: Upright, rather stout, usually hairy annual herb 12–32 in. (3–8 dm) high; stems slender, branched in upper portion. **Flower** to ⅝ in. (16 mm) across; petals 4, yellow, spreading flat to form cross-shape. Flowers numerous, in short, dense, elongating, terminal, clusterlike spike. Fruit present in lower portion of spike while terminal buds still unopened. **Leaves** 1–6 in. (25–150 mm) long, ½–3⅛ in. (13–80 mm) wide, alternate; lower leaves stalked, the blade cut into several lobes with terminal lobe rounded, toothed, larger than side lobes; upper leaves stalkless, lobed, sharply toothed, or entire.

Habitat: Various soils in disturbed sites, abandoned areas and cultivated croplands. In NE, SE, SC, EP.

Note: Charlock is another of the mustards native to Eurasia, but now a naturalized escape. Like India mustard, it often forms large colonies and becomes a "pest" or "weed" in cultivated areas. Many of our food crops belong to this genus, including cabbage, cauliflower, broccoli, turnip, rutabaga and Brussels sprout.

163

MUSTARD

TANSY MUSTARD (*Descurainia pinnata*)
Mustard Family (Brassicaceae)

Bloom Period: February–April

Description: Upright, usually densely hairy annual to 32 in. (8 dm); stems solitary or several from base, usually branched. Plant with glandular hairs and sticky to the touch. **Flower** to 3/16 in. (5 mm) across, whitish to yellow; petals 4, narrowed at base, broader in tip portion. Flowers numerous, in rather flat-topped, elongating, terminal spikes (racemes). **Leaves** 3/4–43/4 in. (2–12 cm) long, alternate, blue-green, usually densely hairy. Lower leaves finely divided into numerous segments; upper leaves smaller and less parted.

Habitat: Sandy soils in abandoned areas, old fields and prairies. Throughout.

Note: Tansy mustard resembles true tansy (*Tanacetum vulgare*), a member of the sunflower family, having somewhat similar leaves. In Mexico, tansy mustard is used as a wild food source as well as a medicine. It is sold for treatment of chronic cough and is said to clear the lungs. American Indians reportedly roasted the seeds and added them to other foods.

PLAINS WALLFLOWER (*Erysimum asperum*)
Mustard Family (Brassicaceae)

Bloom Period: April–July

Description: Stiffly upright, hairy biennial or perennial herb 6–14 in. (15–35 cm) high; stem usually solitary, widely branching in upper portion. **Flower** to 2 in. (5 cm) across; petals 4, yellow to orange-red, very slender in basal portion. **Leaves** 1–5 in. (25–125 mm) long, very narrow, numerous, crowded along stem; margins entire to remotely toothed.

Habitat: Sandy or clay soils in prairies, plains, open woodlands, on hillsides and bluffs. In NC, PH, FW.

Note: Plains wallflower is one of the largest and showiest of the mustards. Traditionally, the dried plant was crushed, mixed with a small amount of water and the paste applied to the forehead and temples for relief of headache.

WESTERN WALLFLOWER

(Worthington)

FENDLER BLADDERPOD

(Tveten)

WESTERN WALLFLOWER (*Erysimum capitatum*)
Mustard Family (Brassicaceae)

Bloom Period: March–July

Description: Upright, coarse, densely hairy biennial or perennial herb 16–40 in. (4–10 dm) high; stem solitary, branched in upper portion. **Flower** to 1 in. (25 mm) across; petals 4, spreading flat, yellow to orange-red or brownish. Flowers numerous, short-stalked, densely crowded in elongating terminal cluster. **Leaves** 1–5 in. (25–125 mm) long, alternate, clustered at base and scattered along stem; margins entire to finely toothed.

Habitat: Dry sandy or rocky soils on open flats, along rock outcrops, banks, slopes, dry stream beds, hillsides and wooded mountain slopes. In all except NE, SE, CT, ST.

Note: Western wallflower is extremely variable in size and flower color. It is very similar to the cultivated wallflower (*Cheiranthus* spp.) and is equally showy in a wildflower garden, often forming low mounds of solid color when in full bloom. Closely related to plains wallflower, this species differs in having upright, instead of widely spreading, seedpods.

FENDLER BLADDERPOD (*Lesquerella fendleri*)
Mustard Family (Brassicaceae)

Bloom Period: March–June

Description: Low, upright or flatly sprawling, hairy perennial herb 1–16 in. (2.5–40 cm) high; stems usually several, forming tufts or clumps, sometimes branched. Plant appears silvery-gray. **Flower** to 1 in. (2.5 cm) across, bright yellow, stalked; petals 4, widely spreading. Flowers numerous, loosely arranged in elongating terminal spike. The small, round fruiting pods stand erect, becoming mature in basal portion of spike while flowers continue opening in tip portion. **Leaves** to 4 in. (10 cm) long, to ½ in. (13 mm) wide, alternate, stalked, thin; margins entire to coarsely toothed.

Habitat: Dry sandy or rocky, especially calcareous, soils in arid plains, grasslands and deserts. In PH, EP, FW.

Note: Fendler bladderpod is one of the first wildflowers to bloom in the spring, and its spikes of gold are most showy against the barren areas where it usually occurs. The common names of bladderpod and *popweed* are given this plant because the inflated ball-like fruits will pop loudly when stepped on or crushed.

CLOTH-OF-GOLD

CLOTH-OF-GOLD (*Lesquerella gracilis*)
Mustard Family (Brassicaceae)

Bloom Period: March–May

Description: Upright or sprawling, hairy annual to 20 in. (5 dm); stems several, usually branched; younger portions of plant gray-colored with appressed hairs, older portion sparsely hairy and green. **Flower** about ¾ in. (2 cm) across; petals 4, yellow, sometimes streaked with orange near base. Flowers numerous, stalked, forming short, dense elongating terminal spike. Fruit stalks straight, upright. **Leaves** ⅜–2 in. (1–5 cm) long, alternate, stalkless, commonly coarsely toothed.

Habitat: Sandy but mostly calcareous clay soils in prairies, plains, disturbed areas, pastures, edges of fields and woodlands. In all except FW.

Note: Cloth-of-gold is a most descriptive name for this plant, for often it forms solid sheets of golden yellow across large open areas in earliest spring. The small, roundish, ball-like fruit is eaten by larvae of the falcate orangetip butterfly.

TEXAS SELENIA (*Selenia dissecta*)
Mustard Family (Brassicaceae)

Bloom Period: February–June

Description: Low, upright, smooth, winter annual from well-developed root; flowering stem very short, mostly hardly above the leaves. **Flower** about 1 in. (2.5 cm) across, fragrant, solitary or few at top of stalk; petals 4, yellow, often striped with green near base, spreading flat. Flowers usually numerous and forming a mound hardly exceeding foliage. **Leaves** to 4 in. (1 dm) long, from root, stalked; blade deeply lobed, the lobes narrow, opposite.

Habitat: Deep, moist, sandy soils in low areas and edges of playa lakes. In FW.

Note: Where garden conditions are favorable, this plant is attractive used as an edging. The large, flat seedpods stand erect and add interest to the plant after the flowers have withered.

JONES SELENIA (Mahler)

BROOM WHITLOW-WORT (Darby)

JONES SELENIA (*Selenia jonesii*)
Mustard Family (Brassicaceae)

Bloom Period: March–April

Description: Low, sprawling, smooth winter annual; stem branching at base, the branches leafy, lying on ground, to 12 in. (3 dm) long. **Flower** about ½ in. (13 mm) across, yellow, fragrant; petals 4. Flowers several on stems in loose, terminal, leafy-bracted spikelike raceme from upper leaf axils or few from center of plant. **Leaves** to 4 in. (1 dm) long, mostly basal, alternate, stalked, the blade divided into small lobes or segments.

Habitat: Moist sandy, gravelly or calcareous soils in depressions, swales and buffalo wallows on prairies and plateaus. In PH, EP.

Note: Jones selenia is limited to portions of west Texas, but is often found in large masses and is quite showy. The genus name is derived from the Greek word *selene* for "the moon," and refers to the strongly winged, flattened and somewhat moon-shaped seeds.

BROOM WHITLOW-WORT (*Paronychia virginica* var. *scoparia*)
Pink Family (Caryophyllaceae)

Bloom Period: July–November

Description: Upright to sprawling, stiff, wiry perennial to 16 in. (4 dm); stems numerous from base, forming tufts or mats, branching from near base. Plant turns yellowish or yellowish-brown in age. **Flower** about ⅛ in. (3 mm) long, yellowish to brown; petals absent; sepals 5, petallike, united at base, appearing deeply 5-lobed; lobes narrow, 3-ribbed, sharply pointed at tip. **Leaves** ⅝–1 in. (16–25 mm) long, almost threadlike in width, opposite, erect, 2-grooved beneath. Leaves subtended by long-tapering, silvery, leaflike bracts.

Habitat: Dry gravelly or rocky soils on rock outcrops, hillsides and slopes. In NC, PH, EP.

Note: The "scaly" or "scruffy" appearing plants of this genus were once used in the treatment of a disease known as "whitlow," which affected the fingernails, causing them to look scaly. It was once believed that a plant or any part of a plant which resembled a part of the body was to be used in the treatment of an illness in that particular body part. This early practice of medicine was called the "doctrine of signatures."

YELLOW STONECROP (Cheatham)

YELLOW STONECROP (*Sedum nuttallianum*)
Orpine Family (Crassulaceae)

Bloom Period: April–July

Description: Low, smooth, succulent annual 2–3⅛ in. (5–8 cm) high; stem solitary, usually branching at base, forking in upper portion with horizontal flowering branches. **Flower** to ⁵⁄₁₆ in. (8 mm) across, bright yellow, solitary; petals 5, pointed at tip. Flowers numerous, in leaf axils along upper side of flowering branches. **Leaves** ¼–½ in. (6–13 mm) long, alternate, stalkless, numerous, thick, pale green, entire.

Habitat: Deep sandy or clay soils, but especially limestone, sandstone and granite, of pastures, prairies, hillsides and slopes. In NE, SE, EP.

Note: Many cultivated plants belong to this family, most of them having thick, succulent leaves. Yellow stonecrop is an excellent plant for the wildflower garden when used as a cover plant or scattered between rocks or stones. The genus name is from the Latin *sedere*, meaning "to sit," and is so called because of its low growth and its habit of sprawling over and among rocks.

BUFFALO GOURD (*Cucurbita foetidissima*)
Gourd Family (Cucurbitaceae)

Bloom Period: May–August

Description: Large, coarse, rough-hairy, trailing or widely spreading perennial vine from huge tuberous root; stems solitary to several, to 18 ft. (6 m) or more long. Herbage has most unpleasant odor when disturbed. **Flower** 2⅜–4 in. (6–10 cm) long, yellow to orange, bell-shaped, 5-lobed at rim, the lobes recurved at tips. Male and female flowers separate but on same plant, the female flowers pleasantly scented. Flowers solitary, stalked, from axils of leaves. **Leaves** to 12 in. (3 dm) long, alternate, coarse, thick, grayish-green, rounded or lobed at base, strongly veined on lower surface, rough to the touch.

Habitat: Sandy or gravelly soils in disturbed areas, rangelands, chaparral, along railroad embankments, stream banks and fencerows. In all except NE, SE.

Note: Buffalo gourd is a rank and rampant vine that often covers surrounding vegetation or supports such as fences, wood or junk piles. The fruit is a small gourd which reportedly was boiled and eaten by Indians. The crushed roots were used in washing clothes. The buffalo gourd is related to several cultivated crops, including bottle gourds, luffas, muskmelons, watermelons, pumpkins, squashes and cucumbers.

PLAINS WILD INDIGO

GREEN WILD INDIGO   (D. Williams)

PLAINS WILD INDIGO (*Baptisia leucophaea*)
Legume Family (Fabaceae)

Bloom Period: March–April

Description: Upright, smooth perennial to 30 in. (7.5 dm); stem solitary, much-branched and forming low, bushy mound. **Flower** to ¾ in. (2 cm) long, creamy to dark yellow; petals 5, upper petal wide-spreading, notched at tip. Flowers numerous, in long horizontal or curved raceme near base of plant, sometimes lying on ground; each flower subtended by large, leaflike bract. **Leaves** alternate, short-stalked, the blade divided into 3 leaflets with each leaflet 1⅛–4 in. (3–10 cm) long. Two large stipules at base of leaves very leaflike and the whole appearing as 5 leaflets.

Habitat: Sandy soils in prairies, pastures and open woodlands. In all except EP, ST, FW.

Note: Late in the summer the entire plant turns blackish or silver-gray, breaks off at ground level and tumbles about in the wind. Roots of this plant were formerly used as toothbrushes. They can also be boiled to produce a blue dye for fabric or woolen yarn. A stimulant and astringent decoction can be made from the leaves and branches.

GREEN WILD INDIGO (*Baptisia sphaerocarpa*)
Legume Family (Fabaceae)

Bloom Period: April–May

Description: Upright, stout, tough, usually smooth perennial to 3 ft. (1 m), often lower; stems solitary or several, bushy-branched in upper portion. **Flower** to 1 in. (25 mm) long, dark yellow or light orange, short-stalked; petals 5, the upper petal or banner wide-spreading. Flowers 15–20, in slender, upright, terminal or axillary racemes. **Leaves** alternate, firm, bluish-green, the blade divided into 3 leaflets, each leaflet to 3½ in. (89 mm) long; upper leaves often reduced to 1 or 2 leaflets.

Habitat: Loamy, sandy or silty soils in prairies, pastures and edges of woodlands. In NE, SE, NC, SC.

Note: Green wild indigo is a common plant of the prairies, the slender spikes of golden yellow flowers very conspicuous above the blue-green foliage. After frost, the plant turns a dark gray or silvery color, breaks off at ground level and becomes a "tumbleweed," blowing about in the wind. The spikes of large, woody, globelike fruits are often used in dried arrangements.

JAMES RUSH-PEA

PARTRIDGE PEA

JAMES RUSH-PEA (*Caesalpinia jamesii*)
Legume Family (Fabaceae)

Bloom Period: May–September

Description: Upright or widely sprawling, sticky-hairy herbaceous perennial 8–16 in. (2–4 dm) high from long, woody, spindle-shaped root; stems usually several from base, somewhat woody in lower portion. Plants, especially leaves, have orange glands scattered over surface. **Flower** ½ in. (13 mm) or more across, yellow; petals 5, with glands on outer surface, the uppermost larger, somewhat cupped, marked with red at base; stamens 10, red. Flowers 5–15, in loose terminal spikes. **Leaves** alternate, blue-green, the blade twice divided into segments, the ultimate divisions 5–10 pairs, to ³⁄₁₆ in. (5 mm) long, hairy and with glands on lower surface.

Habitat: Dry, loose, sandy, gravelly or alluvial soils of plains, grasslands, mesas and dunes. In NC, PH, EP, FW.

Note: A related species is the lovely yellow-flowered bird of paradise (*C. gilliesii*), a wild shrub of the Southwest that is often cultivated throughout the state. It is a much larger plant and has larger flowers. The genus is sometimes included in the genus *Hoffmanseggia*.

PARTRIDGE PEA (*Cassia fasciculata*)
Legume Family (Fabaceae)

Bloom Period: June–October

Description: Upright, smooth annual 1–5 ft. (3–15 dm) high; stem usually slender and unbranched in dense stands, but much-branched when not crowded. **Flower** to 1½ in. (38 mm) across, petals 5, bright yellow, unequal in size; upper 3 petals red-spotted at base, lower petal prominently cupped; the other petal broad, spreading flat. Flowers in short cluster from leaf axil, with only 1 flower opening at a time, so appearing solitary. Flowers usually wither by midday. **Leaves** alternate, divided into 8–15 opposite pairs of small leaflets. Foliage somewhat sensitive, partially closing when touched.

Habitat: Mainly sandy soils in old fields, pastures and open woodlands. In all except PH, EP, ST, FW.

Note: Partridge pea produces a nectar in small orange glands at the base of each leaf. Ants seeking this nectar often form a continuous trail along the stem. The adult common sulfur butterfly lays its eggs on the leaves, and the larvae use the leaves as a food source. The plant's flat brown seeds are an important food for many game and song birds.

LINDHEIMER SENNA (Cheatham)

TWO-LEAVED SENNA (Wilbanks)

LINDHEIMER SENNA (*Cassia lindheimeriana*)
Legume Family (Fabaceae)

Bloom Period: June–October

Description: Upright, velvety-hairy, bushy perennial herb 3–6 ft. (1–2 m) high from woody root; stems 1 to several, branching in upper portion. **Flower** 1¼ in. (32 mm) or more across, yellow; petals 5, somewhat unequal, wide-spreading. Flowers few to several in spikelike racemes about as long as the leaves; racemes borne terminally and in upper leaf axils. **Leaves** alternate, spirally arranged around stem, the blade divided into 4–8 pairs of leaflets; each leaflet 1–2 in. (2.5–5 cm) long, ⅜–¾ in. (1–2 cm) wide, unequal at base, densely covered with shiny, silklike hairs.

Habitat: Dry, rocky limestone soils on hills, slopes or mesas. In EP, ST, FW.

Note: Plants of Lindheimer senna grow either singly or sparsely scattered, usually in small areas. It is very effective in the wildflower garden, especially when used as a background or specimen plant. As with many other sennas, this species is a strong laxative when taken internally, usually as a tea brewed from the dried leaves.

TWO-LEAVED SENNA (*Cassia roemeriana*)
Legume Family (Fabaceae)

Bloom Period: April–September

Description: Upright to somewhat sprawling perennial to 2 ft. (6 dm); stems several, rising from thick root. **Flower** 1⅛ in. (3 cm) or more across, yellow, usually marked with brown veins; petals 5, unequal in size, wide-spreading. Flowers short-stalked, in clusters of 2–6 from leaf axils in upper portion of plant. **Leaves** 1–2 in. (25–50 mm) long, alternate, long-stalked, uniquely divided into 2 leaflets, the leaflets having unequal sides.

Habitat: Poor, dry, limestone or clayey soils in fields, open woodlands, and on hillsides and slopes. In all except NE, SE, SC, ST.

Note: Easily grown from seed, this species makes a good perennial for the garden in areas where it grows naturally. The plant bears the name of Ferdinand Roemer, a German geologist and naturalist who collected specimens in the New Braunfels area, 1845–47. Sennas form a large group with many species being noted for medicinal uses.

GOLDEN DALEA (Darby)

DWARF DALEA (Cheatham)

GOLDEN DALEA (*Dalea aurea*)
Legume Family (Fabaceae)

Bloom Period: April–June

Description: Upright, clumped, silky-hairy perennial herb 12–20 in. (3–5 dm) high, from woody base; stems one to several, slender, leafy. **Flower** about ⅜ in. (1 cm) long, yellow, the 5 petals irregularly attached at base. Flowers numerous, in spike, opening few at a time, usually forming circle around spike. Spike thick, silky-gray with soft hairs, elongating as flowers open. **Leaves** ¾–2 in. (2–5 cm) long, stalked, divided into usually 5 leaflets, the leaflets 5/16–⅝ in. (8–15 mm) long, densely silky-hairy, dotted with glands containing a fragrant, volatile oil.

Habitat: Sandy or calcareous soils in prairies, openings and on hillsides and slopes. In all except NE, SE, SC.

Note: The *Daleas* are named for Samuel Dale, an 18th century English botanist. The flowers are cross-pollinated by bees seeking nectar. Foliage is rather sparse, perhaps enabling the plant to better withstand drought.

DWARF DALEA (*Dalea nana*)
Legume Family (Fabaceae)

Bloom Period: May–October

Description: Low, upright, sprawling or trailing, hairy perennial herb 4–16 in. (1–4 dm) high; stems solitary or several. Herbage covered with long, silky hairs. **Flower** to ¾ in. (2 cm) across, yellow fading rose-colored; petals 5, irregularly placed, narrowed in basal portion. Flowers numerous, densely congested in thick, conelike cluster, a few opening at a time and forming circle around cone. **Leaves** ¾–1⅛ in. (2–3 cm) long, alternate, short-stalked, dotted with small glands, the blade divided into 5–9 narrow leaflets.

Habitat: Various soils in prairies, plains, rangelands, chaparral and along rocky slopes. In all except NE, SE, SC.

Note: Dwarf dalea shows a preference for dry, almost desertlike places, where the yellow flowers make quite a show against the stark, barren soils. Several shrubby species of *Dalea* occur in the state, and these play host to the parasitic flowering plant *Pilostyles thurberi*. For most of the year this parasite remains under the bark of the shrub, then in early summer produces tiny yellowish-brown flowers which burst through the bark, are pollinated, then disappear, leaving the remainder of the plant again concealed beneath the bark.

RUSH-PEA

SWEET CLOVER

INDIAN RUSH-PEA (*Hoffmanseggia glauca*)
Legume Family (Fabaceae)

Bloom Period: March–September

Description: Upright, low, hairy perennial herb 4–12 in. (1–3 dm) high, from large tuberous roots; stems usually several. Plants with glandular hairs throughout and somewhat sticky to the touch. **Flower** to 1 in. (2.5 cm) across, bright yellow; petals 5, the uppermost dissimilar in shape, marked with orange spots and stripes. Flowers 5–15, in terminal spikes (racemes). **Leaves** alternate, divided into 5–11 primary leaf segments, these again divided into 4–11 pairs of smaller leaflets.

Habitat: Various soils in plains, deserts, rangelands, along open slopes, hillsides and bluffs. In all except NE, SE, SC.

Note: Indian rush-pea usually grows in scattered colonies. It forms large tubers about 6 inches underground which are sometimes used as food for hogs, thus giving it another common name, *hog-peanut*. These tubers were gathered, roasted and eaten by Western Indian tribes. A common Spanish name is *camote de ratón*, meaning "mouse's sweet potato." In irrigated croplands, this plant frequently becomes a troublesome "weed" because of its large, tenacious roots.

YELLOW SWEET CLOVER (*Melilotus officinalis*)
Legume Family (Fabaceae)

Bloom Period: May–October

Description: Upright, mostly smooth biennial 2–5 ft. (6–15 dm) high; stem solitary, open and loosely branched in upper portion. **Flower** to ¼ in. (6 mm) long, yellow; petals 5, the uppermost petal or banner partially folded forward. Flowers numerous and crowded in slender, spikelike raceme 2–6 in. (5–15 cm) long from leaf axils. **Leaves** alternate, stalked, the blade divided into 3 narrow leaflets with each leaflet ½–1 in. (13–25 mm) long; margins finely toothed.

Habitat: Almost all soils in abandoned areas, fields, open bottomlands or uplands. Throughout.

Note: Naturalized from Europe, yellow sweet clover is considered a "weedy" species in North America. It often grows in the same areas as white sweet clover (*M. albus*). Both plants are widely cultivated as cover crops to enrich the soil with nitrogen. The leaves of yellow sweet clover have the fragrance of vanilla when crushed or dried, and are often used in making sachets.

YELLOW-PUFF

RATTLEBUSH

YELLOW-PUFF (*Neptunia lutea*)
Legume Family (Fabaceae)

Bloom Period: April–October

Description: Trailing or sprawling vinelike perennial; stem much-branched, the branches elongating to 6 ft. (2 m) long. Plant covered with soft spines but not prickly or noxious to the touch. **Flower** minute, yellow, often fragrant; petals 5, united; stamens conspicuously exserted. Flowers 30–60, densely crowded in slightly elongated terminal cluster on long, slender stalk from leaf axils. **Leaves** alternate, stalked, the blade divided into 2–11 pairs of opposite segments, the segments again divided into 8–18 pairs of tiny leaflets. Leaflets conspicuously veined on lower surface.

Habitat: Various soils in pastures, prairies, openings in thickets and woodlands. In all except PH, EP.

Note: Leaves of this plant are sensitive; they close at night, during cloudy weather and especially when touched. Yellow-puff makes a most attractive ground cover and can be kept trimmed quite low if needed.

RATTLEBUSH (*Sesbania drummondii*)
Legume Family (Fabaceae)

Bloom Period: May–October

Description: Upright, robust, conspicuously dark green, herbaceous perennial 2–10 ft. (6–30 dm) high; stems solitary or few, from woody base, usually much-branched in upper portion, the branches thin, widely spreading. Plants die back to ground level each winter. **Flower** about ½ in. (1.3 cm) long, orange-yellow, often lined with red; petals 5, the upper petal or banner upright, longer than other petals. Flowers few to several, long-stalked, loosely clustered in elongated, drooping spike from leaf axils. **Leaves** 4–8 in. (1–2 dm) long, alternate, short-stalked, the blade once divided into 20–50 segments or leaflets; leaflets mostly ½–1¼ in. (1.3–3.2 cm) long, about ¼ in. (6 mm) wide.

Habitat: Moist or wet soils in swales, ditches, depressions, meadows, and along open edges of ponds, lakes and streams. In NE, SE, SC, ST.

Note: The fruit of rattlebush is a large, conspicuously four-sided pod containing several seeds that are reportedly toxic to livestock. When the pods becomes mature and dry, the seeds loosen inside and will rattle loudly if the plant is moved.

GOAT'S RUE

LOW HOP CLOVER

GOAT'S RUE (*Tephrosia virginiana*)
Legume Family (Fabaceae)

Bloom Period: April–June

Description: Stiffly upright perennial to 28 in. (7 dm), from long, tough root; stems woody at base, usually several and forming clump, seldom branched. Plant conspicuously covered with silvery, silky hairs throughout. **Flower** ½–¾ in. (1.3–2 cm) long; petals 5, the broad upper petal erect, lemon-yellow or cream-colored; the side and lower petals pink to rose, rarely white. Flowers numerous, congested in short, dense, terminal cluster to 3 in. (7.6 cm) long. **Leaves** 2–5½ in. (5–13.8 cm) long, alternate, short-stalked, the blade divided into 8–24 opposite leaflets with 1 terminal leaflet. Leaflets ½–1¼ in. (13–32 mm) long, ⅛–¼ in. (3–6 mm) wide, sharply pointed at tip.

Habitat: Sandy soils in plains, clearings and open pine or hardwood stands. In all except CT, EP, ST, FW.

Note: Roots of this plant contain rotenone, an insecticide and fish poison. In a weakened form, it was much used medicinally by Indians and early settlers. The strong, sinewy roots were boiled by the Cherokee and a weak tea was given to the children to make them strong and muscular. Also called *devil's shoestring* and *catgut*.

LOW HOP CLOVER (*Trifolium campestre*)
Legume Family (Fabaceae)

Bloom Period: May–September

Description: Upright or sprawling annual or biennial less than 2 ft. (6 dm) high; stem weak, much-branched. **Flower** to ¼ in. (6 mm) long, bright yellow; petals 5, the upper petal or banner noticeably longer than other petals and folded forward instead of in usual upright position. Flowers 20–40, congested in small, globelike or elongated head borne at end of long stalk, either terminal or from the leaf axils. Flowers turn brown upon aging and drying. **Leaves** alternate, subtended by leaflike bracts, the blade divided into 3 leaflets with each leaflet ¼–⅝ in. (6–16 mm) long, usually about twice as long as broad, pointed at tip.

Habitat: Sandy soils in lawns, abandoned areas, borders of fields and along woodland edges. In NE, SE, SC.

Note: A native of Europe, low hop clover is now established and widely distributed throughout the state. Although these plants are rather "weedy," they are good soil builders.

GOLDEN CORYDALIS (Worthington)

SOUTHERN CORYDALIS (Cheatham)

GOLDEN CORYDALIS (*Corydalis aurea*)
Fumitory Family (Fumariaceae)

Bloom Period: February–September

Description: Weakly upright to sprawling, smooth, soft, delicate winter annual or biennial to 24 in. (6 dm); stems few to several, few-branched. Plant covered with whitish coating easily removed when handled; contains watery juice. **Flower** ½–¾ in. (1.3–2 cm) long, pale to bright yellow; petals 4, the uppermost petal longest, arching in front, extending into saclike spur at base. Flowers 4–20, in loose, elongating spike, the spike usually shorter than foliage. **Leaves** 3–6 in. (7.6–15 cm) long, alternate; blade divided into 5–7 segments which are divided twice more, the ultimate segments very narrow, to 5 times as long as broad.

Habitat: Sandy or gravelly soils in prairies, plains, burned areas, gravel pits, flats along creeks, road cuts, hillsides, among rocky ledges or brushlands. In NC, PH, EP, FW.

Note: Plants of *Corydalis* are excellent when used in cultivation, the golden flowers providing early color against the delicate, finely cut foliage. Some members of this family are sold as cultivated ornamentals, including Dutchman's breeches and bleeding hearts. The plants are known to contain eight alkaloids and are reportedly toxic to livestock. Golden corydalis has been used in the treatment of arthritis. Also called *golden smoke* and *scrambled eggs*.

SOUTHERN CORYDALIS (*Corydalis micrantha*)
Fumitory Family (Fumariaceae)

Bloom Period: February–April

Description: Upright to sprawling or trailing, delicate winter annual to 24 in. (6 dm), often less than 12 in. (3 dm) high; stems solitary to several, containing bitter, watery juice. Herbage has whitish coating which comes off when rubbed. **Flower** to ⅝ in. (16 mm) long, pale yellow; petals 4, the uppermost petal longest, extending into saclike spur at base. Flowers 3–12, intermixed with short, leaflike bracts in an elongated spike (raceme). **Leaves** alternate, the blade divided into 5–7 segments which are divided twice more; ultimate segments to ⅝ in. (16 mm) long.

Habitat: Sandy or clay soils in disturbed areas, abandoned fields, prairies and open woodlands. In all except PH, FW.

Note: Southern corydalis can frequently be seen covering large areas, such as fall-plowed fields, with an almost solid sheet of yellow in early spring. In cultivation, it is most attractive if allowed to trail down a sunny slope or bank or a rock wall.

SPOTTED BEEBALM (Tveten)

FLOATING BLADDERWORT

SPOTTED BEEBALM (*Monarda punctata*)
Mint Family (Lamiaceae)

Bloom Period: May–August

Description: Upright, hairy perennial to 3 ft. (1 m), but usually much lower; stems 4-angled, solitary or few from base and forming clump, commonly branched in upper portion. **Flower** ¾–1 in. (20–25 mm) long, yellowish or rarely pinkish, spotted with dark maroon, hairy, tubular in basal portion, prominently 2-lipped; upper lip slender, unlobed, cupped forward; lower lip 3-lobed; stamens 2, arched beneath upper lip and not exserted. Flowers many, in whorls, forming dense, elongated spike at end of stem or from leaf axils. Each whorl subtended by large, conspicuous, whitish or yellowish purple-tinged leaflike bracts. **Leaves** ⅝–3¾ in.(16–95 mm) long, much varied in size, opposite, usually long-tapering into short stalk, pale green, shallowly toothed to entire.

Habitat: Dry, usually sandy or rocky soils in abandoned areas, pastures, openings and edges of woodlands. Throughout.

Note: Noticeably aromatic, spotted beebalm contains the antiseptic drug thymol. It is not grazed by cattle or browsed by wildlife and often forms extensive stands.

FLOATING BLADDERWORT (*Utricularia radiata*)
Bladderwort Family (Lentibulariaceae)

Bloom Period: March–July

Description: Free-floating, smooth, carnivorous aquatic perennial to 8 in. (2 dm); stem with 6–10 branches, the branches somewhat inflated and floating, whorled at tip of stem like spokes of wagon wheel, divided at tips into numerous threadlike segments; flower stalk upright, extending above water. **Flower** about ⅝ in. (1.6 cm) across, yellow, 2-lipped; upper lip broad, upright; lower lip 3-lobed, extending basally into curved spur and having large, conspicuous projection or hump on top almost closing throat; lower lobe with small spur at tip. Flowers 3 or 4, in terminal portion of leafless stalk. **Leaves** below water surface, alternate, delicate, repeatedly divided into numerous threadlike segments bearing small bladders.

Habitat: Aquatic, floating on water in ponds, ditches, lakes, marshes and baygalls. In NE, SE, SC.

Note: The small bladders along the threadlike leaves are equipped with sensitive hairs around the opening, and when microscopic organisms touch these "trigger" hairs, the bladder opens, sucking the prey inside. The plant then secretes certain enzymes which dissolve the organism into nutrients used by the plant.

OOT

-FLOWERED ONION

COLICROOT (*Aletris aurea*)
Lily Family (Liliaceae)

Bloom Period: May–July

Description: Stiffly upright, smooth perennial 1–3 ft. (3–9 dm) high; flowering stem unbranched. Plant contains bitter juice. **Flower** about ¼ in. (6 mm) long; petallike segments 6, orange-yellow, united at base into short tube, 6-lobed at tip; outer surface of tube wrinkled and roughened with small projections and feeling mealy to the touch. Flowers many, in very slender spikelike raceme at top of long, slender stalk. **Leaves** to 4¾ in. (12 cm) long, mostly in flat basal rosette; blade yellow-green, flat, thin, soft, pliable; leaves along stem much smaller, bractlike.

Habitat: Moist acid soils in pinelands, savannahs and edges of bogs. In SE.

Note: Colicroot is rather restricted in its range in Texas, but where it does occur, it often forms almost solid stands, and the spikes of oddly shaped yellow flowers are quite spectacular. The roots of this plant are very bitter, but have been used in making tonics for stomach ailments and as a stimulant. In Appalachia a mixture of the dried root and brandy or whisky is drunk as a treatment for rheumatism.

YELLOW-FLOWERED ONION (*Allium coryi*)
Lily Family (Liliaceae)

Bloom Period: April–May

Description: Upright, smooth perennial to 12 in. (3 dm); flowering stems unbranched, from bulb. **Flower** ¼–⅜ in. (6–9 mm) long or high, bright yellow sometimes tinged with red on outer surface, the 6 segments all petallike, rather wide-spreading. Flowers 10–25, long-stalked, in solitary cluster at top of long, slender stem. **Leaves** to 12 in. (3 dm) long, very narrow, 3 or 4, from bulb, green at time of flowering.

Habitat: Rocky, often limestone soils in plains or on hillsides and mountain slopes. In EP, FW.

Note: While this plant is endemic to Texas and found only in some western portions of the state, it often forms large colonies and adds spots of gold to the hills and slopes. The herbage of wild onions is often grazed by cows, causing the milk to be tainted with an onion or garlic flavor.

YELLOW SUNNY-BELL

STIFF-STEM FLAX

YELLOW SUNNY-BELL (*Schoenolirion croceum*)
Lily Family (Liliaceae)

Bloom Period: March–May

Description: Upright, slender, smooth perennial to 18 in. (45 cm), frequently lower; stems solitary or few, from bulblike base. **Flower** to ⅝ in. (16 mm) or more across, bright-yellow often tinged with red, the 6 segments all petallike, distinctively 3- to 5-veined, wide-spreading. Flowers numerous, stalked, in elongating terminal spikelike raceme. **Leaves** 1–16 in. (2.5–40 cm) long, to 3/16 in. (5 mm) wide, alternate, basal and rather tufted, grasslike, somewhat rigid, ribbed, flat.

Habitat: Wet, mostly acid soils in pinelands, savannahs, edges of bogs and on seepage slopes. In SE, SC.

Note: This low herb forms large colonies of somewhat thinly scattered plants but when in full flower makes an impressive display. The bloom period is rather brief, but the racemes of lovely golden stars are most attractive when used in small clumps in a wildflower planting where acid soils are available.

STIFF-STEM FLAX (*Linum rigidum* var. *berlandieri*)
Flax Family (Linaceae)

Bloom Period: February–September

Description: Stiffly upright, thin, smooth annual 8–20 in. (2–5 dm) high; stem solitary, branched in upper portion, the slender branches prominently angled or winged. **Flower** to 1½ in. (3.8 mm) across, yellow or copper-colored, often with dark reddish center; petals 5, cupped, swirled in bud, falling early. Flowers few, forming open terminal cluster. **Leaves** to 1¼ in. (32 mm) long, about ⅛ in. (3 mm) wide, alternate, stalkless, upright, rigid.

Habitat: Sandy, gravelly, clay-loam or chalky soils in prairies, pastures, and edges of woodlands. Throughout.

Note: *Linum* is Latin for "flax." The flax plants are important producers of fiber from which cloth, thread and cord are manufactured; oil is extracted from the seeds. The words *linen*, *linseed* and *lingerie* are all derived from the word *linum*.

PRAIRIE FLAX

YELLOW PRAIRIE FLAX (*Linum sulcatum*)
Flax Family (Linaceae)

Bloom Period: May–August

Description: Upright, smooth, slender, delicate annual 8–32 in. (2–8 dm) high; stem usually solitary, widely branched in upper portion, rigid, grooved, sharply angled or winged. **Flower** to ¾ in. (2 cm) or more across; petals 5, pale-yellow, commonly not red-tinged at base; swirled in bud, soon falling. Flowers few, in loose, stalked clusters at ends of branches. **Leaves** ⅜–1⅛ in. (1–3 cm) long, narrow, mostly alternate, stalkless; margins entire. Lower leaves soon fall and leave stem bare.

Habitat: Sandy, gravelly soils on prairies, in open fields and woodland openings and edges. In NC, PH, EP, FW.

Note: Yellow flax bears many flowers during its bloom period, but there are never many open at any one time. The flowers open early in the morning and last for only one day. They seem to be most fragile and very delicately attached, the petals falling if an attempt is made to break the stems. The species name *sulcatum* is from the Latin *sulcatus* meaning "furrowed" and refers to the grooved or furrowed stems.

STINGING CEVALLIA (*Cevallia sinuata*)
Stickleaf Family (Loasaceae)

Bloom Period: June–October

Description: Low, upright to widely spreading, rough-hairy perennial to 24 in. (6 dm); stems several, much-branched and forming clump; stems brittle, with whitish and papery outer surface that peels or flakes. Entire plant armed with stinging hairs. **Flower** to ⁵⁄₁₆ in. (8 mm) high; sepals 5, petallike, reddish on outer surface; petals 5, very narrow, hairy, yellow to orangish; stamens 5, broad. Flowers few to several, tightly congested in roundish clusters at ends of long stalks opposite the leaves, opening in the morning. **Leaves** 1–2 in. (25–50 mm) long, alternate, stalkless or nearly so, covered with stinging hairs; margins wavy to opposite-lobed or coarsely toothed.

Habitat: Dry rocky or gravelly soils in plains, open areas, slopes and hillsides. In all except NE, SE, SC, CT.

Note: The flowers of this plant are very interesting, but do not lend themselves to close inspection due to the noxious stinging hairs covering the plant. These hairs, which look like tiny "glass trees" under a hand lens, contain formic acid and can produce a severe rash on the skin of those sensitive to it.

ROCK-NETTLE   (Worthington)

SAND LILY   (Young)

ROCK-NETTLE (*Eucnide bartonioides*)
Stickleaf Family (Loasaceae)

Bloom Period: May–August

Description: Sprawling or vinelike, succulent, hairy perennial; stems solitary or few, brittle, woody at base, much-branched. **Flower** to 3⅛ in. (8 cm) across, light-yellow; petals 5, joined near base; stamens numerous, to 1 in. (2.5 cm) long, prominently exserted, attached to base of petals and falling with them. Flowers open in late afternoon. **Leaves** 2–4 in. (5–10 cm) long, alternate, long-stalked, covered with hooked and stinging hairs; margins slightly lobed or coarsely toothed.

Habitat: Dry, gravelly, limestone or calcareous soils on slopes or bluffs. In EP, ST, FW.

Note: The hooked hairs on the leaves of this plant readily become attached to the clothing of anyone passing by, and the leaves are extremely difficult to remove. Rock-nettle makes an admirable novelty plant for the rock or desert garden but should not be planted near paths or walkways.

SAND LILY (*Mentzelia nuda*)
Stickleaf Family (Loasaceae)

Bloom Period: May–November

Description: Stiffly upright, rough-hairy herbaceous perennial to 3 ft. (1 m); stems solitary to several, rigid, ashy-white, branched above the middle. **Flower** to 2⅜ in. (6 cm) across; petals 10, pale yellow to greenish or white; stamens many, of different lengths. Flowers mostly solitary, from leaf axils. **Leaves** 1–2 in. (2.5–5 cm) long, alternate, mostly stalkless, both surfaces covered with stiff, hooked hairs; margins irregularly toothed or shallowly lobed.

Habitat: Deep, dry, usually sandy soils on prairies, plains, grasslands, rocky hillsides and slopes. In NC, PH, EP, ST, FW.

Note: Sand lily, like other *Mentzelia* species, has rough, sandpapery leaves which easily become attached to clothing. The flowers open in late afternoon and close the following day. Other common names include *poor-man's-patches* and *starflower*.

STICKLEAF (Cheatham)

PRAIRIE STICKLEAF (Wesby)

STICKLEAF (*Mentzelia oligosperma*)
Stickleaf Family (Loasaceae)

Bloom Period: April–November

Description: Upright to sprawling, rough-hairy perennial to 1½ ft. (45 cm); stem straw-colored to ashy-white, much-branched with the branches wide-spreading and forming mats or clumps. **Flower** ½–1 in. (13–25 mm) across, yellow-orange to salmon-yellow; petals 5. Flowers solitary from leaf axils or in few-flowered terminal clusters. **Leaves** ⅜–2⅜ in. (1–6 cm) long, alternate, stalkless, entire to distinctly 3-lobed, the margins irregularly toothed.

Habitat: Sandy, chalky or limestone soils in open areas, edges of woodlands, along bluffs, on hillsides and slopes, and on beach shell. In all except NE, SE, SC, ST.

Note: Unlike the other species of this genus, the flowers of stickleaf open in early morning instead of late evening. They gradually close or wither with the intense heat of afternoon. Also known as *chicken-thief*.

PRAIRIE STICKLEAF (*Mentzelia reverchonii*)
Stickleaf Family (Loasaceae)

Bloom Period: March–October

Description: Upright, hairy, herbaceous perennial herb to 36 in. (1 m); stems solitary or few, much-branched but open. **Flower** to 2¼ in. (5.7 cm) across, yellow; petals 10, narrowed at base, widest near middle; stamens numerous. **Leaves** 1⅛–4 in. (3–10 cm) long, alternate, covered on both surfaces with barbed hairs; margins shallowly lobed to coarsely or finely toothed; upper leaves somewhat clasping stem; rosette leaves with short, blunt lobes.

Habitat: Dry, gravelly limestone soils in rangelands, plains, on hillsides and slopes. In PH, EP, ST, FW.

Note: The leaves of prairie stickleaf are easily detached from the plant and the barbed hairs enable it to cling closely to clothing and hair of animals. This clinging characteristic gives the plant the common name of *buena mujer*, meaning "good woman." The seeds may be roasted and eaten. The flowers open in late afternoon and remain open during the night, closing during the day.

INDIAN MALLOW (Cheatham)

BASTARDIA (Cheatham)

INDIAN MALLOW (*Abutilon fruticosa*)
Mallow Family (Malvaceae)

Bloom Period: March–December

Description: Upright, hairy perennial 1–6 ft. (3–18 dm) high, more commonly 2–3 ft. (6–9 dm) high, the stem unbranched to much-branched. **Flower** ¾–1 in. (18–25 mm) across, the 5 petals yellow to orange or reddish; stamens numerous, united in a tube around the style and forming short column. Flowers solitary or sometimes several, on slender branches from leaf axils or in terminal clusters. **Leaves** to 4 in. (10 cm) long, alternate, short-stalked; blade thickish, gray in color with fine, star-shaped hairs, heart-shaped at base, sharply pointed at tip, the margins irregularly toothed. Upper leaves much smaller.

Habitat: Dry, mostly calcareous soils of prairies, chaparral and open woodlands, and on rocky cliffs and slopes. In all except NE, SE.

Note: The tough fibers from the stems of Indian mallow can be used as cordage in weaving or making rope. The plants are readily eaten by deer, sheep and goats and are quickly eliminated from grazed rangelands. Another common name for this plant is *pelotazo*. Several other species of *Abutilon* are also known as Indian mallow.

BASTARDIA (*Bastardia viscosa*)
Mallow Family (Malvaceae)

Bloom Period: Throughout year

Description: Upright, finely hairy perennial to 3 ft. (1 m); stem solitary, branched, somewhat woody at base. Plant covered with soft, often sticky hairs, especially in upper portion. **Flower** ½ in. (13 mm) or more across; petals 5, yellow; stamens united into column, divided into several hairlike segments at tip. Flowers long-stalked, solitary or few in axils of leaves. **Leaves** to 3⅛ in. (8 cm) long, alternate, long-stalked; blade paler on lower surface, covered with star-shaped hairs; margins irregularly toothed.

Habitat: Clay soils in thickets, palm groves and chaparral. In ST.

Note: Bastardia is a plant of Mexico and South America, reaching its northernmost limit in the Rio Grande Valley, where its yellow flowers are a common sight throughout the year. The plant may be confused with *Sida* spp., but can be differentiated by the fruit.

COPPER-MALLOW

(Darby)

COPPER-MALLOW (*Sphaeralcea angustifolia*)
Mallow Family (Malvaceae)

Bloom Period: Throughout year

Description: Upright, stout, hairy perennial herb 1–6 ft. (3–18 dm) high from woody root; stems few to numerous, mostly unbranched. Plant appearing ashy-gray from thick covering of star-shaped hairs. **Flower** about ¾ in. (2 cm) across, dark yellow or orange to pink or lavender; petals 5, slightly cupped, unequally and shallowly lobed at the tip; stamens numerous, united halfway up their length, forming slender column. Flowers in clusters from upper leaf axils, opening 1 or 2 at a time in each cluster and forming an elongating terminal spike. **Leaves** 1½–3 in. (3.8–7.6 cm) long, alternate, long-stalked, thick, rather angular at base, the margins toothed.

Habitat: Sandy or rocky soils, mostly limestone and gypsum, in plains, brushlands, rangelands, on hillsides and slopes. In NC, PH, EP, FW.

Note: Copper-mallow does well in cultivation, the soft, grayish-green foliage a rich contrast to the brightly colored, hollyhock-like flowers. In the wild, the plants are browsed by deer. Some species of *Sphaeralcea* were used by Western tribes of Indians as remedies for various ills.

CALICHE GLOBE-MALLOW (*Sphaeralcea coccinea*)
Mallow Family (Malvaceae)

Bloom Period: May–October

Description: Upright or occasionally sprawling, densely white-hairy perennial herb to about 32 in. (8 dm); stems usually several, woody and tough at base. **Flower** to 1½ in. (38 mm) across, orangy-pink to orangy-red; petals 5, swirled in bud, somewhat cupped when open; with many anthers. Each flower subtended by dark red, conspicuous, lobed or cut leaflike bract. Flowers few, in open, branching cluster. **Leaves** to 2 in. (5 cm) long, about as wide, alternate, long-stalked, thin, deeply notched at base, shallowly 3-lobed or 3-parted; margins irregularly toothed.

Habitat: Mostly caliche or clay soils in plains, prairies, open areas, along hillsides and canyon slopes. In FW.

Note: In areas of caliche, this is a very common wildflower. In the shade it forms thin, bright-green, shallowly lobed leaves; in the sun it has thick, white-hairy, often deeply lobed leaves.

VELVETLEAF (Miller)

SPATTERDOCK

VELVETLEAF (*Wissadula holosericea*)
Mallow Family (Malvaceae)

Bloom Period: April–December

Description: Upright, densely hairy, strongly scented perennial herb to 4 ft. (12 dm); stems solitary or few, somewhat woody at base, much-branched. Plant appears downy or velvety and pale or light-colored from the dense, star-shaped hairs. **Flower** 1½–2 in. (38–50 mm) across, yellow or orange; petals 5. Flowers solitary in leaf axils in lower portion of stem, later in terminal clusters. **Leaves** to 8 in. (2 dm) long, often about as broad, long-stalked, alternate, thick, prominently veined beneath, indented at base; margins toothed or sometimes 3-lobed.

Habitat: Dry sandy, rocky or loamy clay soils in plains, woodland openings and on hillsides and slopes. In CT, EP, ST, FW.

Note: Velvetleaf much resembles the closely related *Abutilons*, but is larger and has a partition in the fruit segments. The flowers of velvetleaf are edible, and can be eaten raw in salads or dipped in batter and fried. A tea from the flowers reportedly eases headache discomfort.

SPATTERDOCK (*Nuphar luteum* subsp. *macrophyllum*)
Water-Lily Family (Nymphaeaceae)

Bloom Period: March–October

Description: Floating, perennial aquatic with long, branching, spongy roots, rooted in mud; flowering stems unbranched, from roots, with numerous minute air cavities. **Flower** to 1¾ in. (45 mm) across, to 1 in. (25 mm) high, waxy yellow, somewhat greenish on outer surface; sepals 4–6, petallike, rather thick, rounded, prominently cupped; petals numerous, very small, stamenlike, mixed with the numerous stamens; anthers yellow, sometimes red-tinged. Flowers solitary, floating or slightly emergent, terminal on long, slender, leafless stalk from roots. **Leaves** to 12 in. (3 dm) long or more, to 10 in. (25 cm) wide, containing numerous minute air cavities, long-stalked from root; blade floating on water or emergent and erect, smooth on upper surface, usually hairy on lower surface, deeply cut at base.

Habitat: In water or mud in slow streams, ponds, shallow lakes, marshes or springs. In NE, SE, SC, EP.

Note: The flowers of spatterdock, also commonly called *cow lily* and *yellow pond-lily*, never open fully, always appearing as half-opened buds. Stands of spatterdock are important as breeding grounds and as protective habitat for numerous forms of aquatic life. In some areas, it can spread rapidly under favorable conditions and can cause serious drainage problems by slowing down the normal flow of water by the accumulation of debris and silt.

REDBUD

SQUARE-BUD DAY PRIMROSE (Wasby)

REDBUD (*Menodora heterophylla*)
Olive Family (Oleaceae)

Bloom Period: February–December

Description: Low, spreading perennial to 10 in. (25 cm), but usually much lower; stems numerous, slender, slightly angled, very leafy, forming clumps or mats. **Flower** about 1 in. (25 mm) across; petals 5–6, united at base, light-yellow on inner surface; 3 petals red on outer surface. Flowers long-stalked, solitary from leaf axils. **Leaves** to 1⅝ in. (4.1 cm) long, to 1⅛ in. (3 cm) wide, opposite, numerous, crowded, the blade entire or deeply cut into 3–7 lobes or segments.

Habitat: Sand, loam, clay, gravel or chalky soils in pastures, lawns, chaparral, on rocky outcrops, hillsides and slopes. In NC, CT, PH, EP, ST.

Note: Redbud is a rather low plant, but when in bloom is quite showy. The three outer petals, which are red on the outside, enclose the unopened flowers, forming red-colored buds among the open yellow-colored flowers. The paired fruits are like small, round peas, the top portion opening like a lid to release the seed.

SQUARE-BUD DAY-PRIMROSE (*Calylophus drummondianus*)
Evening-Primrose Family (Onagraceae)

Bloom Period: March–July

Description: Upright to somewhat sprawling or reclining, annual or perennial herb 4–20 in. (1–5 dm) high; stems solitary to several and forming bushy clump, sometimes woody near base, slender, soon becoming reddish or straw-colored. **Flower** 2 in. (5 cm) or more across, yellow; petals 4, broad, wrinkled or crinkled. Flowers several, borne in axils of upper leaves, opening near sunrise and remaining open during the day. **Leaves** ⅜–3⅛ in. (1–8 cm) long, ³⁄₁₆–⅝ in. (5–16 mm) wide, alternate, stalkless or almost so; margins entire to spiny-toothed.

Habitat: Sandy or rocky soils in open areas of prairies, plains, hillsides and slopes. In NC, EP.

Note: Square-bud day-primrose is distinguished from the evening primroses (*Oenothera* spp.) by the raised or winged midnerve of the leaflike sepals which enclose the bud, giving it a four-angled or square look; and by the flowers, which remain open during the day. The stigma of the subspecies *drummondianus* is black, and quite conspicuous in the center of the flower.

WATER-PRIMROSE

WATER-PRIMROSE (*Ludwigia peploides*)
Evening-Primrose Family (Onagraceae)

Bloom Period: April–November

Description: Creeping, trailing or floating, mostly smooth herbaceous perennial; stems many, much-branched or forking and rooting at the joints (nodes). **Flower** to 1½ in. (38 mm) across, long-stalked, yellow; petals 5; stamens 10. Flowers borne in axils of upper leaves. **Leaves** ¾–3⅛ in. (2–8 cm) long, to 1½ in. (38 mm) wide, alternate, stalked, dark green and shiny, usually narrowed at both ends, the margins entire.

Habitat: In mud, often floating on water, in ditches, swales, depressions, along banks and edges of water in streams, ponds and lakes. In all except EP, FW.

Note: Water-primrose is a common wildflower around streams and lakes, often forming large mats or wide bands along the banks. Another common name is *primrose-willow* from the flowers' resemblance to primroses and the leaves' looking much like willow. A Spanish common name is *verdolaga de agua*. The former name for this genus was *Jussiaea*, a word commemorating Bernard de Jussieu, the founder of the "natural system of botany."

BEACH EVENING PRIMROSE (*Oenothera drummondii*)
Evening-Primrose Family (Onagraceae)

Bloom Period: March–December

Description: Upright to sprawling, densely hairy perennial to 3 ft. (1 m); stems usually many, woody at base. **Flower** to 3⅛ in. (8 cm) across, yellow fading reddish; petals 4; mature buds upright. Flowers few to several, from upper leaf axils, opening in late afternoon, closing in early morning. **Leaves** ⅜–2¾ in. (1–7 cm) long, ³⁄₁₆–⅝ in. (5–16 mm) wide, alternate, stalked, densely white-downy; margins entire or remotely toothed or lobed.

Habitat: Deep sandy soils of Gulf Coast, bay shores, beaches, island dunes and barrens. In CT.

Note: Beach evening primrose is a Texas species of the Gulf Coast but has been introduced and has become naturalized in some areas in Florida and coastal North Carolina. This group of plants is reported to be useful in treating sore throat and eye diseases.

MISSOURI PRIMROSE (Cheatham)

MISSOURI PRIMROSE (*Oenothera missouriensis*)
Evening-Primrose Family (Onagraceae)

Bloom Period: April–August

Description: Low, upright or trailing, gray-hairy perennial 6–24 in. (15–60 cm) high or long; stems usually several, often much-branched. **Flower** to 4 in. (10 cm) or more across; yellow sometimes fading reddish; petals 4, broad, somewhat cupped; stalk-like floral tube 4–6 in. (10–15 cm) long, hollow; young buds red-dotted, drooping, later becoming upright. Flowers many, from upper leaf axils, opening in afternoon, closing the next morning. Fruit broadly and conspicuously winged. **Leaves** 1⅛–4 in. (3–10 cm) long, ³⁄₁₆–1¼ in. (5–32 mm) wide, alternate, tapered at base to short stalk, rather thick in texture; margins entire, wavy or remotely toothed.

Habitat: Dry, thin, rocky, exposed calcareous soils on prairies, cliffs, hillsides and slopes. In NC, CT, PH, EP.

Note: The name *Missouri* comes from the Illinois Indian word *Emissourita*, meaning "dwellers on the Big Muddy," and was given by the Illinois to a tribe of Siouan Indians that lived on this river. In the naming of this plant, the word *Missouri* was Latinized by adding "ensis," and signifies in this instance that the specimen was first collected in the state of Missouri.

STEMLESS EVENING PRIMROSE (*Oenothera triloba*)
Evening-Primrose Family (Onagraceae)

Bloom Period: February–May

Description: Low, smooth or somewhat hairy winter annual to 8 in. (2 dm); stem very short or nonexistent. **Flower** to 3 in. (76 mm) across, pale-yellow; petals 4, broad; mature buds upright. Flowers open near sunset, close about noon the following day. **Leaves** 1⅛–12 in. (3–30 cm) long, ⅜–1⅝ in. (1–4.1 cm) wide, in basal rosette, long-stalked, the blade deeply and irregularly cut.

Habitat: Mostly clay or calcareous soils of prairies, flats, floodplains, slopes and hillsides. In all except NE, SE.

Note: The four petals of each flower are borne on a long, slender tube, with the seed-producing section (ovaries) nestled among the leafstalks at ground level. The leaves wither away as the fruit matures, leaving a seed-cluster somewhat resembling a pinecone.

YELLOW WOOD-SORREL

MEXICAN POPPY (D. Williams)

YELLOW WOOD-SORREL (*Oxalis dillenii*)
Wood-Sorrel Family (Oxalidaceae)

Bloom Period: February–November

Description: Upright or sprawling perennial to 16 in. (4 dm), but usually much lower; stem solitary or much-branched at base and forming small tufts or clumps. **Flower** to 1 in. (25 mm) across, commonly smaller, yellow; petals 5, opening flat. Flowers 2–9, clustered on stalks longer than the leaves, nodding before and after blooming, remaining open only during warm or sunny weather. **Leaves** alternate, long-stalked, the blade divided into 3 leaflets. Each leaflet to ½ in. (13 mm) long, notched at tip, sensitive and folding downward at night and during cool or cloudy weather.

Habitat: Almost all soils and habitats but especially lawns, gardens, pastures, prairies, canyons, river bottoms and woodlands. In all except PH, FW.

Note: Leaves of yellow wood-sorrel have a tart but agreeable taste, are high in vitamin C and make an excellent addition to other salad greens. The sour or tart taste comes from oxalic acid crystals in the sap of the plant, and the leaves should not be eaten in excessive quantities.

MEXICAN POPPY (*Argemone mexicana*)
Poppy Family (Papaveraceae)

Bloom Period: March–October

Description: Upright, somewhat prickly annual to about 32 in. (8 dm); stems mostly solitary, often branched from near base, bearing few, somewhat reflexed, prickles. Herbage has whitish coating which comes off when rubbed. Plants contain a bright yellow juice or latex. **Flower** to 2½ in. (6.3 cm) across, short-stalked, the 6 petals bright or pale yellow, somewhat crinkled; stamens conspicuous, usually only 50–60. Flowers few in terminal clusters. **Leaves** 1–3⅛ in. (2.5–8 cm) long, alternate, unstalked, the middle and upper ones clasping stem, deeply lobed, with conspicuous light-blue markings and prickles over the veins; margins with spine-tipped teeth.

Habitat: Sandy, gravelly or rocky soils of disturbed sites, pastures, open areas, slopes and hillsides. In SC, CT, EP, ST.

Note: A native of the West Indies, Mexican poppy has long been introduced into Mexico and parts of the United States. It is often cultivated for the attractive flowers. Oil from the seed is used in painters' oil. The plant contains narcotic properties and its latex is used by Guatemalan Indians in treating eye afflictions. Also known as *yellow prickly poppy*.

MEXICAN GOLD POPPY (Darby)

LARGE BUTTERCUP

MEXICAN GOLD POPPY (*Eschscholzia mexicana*)
Poppy Family (Papaveraceae)

Bloom Period: March–May

Description: Low, upright or somewhat sprawling, smooth annual to 16 in. (4 dm); stems solitary or several, leafy, branching in upper portion. Herbage pale bluish-green. Plant has yellowish sap. **Flower** ¾–1½ in. (2–3.8 cm) across, orange to gold or bright yellow; petals 4, cupped. Flowers solitary, erect, at tip of long stalks or few in loose clusters at ends of branches. **Leaves** about 2 in. (5 cm) long, to 2 in. (5 cm) wide, alternate, long-stalked, the blade deeply divided into narrow segments.

Habitat: Dry rocky or gravelly soils on hillsides and mountain slopes. In FW.

Note: Mexican gold poppy is not exceptionally common in Texas, but the plants usually form large colonies that are truly spectacular. More commonly seen in Mexico, it is known there as *amapola del campo*, meaning "poppy of the field."

LARGE BUTTERCUP (*Ranunculus macranthus*)
Crowfoot Family (Ranunculaceae)

Bloom Period: March–June

Description: Upright to sprawling, herbaceous perennial from stout roots; stems to 3 ft. (1 m) long but usually much shorter and appearing clumplike or tufted when first flowering, elongating in age and becoming more loosely sprawling. **Flower** ½–1¼ in. (13–32 mm) across, golden-yellow, long-stalked, fragrant; petals 8–20, somewhat glossy, cupped and appearing as semidouble flower. **Leaves** (basal) 1½–9 in. (3.8–23 cm) long, 1¼–10 in. (3.2–25 cm) wide, long-stalked, the blade usually deeply cut into 3–7 leaflets, the leaflets entire, toothed or lobed. Stem leaves much smaller, stalkless and clasping stem, deeply cut or entire.

Habitat: Rich, wet soils in ditches, drainage areas, mud flats, low woodlands, ravines, seepage areas and along creek banks. In all except NE, SE, PH.

Note: This is our largest-flowered native buttercup and is quite showy. It is easily raised from seed and well worth cultivating in the wildflower garden. All species of *Ranunculus* should be handled carefully, since the juice sometimes causes a rash of small blisters on the skin. The genus name means "little frog," perhaps given to these plants because they prefer wet habitats.

LEMON PAINTBRUSH (Simpson)

WOOD BETONY

LEMON PAINTBRUSH (*Castilleja purpurea* var. *citrina*)
Figwort Family (Scrophulariaceae)

Bloom Period: April–May

Description: Upright, densely hairy perennial herb 8–12 in. (2–3 dm) or more high; stems several, slender, very leafy, forming clump. **Flower** to 1⅝ in. (4.1 cm) long, pale greenish-yellow, tubular, very slender, 2-lipped; lower lip long, widely flaring. Flowers subtended by conspicuous greenish-yellow to bright-yellow leaflike bracts. Flowers and bracts numerous, the whole forming showy terminal spike. **Leaves** to 2½ in. (6.3 cm) long, alternate, stalkless, with 1 or 2 pairs of lobes.

Habitat: Sandy or rocky calcareous soils in prairies, grasslands and on hillsides and slopes. In NC, PH, EP.

Note: Other common names for this plant are *lemon painted-cup* and *citron paintbrush*, all referring to the yellow-colored flowers and bracts. The varietal name is from the Latin *citrus* meaning "citron tree" or *citrinus* meaning "lemon-colored." This species is represented in Texas by the three distinct color phases of red, yellow and purple, with each color representing a different variety.

WOOD BETONY (*Pedicularis canadensis*)
Figwort Family (Scrophulariaceae)

Bloom Period: March–May

Description: Upright, soft-hairy perennial 4–16 in. (1–4 dm) high; stems solitary, unbranched. Plants usually numerous, forming dense colonies. **Flower** to almost 1 in. (25 mm) long, cream to yellow, sometimes reddish, tubular, 2-lipped; upper lip flattened, curved forward and forming hood; lower lip 3-lobed, spreading or curved downward. Flowers few to many, in short, dense, terminal spike elongating in fruit. Small, leaflike bracts subtend each flower. **Leaves** 3–5 in. (7.6–12.7 cm) long, opposite or alternate, mostly basal, much smaller and fewer along upper portion of stem, deeply divided into lobes or toothed segments.

Habitat: Rich loamy or sandy soils in prairies, woodland openings, along forest edges and seepage slopes. In NE, SE, SC.

Note: Wood betony is semiparasitic on the roots of other plants. The flowers are rich in both nectar and pollen and are an early food source for numerous insects. Another common name is *lousewort*; in ancient times it was said that cattle grazing among this plant would become infested with lice. In describing the plants, early botanist and physician John Gerald wrote in his famous Herbal of 1597: "It filleth sheep and other cattle, that feed in meadows where this groweth, full of lice."

219

COMMON MULLEIN (Wesby)

COMMON MULLEIN (*Verbascum thapsus*)
Figwort Family (Scrophulariaceae)

Bloom Period: March–November

Description: Stiffly upright, coarse, stout, densely hairy perennial to 6 ft. (2 m); stems usually solitary, polelike. **Flower** ¾–1⅛ in. (2–3 cm) across, yellow; petals 5, united; stamens 5, the anthers red. Flowers numerous, densely crowded in thick spikelike raceme 6–36 in. (1.5–9 dm) long. **Leaves** 4–16 in. (1–4 dm) long, mostly clustered at base, alternate, stalkless, basally extending down stem as wings, soft, prominently veined, densely covered with feltlike gray hair. Upper leaves progressively smaller.

Habitat: Various soils and in almost all situations, but especially in pastures and disturbed areas. Throughout.

Note: Common mullein is known by numerous common names (*flannel leaf, Indian tobacco, Jupiter's staff* and *velvet dock*, to name a few), and the historical uses made of the plant are almost as many. It provided a leaf tea for colds, its hot vapors were inhaled for throat irritation, and the leaves were soaked in hot vinegar and water to form a poultice applied to external irritations. In Mexico, the dried leaves were smoked to treat asthma. The dried stalks were once dipped in wax and used as candles.

DOWNY GROUND-CHERRY (*Physalis pubescens*)
Nightshade Family (Solanaceae)

Bloom Period: April–December

Description: Upright, usually hairy annual herb 3⅛–36 in. (8–90 cm) high; stem usually solitary, much-branched in upper portion. **Flower** ⁵⁄₁₆–⅜ in. (8–10 mm) long, ⅜–⅝ in. (10–16 mm) wide, yellowish or greenish-yellow, dark-spotted or blotched at base, stalked, solitary from leaf axils; petals 5, united into widely spreading bell-shape; anthers bluish or violet. **Leaves** ¾–3½ in. (2–9 cm) long, ¾–1⅝ in. (2–4.1 cm) wide, alternate, long-stalked, the margins entire to irregularly several-toothed.

Habitat: Moist, usually shady, sandy or loamy soils in open woodlands and thickets, stream bottoms, along stream and river banks. In all except NC, PH, FW.

Note: The genus name *Physalis* is a Greek word meaning "bladder" or "bubble" and refers to the ripened fruit of this plant. The five sepals, which are united only at their base at time of flowering, slowly grow together their entire length until forming an inflated pod or "bubble" around the small, ripened fruit. In this species, the pod is prominently five-angled and covered with soft hairs.

BUFFALO BUR (Cheatham)

BUFFALO BUR (*Solanum rostratum*)
Nightshade Family (Solanaceae)

Bloom Period: April–October

Description: Low, spreading or sprawling, bristly annual 16–32 in.
(4–8 dm) high, densely covered with golden-yellow prickles;
stem solitary or few from base, much-branched in upper portion. **Flower** to 1 in. (25 mm) across; petals 5, bright yellow,
united at base, 5-lobed at rim, the lobes usually widely spreading; anthers usually held tightly upright in column. Flowers
clustered at ends of branches or from leaf axils. **Leaves** 2–6 in.
(5–15 cm) long, deeply parted into irregular segments, the segments again divided or lobed and very spiny.

Habitat: Various soils in abandoned areas, overgrazed pastures,
cultivated fields and flats. Throughout.

Note: The fruit of buffalo bur is a berry enclosed by a conspicuously spiny covering. The common name recalls the time
when buffalo roamed the prairies and wallowed in areas where
this plant grew profusely, getting the burs matted in their
shaggy coats. Although many wild species of Solanaceae are poisonous, many cultivated crops also belong to the nightshades,
including tomatoes, potatoes, eggplant and tobacco.

RED FLOWERS

TUBE-TONGUE (Wesby)

SPREADING DOGBANE (Cheatham)

TUBE-TONGUE (*Siphonoglossa pilosella*)
Acanthus Family (Acanthaceae)

Bloom Period: February–December

Description: Low, upright or sprawling, hairy perennial herb to 12 in. (3 dm) high from woody base; stems usually several from base, weak, with evenly scattered hairs. **Flower** to 1 in. (25 mm) long, white to rose or pale violet to dark lavender, 2-lipped; upper lip small, narrow, turned backward, notched at tip; lower lip large, to ½ in. (13 mm) across, 3-lobed, purple-dotted and with white spot in throat of tube. Flowers solitary or few, borne in axils of upper leaves. **Leaves** ⅜–1⅝ in. (1–4.1 cm) long, to ¾ in. (2 cm) wide, opposite, stalkless or almost so, entire.

Habitat: Dry rocky or gravelly soils, often shaded, in pastures, woodlands, chaparral and along hills, slopes and stream banks. In CT, ST, FW.

Note: This low-growing perennial resembles members of the mint family. It is valuable for use as a border plant and also acts as a good soil binder, usually growing best where there is little competition. The plants produce a profusion of flowers throughout the summer, but the blossoms have a tendency to fall soon after opening. Also called *false-honeysuckle* because of its similarity to true honeysuckle (*Lonicera* spp.).

SPREADING DOGBANE (*Apocynum androsaemifolium*)
Dogbane Family (Apocynaceae)

Bloom Period: April–July

Description: Upright to somewhat sprawling, smooth herbaceous perennial to 20 in. (5 dm); stems usually solitary, widely branching and bushy. Plant contains milky juice. **Flower** ¼–½ in. (6–13 mm) long, fragrant, pink or white, with darker pink lines, bell-shaped, deeply 5-lobed at rim, the lobes wide-spreading or curving backward. Flowers short-stalked, in clusters at ends of stems or from leaf axils. **Leaves** to 4 in. (10 cm) long, to 2⅜ in. (6 cm) wide, opposite, stalked, drooping, dark-green.

Habitat: Dry or moist sandy soils of thickets, openings and edges of woodlands, hillsides and slopes. In FW.

Note: Spreading dogbane contains several potent and toxic chemicals, but in mild form it has been used for various ailments, including chronic liver complaints, typhoid fever, stomach disorders, and localized pain and swelling. The stems yield an excellent fiber that can be used as cordage. Descriptive common names range from *Indian hemp*, *bitterroot* and *colic-root* to *honey bloom* and *wandering milkweed*.

SHOWY MILKWEED (Cheatham)

BUTTERFLY WEED

SHOWY MILKWEED (*Asclepias speciosa*)
Milkweed Family (Asclepiadaceae)

Bloom Period: May–September

Description: Upright, stout, herbaceous perennial 24–40 in. (6–10 dm) high; stems few to several, unbranched. Plant densely white-hairy throughout. **Flower** about ¾ in. (2 cm) across, pinkish to rose-purple, deeply 5-lobed, the lobes bent backward. Flowers several to many, long-stalked, in solitary clusters from upper leaf axils. **Leaves** 4–8 in. (10–20 cm) long, 1⅛–5½ in. (3–14 cm) wide, opposite, short-stalked, firm, with conspicuous veins from midrib to margins.

Habitat: Almost all soils and sites. In PH.

Note: Showy milkweed has the largest flowers of any of our wild milkweeds. Generally it is a more northerly U.S. species but is becoming quite common in northern Texas, and in some instances has become "weedy" in cultivated fields and other disturbed areas. Most milkweeds contain poisonous glycosides, and the larvae of the monarch butterfly, which use this genus as their only food source, absorb the chemicals and are therefore toxic to predators.

BUTTERFLY WEED (*Asclepias tuberosa*)
Milkweed Family (Asclepiadaceae)

Bloom Period: April–September

Description: Upright to sprawling, usually clump-forming hairy perennial to 3 ft. (1 m); stems often branched in upper portion. Plant contains watery juice, not the milky sap of other *Asclepias*. **Flower** less than ½ in. (13 mm) across, orange to orange-red or occasionally yellow, deeply 5-lobed, the lobes reflexed or curved downward. Flowers numerous and forming rounded terminal clusters. **Leaves** to 4¼ in. (108 mm) long, 1¼ in. (32 mm) wide, alternate, numerous, somewhat crowded, rounded to sharp-pointed at tip; margins wavy or sometimes rolled toward lower surface.

Habitat: Various soils in prairies, fields, thickets, dunes, open woods and hillsides. Throughout.

Note: The floral parts of the milkweeds are highly modified and complex. The pollen is a waxlike, glandular mass contained in a V-shaped structure which often becomes attached to the feet of foraging insects and is later deposited on other flowers. Sometimes an insect's leg is caught in the "V," trapping the insect. The flowers are a rich source of nectar and a favorite of butterflies, bees and beelike flies. The seeds and roots make a gentle laxative, and a root tea has been used for heart trouble. Also called *pleurisy root*.

NG THISTLE

NODDING THISTLE (*Carduus nutans*)
Sunflower Family (Asteraceae)

Bloom Period: May–July

Description: Upright, stout herbaceous biennial 16–80 in. (4–20 dm) high; stems few from base, spiny-winged, often with cobweb-like covering. **Flower** head to 2½ in. (63 mm) across, nodding, usually solitary at ends of leafless branches; ray flowers absent; disk flowers numerous, pink to rose-purple. Head surrounded by broad, purple, leaflike, spine-tipped bracts, the outer and middle ones turning downward. **Leaves** to 10 in. (25 cm) long, alternate, the blade deeply lobed, very spiny, the base extending down stem as spiny wing.

Habitat: Various soils in disturbed areas, pastures, edges of fields and on hillsides. In PH, EP.

Note: Nodding thistle, also called *musk thistle* and *plumless thistle*, is an Old World genus introduced from Europe. It has spread rapidly westward and in some rangeland areas has become a "problem" species. The Latin word *carduus* was early used for a common thistle, and *nutans*, also Latin, means "nodding."

PURPLE CONEFLOWER (*Echinacea sanguinea*)
Sunflower Family (Asteraceae)

Bloom Period: May–June

Description: Stiffly upright, slender, usually rough-hairy perennial 1½–3 ft. (4.5–9 dm) high; stems solitary or several and clumplike, usually unbranched. **Flower** head to 1 in. (25 mm) across, to 3½ in. (89 mm) long, solitary on long, leafless stalk; ray flowers several, pale to dark rose-pink, drooping; disk flowers numerous, purplish or brownish, mixed with stiff, sharp-pointed scales (chaff). **Leaves** 4–9½ in. (10–24 cm) long, alternate, mostly toward base, rough to the touch, entire; lower leaves stalked; upper leaves becoming smaller, stalkless.

Habitat: Sandy or gravelly soils of prairies, hillsides, slopes and pine-hardwood forests. In NE, SE, CT.

Note: The pink-flowered coneflowers have long been in cultivation and are readily available from most nurseries. They also may be started by root division. The stiff, sharp-pointed chaff which protrudes beyond the disk flowers gives this genus its name, coming from the Greek word *echinos*, meaning "hedgehog." The roots contain the drug echinacea and Indians used a decoction as a blood purifier, as a wash for wounds, and as a gargle for sore throat. It is used today in the treatment of septicemia.

231

RED GAILLARDIA

INDIAN BLANKET (Tveten)

RED GAILLARDIA (*Gaillardia amblyodon*)
Sunflower Family (Asteraceae)

Bloom Period: April–October

Description: Upright or sprawling, hairy annual 12–20 in. (3–5 dm) high; stems usually solitary, widely branching, leafy. **Flower** head to 2¾ in. (7 cm) across, solitary at tip of leafy stalk; ray flowers 10–20, dark red, 3-toothed at tip; disk flowers numerous, reddish-brown. **Leaves** 1⅛–2¾ in. (3–7 cm) long, alternate, stalkless and with small lobes at base which partly clasp stem; margins entire or with small teeth.

Habitat: Deep sandy soils in prairies, old fields, pastures and woodland openings. In SE, SC, CT, ST.

Note: Red gaillardia is endemic, but where it occurs it forms large masses, often covering many acres or miles. This is one of the earliest gaillardias to bloom, with the colorful flowers continuing into early fall. These plants are excellent for garden plantings and are easily cultivated, but must be started from seed.

INDIAN BLANKET (*Gaillardia pulchella*)
Sunflower Family (Asteraceae)

Bloom Period: February–December

Description: Upright to sprawling hairy annual 1–2 ft. (3–6 dm) high; stem usually much-branched, becoming woody at base late in season. **Flower** heads 1⅝–2⅛ in. (41–55 mm) across, solitary at tips of long slender stalks; ray flowers 8–10, shades of red tipped with yellow, 3-lobed at tip, wide-spreading; disk flowers numerous, purplish-red or brownish. **Leaves** ¾–3¼ in. (20–83 mm) long, ¼–¾ in. (6–18 mm) wide, alternate, short-stalked or stalkless and clasping basally; margins entire to coarsely toothed or lobed.

Habitat: Sandy or somewhat clayey soils of prairies, fields and woodland openings and in sand or shell along the coast. Throughout.

Note: This and *G. amblyodon* are the only annual gaillardias in Texas; all others are perennial. Indian blanket is much used in cultivation and seeds are available commercially. It is also commonly called *firewheel*.

SMALL PALAFOXIA   (Miller)

HOOKER PALAFOXIA

SMALL PALAFOXIA (*Palafoxia callosa*)
Sunflower Family (Asteraceae)

Bloom Period: June–October

Description: Upright, slender annual to 20 in. (5 dm); stem usually solitary, branched in upper portion. Upper branches slender, densely glandular with purple-tipped hairs and sticky to the touch. **Flower** head about ½ in. (1.3 cm) across, light to dark pink or purple, solitary, terminal on slender stalks; ray flowers absent; disk flowers 7–12, deeply 5-lobed. **Leaves** to 2 in. (5 cm) long, to ¼ in. (6 mm) wide, alternate, stalkless or almost so, surfaces somewhat rough to the touch. Upper leaves smaller, becoming bractlike in flowering portion of stem.

Habitat: Calcareous soils of abandoned areas, pastures, old fields, hillsides and gravel-bars. In NC, EP.

Note: Small palafoxia is so common in some areas that it is considered one of the "weedy" species. It often covers large areas and is hard to eradicate due to its numerous and easily distributed seed.

HOOKER PALAFOXIA (*Palafoxia hookeriana*)
Sunflower Family (Asteraceae)

Bloom Period: July–November

Description: Stiffly upright, rather stout, hairy annual 2–4 ft. (6–12 dm) high; stem solitary, branching from near middle, with gland-tipped hairs in upper portion, sticky to the touch. **Flower** head 1⅛–1¼ in. (30–45 mm) across, solitary at ends of branches; ray flowers 8–12, pale to dark rose, deeply 3-lobed at tip; disk flowers numerous, most often a darker rose. Heads usually many, forming loose terminal cluster. **Leaves** 1⅛–2¾ in. (3–7 cm) long, ⅛–¾ in. (3–20 mm) wide, alternate, short-stalked, entire.

Habitat: Deep, dry, sandy soils in prairies, disturbed areas, pastures, woodland openings and edges, and along hillsides and slopes. In SE, SC, CT, ST.

Note: Hooker palafoxia is one of our most beautiful wildflowers, the large terminal cluster of flowers forming a bouquet in itself. In cultivation, the plants bloom over a long period if not allowed to set seed. However, to be assured of plants each year, let the last flowers of the season mature and self-sow.

ROSE PALAFOXIA (Koros)

ROSE PALAFOXIA (*Palafoxia rosea*)
Sunflower Family (Asteraceae)

Bloom Period: June–October

Description: Upright, thin, rather delicate, hairy annual 1–2 ft. (3–6 dm) high; stem usually solitary, widely branched, the branches slender, stiff, wiry. Plant has glandular hairs; sticky to the touch. **Flower** head about 1 in. (2.5 cm) across; ray flowers absent; disk flowers 12–25, pink to rose, deeply 5-lobed, the lobes wide-spreading. Heads solitary at ends of short, leafless, glandular stalks, forming loose terminal cluster. **Leaves** slender, alternate, to ¼ in. (6 mm) wide, stalked, firm, entire.

Habitat: Sandy soils of prairies, plains, brushlands, woodland edges and open hillsides. In NE, SE, SC, ST.

Note: This plant is easily grown from fall-sown seed and is a beautiful addition in summer wildflower plantings. It is best used for massed plantings, groupings or background specimens. The flowers produce abundant nectar and pollen, attracting small insects, especially butterflies.

SAND PALAFOXIA (*Palafoxia sphacelata*)
Sunflower Family (Asteraceae)

Bloom Period: May–October

Description: Upright, slender, hairy annual to 2 ft. (6 dm); stem solitary, few-branched. Herbage with gland-tipped hairs and sticky to the touch. **Flower** head 1–1½ in. (25–38 mm) across, solitary at tips of slender branches; ray flowers 5–10, pink to rose, deeply 3-lobed or cut at tip; disk flowers numerous, purplish. **Leaves** 1½–3 in. (38–76 mm) long, ⅛–¾ in. (3–20 mm) wide, alternate, stalked; upper leaves smaller.

Habitat: Deep sandy soils in rangeland, plains, deserts and dunes. In PH, FW.

Note: Sand palafoxia is a most attractive wildflower of the arid portions of the state. It adapts well to cultivation and is easily raised from fall-sown seed. Often one or more of the ray flowers will be missing, giving the head an "abnormal" look. It is also called *rayed palafoxia*.

PEONÍA (Tveten)

BROWNFOOT (Worthington)

PEONÍA (*Perezia runcinata*)
Sunflower Family (Asteraceae)

Bloom Period: March–November

Description: Low, upright, perennial herb to 12 in. (3 dm). Plant has no stem but bears several flower stalks from base. **Flower** head to 1 in. (2.5 cm) across, to 1⅛ in. (3 cm) high; ray flowers absent; disk flowers rose-red, pink, lavender or purple, united into tubular shape, 2-lipped at rim; upper lip deeply 2-lobed; lower lip raylike, 3-toothed at tip. Flowers 40–50 in each head; heads 1 or 2, terminal on leafless stalk. **Leaves** 2¾–6 in. (7–15 cm) long, alternate, crowded in basal rosette; margin cut into round, spiny-toothed lobes.

Habitat: Calcareous, limestone or chalky soils in prairies, rangelands, chaparral, and along arroyos and ledges. In EP, ST, FW.

Note: Peonía makes an interesting addition to the garden, and when grown in partial shade puts out many glossy-green leaves and bears numerous flowers. It does not multiply rapidly, so is best started from seed. The plants also can be grown quite successfully in containers.

BROWNFOOT (*Perezia wrightii*)
Sunflower Family (Asteraceae)

Bloom Period: May–November

Description: Upright, hairy perennial 24–52 in. (6–13 dm) high; stems one to several, leafy, from woody base, woolly-tufted beneath soil level. **Flower** head about ⅝ in. (16 mm) high, fragrant; ray flowers absent; disk flowers 8–11, rose-pink to almost white, 2-lipped; upper lip deeply cut into 2 teeth or lobes; lower lip raylike and 3-toothed at tip. Heads crowded in small, terminal clusters or groups, the clusters several, stalked and forming larger terminal cluster. **Leaves** ¾–4¾ in. (2–12 cm) long, alternate, stalkless or almost so, the margins sharply and unevenly spiny-toothed.

Habitat: Dry sandy or clayey loams, rocky limestone or igneous soils, often shaded, in brushy pastures, brushlands, along slopes and hillsides. In CT, EP, ST, FW.

Note: Another common name for this plant is *desert-holly*, which refers to the sharply toothed leaves. The pink flowers are often borne in profusion and have the fragrance of honey. The root was used by Western Indians to make an astringent.

CAMPHOR WEED (Tveten)

MARSH FLEABANE (Darby)

CAMPHOR WEED (*Pluchea camphorata*)
Sunflower Family (Asteraceae)

Bloom Period: July–November

Description: Upright, stout, hairy, aromatic annual or perennial to about 4 ft. (12 dm), usually lower; stem solitary, branching in upper portion. **Flower** head to 5/16 in. (8 mm) high; ray flowers absent; disk flowers several, rose to rose-purple. Heads numerous, crowded in large, showy, somewhat elongated, stalked terminal cluster. **Leaves** 2⅜–6 in. (6–15 cm) long, 1¼–2¾ in. (3.2–7 cm) wide, alternate, stalked; blade dotted with glands on both surfaces; margins entire to sharply toothed.

Habitat: Moist soils in fresh or brackish marshes, shores, ditches, salt marshes or saline areas. In NE, SE, SC, CT, EP.

Note: Foliage of these plants is very aromatic with the fragrance of camphor.

MARSH FLEABANE (*Pluchea purpurascens*)
Sunflower Family (Asteraceae)

Bloom Period: May–December

Description: Stiffly upright, hairy annual herb 1–3 ft. (3–9 dm) high; stem solitary, branching in upper portion. Herbage somewhat aromatic with a fragrance of camphor. **Flower** head about 3/16 in. (5 mm) across; ray flowers absent; disk flowers numerous, rose to rose-purple, tubular. Heads usually crowded in stalked clusters, forming a flat-topped terminal mass. **Leaves** 2-6 in. (5–15 cm) long, alternate, short-stalked or stalkless, entire; margins entire, slightly toothed or scalloped.

Habitat: Rich, moist or wet soils in swales, depressions or meadows and along edges of marshes, creeks, sloughs and lakes. Throughout.

Note: Marsh fleabane probably has some medicinal properties, as two closely related species are reportedly used as stimulants, antispasmodics and diuretics. The plants do well in cultivation and add much color to the late-season garden. The flowers attract small bees and butterflies. The Spanish common name for this plant is *canela*, meaning "cinnamon." It is sometimes used in Mexico for making herb tea.

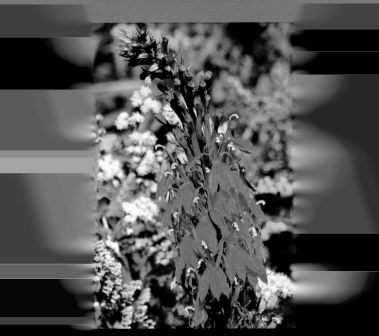

AL FLOWER

MOUNTAIN BEE PLANT

CARDINAL FLOWER (*Lobelia cardinalis*)
Bluebell Family (Campanulaceae)

Bloom Period: May–December

Description: Upright, usually smooth perennial to 6 ft. (2 m), but generally 3 ft (1 m) or less; stems solitary or few from base, usually unbranched but occasionally branched below main flower spike. Plants reproduce by short basal offshoots. **Flower** to 2 in. (5 cm) long, scarlet, dark red or vermilion, tubular, 2-lipped; upper lip deeply 2-lobed with the lobes slender, erect or falling to the side; lower lip 3-lobed, broad; stamens 5, united into slender, prominently exserted tube tipped with conspicuous bluish-gray united anthers. Flowers numerous, in showy terminal spike. **Leaves** 2–8 in. (5–20 cm) long, 1–2 in. (2.5–5 cm) wide, alternate, thin, broadest near base, irregularly and sharply toothed.

Habitat: Rich soils in semishaded moist or wet areas along the edges of streams, lakes, meadows or low woodlands. In all except southern portion of ST.

Note: Cardinal flower is a favorite of hummingbirds, which visit the plants frequently and are their major pollinators. The entire plant contains alkaloids, and while the leaves were used medicinally and for smoking by Indians, many deaths of early settlers occurred through overdose or misuse of the plant derivatives.

ROCKY MOUNTAIN BEE PLANT (*Cleome serrulata*)
Caper Family (Capparidaceae)

Bloom Period: May–September

Description: Upright, smooth, somewhat shrubby annual 8–60 in. (2–15 dm) high; stem usually solitary, branched. Entire plant smells rather unpleasant when touched. **Flower** about ½ in. (1.3 cm) long, bright-pink to purplish or sometimes white; petals 4, unequal, very slender in basal portion, in row on upperside; stamens 6, longer than petals. Flowers many, in dense, elongated terminal spikes. **Leaves** alternate, long-stalked, the blade divided to base into 3 leaflets, each leaflet ¾–2⅜ in. (2–6 cm) long, ³⁄₁₆–⅝ in. (5–16 mm) wide, pointed at both ends; margins minutely toothed or entire.

Habitat: Sandy soils in plains, rangelands, disturbed areas, open woodlands, and on hillsides and mountain slopes. In northeastern portion of PH.

Note: Flowers of these plants produce abundant nectar, attracting numerous insects, especially bees. At one time, they were widely planted as a honey plant, but the bees using them were not as productive as expected. While appearing rather "ragged," the numerous flowering spikes are welcome in the wildflower garden. The plants have been used to treat anemia, insect bites and stomach disorders.

243

MEXICAN CAMPION (Worthington)

GOAT FOOT MORNING GLORY (Ke...)

MEXICAN CAMPION (*Silene laciniata*)
Pink Family (Caryophyllaceae)

Bloom Period: July–October

Description: Upright to sprawling, hairy perennial herb to 3 ft. (1 m); stems one to several, slender, weak, often leaning against other vegetation, few-branched. Plant with glandular hairs throughout, especially in flowering portion, and sticky to the touch. **Flower** to 1 in. (25 mm) across or more, scarlet, solitary or few in cluster at ends of branches; petals 5, usually deeply cut into 4 or more very narrow lobes or segments. **Leaves** to 3⅛ in. (8 cm) long, to 1½ in. (38 mm) wide, very variable, opposite, densely covered with glandular hairs and very sticky; margins entire to finely toothed.

Habitat: Rich, gravelly soils, usually shaded, along hillsides and mountain slopes. In FW.

Note: Mexican campion, also called *fire pink* or *catchfly*, is a beautiful plant of the more mountainous areas. It is often seen along hiking and riding trails. The sticky, fluid-producing hairs often entrap insects which alight or crawl on the plant.

GOAT-FOOT MORNING GLORY (*Ipomoea pes-caprae*)
Morning-Glory Family (Convolvulaceae)

Bloom Period: May–December

Description: Trailing or creeping, smooth perennial vine; stems to 30 ft. (10 m) long, rather thick, almost perfectly straight, closely hugging the sand, rooting at the joints (nodes). **Flower** 2–3⅜ in. (5–9 cm) wide, 2–2¾ in. (5–7 cm) long, rosy or purple, the 5 petals united to form wide-spreading funnel, unevenly wavy at rim. Flowers usually several on stalk from leaf axil, with one flower opening at a time. **Leaves** 1½–4 in. (3.8–10 cm) wide and long; alternate, stalked, the blade thick, leathery, bright green, folded along midrib, deeply notched at tip.

Habitat: Deep sands of the windswept coastal dunes and beaches. In CT.

Note: The deeply rooting stems of goat-foot morning glory are important in helping to stabilize the coastal dunes. One of our most attractive morning glories, it is often found growing with beach morning glory and beach evening primrose. The distinctive leaf shape separates it from all other *Ipomoea*s and gives it its common as well as its scientific name. *Pes* is from the Latin *pediculus* meaning "foot"; *caprae* is derived from the Latin word for "goat."

SALT-MARSH MORNING GLORY

SHARP POD MORNING GLORY

SALT-MARSH MORNING GLORY (*Ipomoea sagittata*)
Morning-Glory Family (Convolvulaceae)

Bloom Period: April–October

Description: Trailing, tightly twining or low-climbing, smooth, herbaceous perennial vine from creeping root; stems slender, to 5 ft. (15 dm) or more long. Plants usually form large colonies. **Flower** to 3⅜ in. (9 cm) long, about as wide, dark rose to red-purple, rarely white, usually solitary, long-stalked, from leaf axils; petals 5, united into widely flaring funnel-shape, essentially unlobed at rim. **Leaves** 1½–4 in. (3.8–10 cm) long, alternate, stalked, the blade deeply lobed at base with the lobes narrow and extending downward.

Habitat: Moist, brackish soils along river and creek banks, on bay and island beaches, dunes, and especially along edges of coastal marshes. In CT.

Note: Salt-marsh morning glory is an unusually attractive and showy plant, but the flowers are usually closed and withered by noon. The species name is derived from the Latin word *sagitta*, meaning "arrow," and refers to the distinctive shape of the leaves.

SHARP-POD MORNING GLORY (*Ipomoea trichocarpa*)
Morning-Glory Family (Convolvulaceae)

Bloom Period: April–December

Description: Twining, low-climbing perennial from large tuberous root; stems one to several, to 15 ft. (5 m) or more long or high. **Flower** to 2 in. (5 cm) long, 2¼ in. (5.7 cm) across, rosy-lavender to purple-rose with dark center, the 5 petals united, funnel-shaped, 5-lobed at rim. Flowers one to several at tip of short stalk rising from axils of leaves. Flowers open in early morning, close about midday. **Leaves** ¾–4 in. (2–10 cm) long, ⅝–3 in. (1.5–7.6 cm) wide, alternate, long-stalked, the blade very variable in outline, from entire and heart-shaped to deeply 3–5 lobed.

Habitat: Various soils in fields, disturbed ground, pastures, thickets, woodland edges and stream bottoms. In all except PH, FW.

Note: A rampant and aggressive grower, sharp-pod morning glory often becomes a troublesome "weed" in cultivated croplands. One or two plants in the garden make a stunning specimen plant when grown in the open on a low support. Also called *coastal morning glory* and *tie vine*.

SCARLET PEA

POWDERPUFF

SCARLET PEA (*Indigofera miniata*)
Legume Family (Fabaceae)

Bloom Period: April–September

Description: Sprawling or trailing, grayish-hairy perennial from woody taproot; stems solitary or several, usually much-branched, from 1–4 ft. (3–12 dm) long. **Flower** to ¾ in. (2 cm) long, brick-red to dark rosy-red; petals 5, the upper petal erect. Flowers 8–25, in terminal spike (raceme), from axils of leaves. Spike longer than subtending leaf. **Leaves** alternate, short-stalked, the blade divided into 5–9 leaflets, rarely more, each leaflet to 1 in. (25 mm) long.

Habitat: Sandy soils in lawns, pastures, woodlands, hillsides, shell islands and sand beaches. In all except FW.

Note: Very abundant and ordinarily quite showy, these legumes usually form a roundish mat of vegetation with the flower spikes arranged in an orange-red ring. Scarlet pea is a prolific bloomer and does very well in the wildflower garden, especially when used as a ground cover. It is relished by deer and also grazed by livestock.

POWDERPUFF (*Mimosa strigillosa*)
Legume Family (Fabaceae)

Bloom Period: April–November

Description: Low, sprawling or trailing perennial; stems annual, to 6 ft. (2 m) long, forming mats, densely covered with stiff bristles, but these not prickly to the touch. **Flower** pink to lavender-rose, fragrant, petals 5, minute; stamens numerous, conspicuously exserted. Flowers numerous, congested in small globelike or somewhat elongated head at tip of leafless stalk. **Leaves** alternate, long-stalked, the blade divided into 4–8 pairs of small segments, these again divided into usually 10–15 pairs of smaller leaflets.

Habitat: Various soils, especially sandy loams, in prairies, grasslands, meadows and forest openings, but mostly in swales or depressions, and along stream and lake edges.

Note: Powderpuff is very similar to the sensitive briers (*Schrankia* spp.), differing mainly in that the spines along stems are not stiff and prickly and that the fruit is a flattened pod instead of the more rounded pod of the *Schrankia*s. The foliage, like the *Schrankia*s', is sensitive to the touch and will quickly fold together when disturbed.

SENSITIVE BRIER

SENSITIVE BRIER (*Schrankia uncinata*)
Legume Family (Fabaceae)

Bloom Period: April–July

Description: Trailing, prickly herbaceous perennial; stems to 3 ft. (1 m) long, usually branched, very prickly with recurved prickles. **Flower** pink to rose, fragrant; petals 5, minute; stamens 8–10, conspicuously exserted. Flowers numerous, congested in small, globelike cluster at tip of leafless stalk. **Leaves** alternate, prickly stalked, the blade divided into 4–8 pairs of small segments, these again divided into 8–15 pairs of smaller leaflets; leaflets prominently veined on lower surface.

Habitat: Sandy soils in prairies, pastures, abandoned areas, openings in woodlands and along woodland edges. In all except EP, ST, FW.

Note: Other common names for this plant include *catclaw*, in reference to the prickly characteristic of the plant, and *shameboy*, referring to the sensitive foliage, which closes when touched. The fruit of sensitive brier is a long, slender pod which is densely covered with prickles; it is attractive when used in dried arrangements.

CRIMSON CLOVER (*Trifolium incarnatum*)
Legume Family (Fabaceae)

Bloom Period: April–June

Description: Upright, soft-hairy annual or winter annual to 18 in. (45 cm); stems usually branched near base. **Flower** to ½ in. (13 mm) long, dark red or scarlet; petals 5, the banner or uppermost petal folded forward and not upright. Flowers numerous, congested in stalked, elongated or cylinderlike terminal clusters. **Leaves** alternate, hairy, long-stalked, the blade divided into 3 leaflets, each leaflet stalkless or essentially so, less than 3 times as long as wide, mostly ⅜–1⅛ in. (1–3 cm) long.

Habitat: Various soils in fields or along roadsides. In NE, SE, SC.

Note: Crimson clover is a native of Europe, used in this country primarily as a late-winter protein-rich forage for cattle and deer. Like other legumes, it helps to enrich the soil because of the nitrogen-fixing bacteria in its roots. It has also been used by the state highway department for roadside beautification and erosion control.

MOUNTAIN PINK (Wesby)

MEADOW PINK

MOUNTAIN PINK (*Centaurium beyrichii*)
Gentian Family (Gentianaceae)

Bloom Period: May–August

Description: Low, upright, slender, delicate annual to 12 in. (3 dm); stems much-branched in upper portion and forming mounds. **Flower** to 1 in. (2.5 cm) across, pink to rose, deeply 5-lobed, the lobes spreading flat. Flowers numerous, in clusters at ends or in forks of the branches. **Leaves** to 1⅛ in. (3 cm) long, to ⅛ in. (3 mm) wide, opposite; uppermost almost hairlike.

Habitat: Gravelly or rocky limestone soils on prairies, hillsides and slopes, and in seepage areas around granite boulders. In NC, PH, EP.

Note: Mountain pink often covers rocky slopes and hillsides with low mounds of beautiful pink in late summer. The plants are just as striking when used as border or specimen plants in the wildflower or rock garden. For best results, sow seed in the fall where they are to grow, as they do not transplant well.

MEADOW PINK (*Sabatia campestris*)
Gentian Family (Gentianaceae)

Bloom Period: March–July

Description: Upright, slender or wide-spreading, smooth annual to 20 in. (5 dm); stem solitary, 4-angled, branched only in upper portion, the branches slender, widely spaced, alternate or forking. **Flower** to 2 in. (5 cm) across, pink to rose with yellow center star; petals 5, united at base, deeply 5-lobed at rim, the lobes to ½ in. (1.3 cm) wide; style 2-branched, elongated, at first lying flat and twisting together concealing stigmas, becoming erect and uncoiling after anthers shed pollen. Flowers solitary at ends of branches and on long stalks from leaf axils. **Leaves** to 1¾ in. (4.5 cm) long, to ¾ in. (2 cm) wide, opposite, stalkless and basally clasping stem.

Habitat: Dry or moist sandy soils in prairies, pastures, rangelands, cedar-oak flats and edges of woodlands.

Note: Meadow pink usually forms large colonies and is often quite spectacular in early spring. Readily self-seeding, it will cover acres of rangeland or form a pink ribbon for miles along roadsides. The plants are easily cultivated and should be used more in garden plantings. For best results, plant seeds in early fall in raked area, and do not cover.

CRAMERIA

SAND BRAZORIA

CRAMERIA (*Krameria lanceolata*)
Ratany Family (Krameriaceae)

Bloom Period: March–September
Description: Trailing, silky-hairy perennial herb from woody base; stems several, slender, branching, eventually elongating to 2 ft. (6 dm) or more. **Flower** to ¾ in. (2 cm) across, reddish-wine, oddly shaped, consisting of 4 or 5 sepals which are colored and appear petallike, and 5 very unequal petals much smaller than the sepals; upper 3 petals united into a 3-lobed, fan-shaped object; other 2 petals greenish, short, broad, thick and glandlike, with 1 on each side of the furry pistil. Flowers solitary, on short, hairy stalk bearing 2 small, leaflike bracts and rising from the axils of the many leaves. **Leaves** to 1 in. (2.5 cm) long, very narrow, alternate, entire, densely covered with silky hairs.
Habitat: Various soils in open areas, pastures, prairies, woodland openings and along hillsides and slopes. Throughout.
Note: The hard, one-seeded, woolly fruit of crameria is covered with barbless spines and gives this plant another common name, *sandbur*.

SAND BRAZORIA (*Brazoria pulcherrima*)
Mint Family (Lamiaceae)

Bloom Period: April–June
Description: Low, upright, hairy annual to 24 in. (6 dm); stem solitary, branched near base, with rounded angles. **Flower** to ⅞ in. (22 mm) long, pinkish-lavender with old-ivory or pale-yellow throat, broadly tubular, 2-lipped at rim; upper lip with 2 rounded and conspicuously toothed lobes; lower lip with 3 small lobes, the lobes often turned under. **Leaves** to 5⅛ in. (13 cm) long, 1 in. (25 mm) wide, opposite, with 5–8 pairs along stem; lower leaves usually withered away at flowering time; upper leaves winged at base; margins sparsely toothed in tip portion.
Habitat: Deep sandy soils in pastures, woodland openings and edges. In SC.
Note: Sand brazoria is an endemic but is found in large masses and is quite common and conspicuous where it occurs. Easily grown in sandy soils, it produces delicately colored flowers that are beautiful in wildflower plantings.

TROPICAL SAGE

PINK MINT

TROPICAL SAGE (*Salvia coccinea*)
Mint Family (Lamiaceae)

Bloom Period: March–December

Description: Strictly upright, hairy perennial 1–3 ft. (3–9 dm) high, often from somewhat woody base; stem 4-angled, usually much-branched in upper portion. **Flower** about 1 in. (2.5 cm) long, bright red to dark scarlet or, rarely, pink to white; 2-lipped with the upper lip narrow, unlobed and extended forward, the lower lip broad, 3-lobed. Flowers in clusters or whorls of 2 to 6; clusters short-stalked, occurring at regular intervals and forming long, slender spike (raceme). **Leaves** to 2⅝ in. (7 cm) long, 2 in. (5 cm) wide, opposite, stalked; blade thin, prominently veined, blunt to rounded at base, rounded or sharp-pointed at tip, bluntly saw-toothed or scalloped on margins.

Habitat: Sandy, loamy or clay soils in chaparral, thickets or woodlands, along stream edges and in floodplains. In all except NE, NC, SC, FW.

Note: Tropical sage is a hardy plant in cultivation and, in part of its range, blooms almost all year. The flowers attract several species of butterflies and are especially well-liked by hummingbirds. Other common names include *scarlet sage, Indian fire* and *mejorana*.

PINK MINT (*Stachys drummondii*)
Mint Family (Lamiaceae)

Bloom Period: February–November

Description: Upright, soft-hairy annual or biennial herb to 3 ft. (1 m); stems solitary or in clumps, 4-angled or square, usually branched from below middle. **Flower** about ⅜ in. (1 cm) long, pink or lavender, somewhat tubular, 2-lipped at rim; upper lip notched; lower lip twice as long as upper one, 3-lobed. Flowers in few-flowered clusters from upper leaf axils and forming long terminal spike. **Leaves** to 4 in. (1 dm) long, opposite, long-stalked; margins with small, rounded teeth.

Habitat: Sandy, gravelly or clayey soils in pastures, palm groves, chaparral, openings and edges of woodlands and thickets. In CT, ST, FW.

Note: Pink mint usually forms large colonies, often in shaded areas, making the entire landscape appear pink or rose-colored. The plants are well worth cultivating and are easily raised from seed sown in November. The flowers provide one of the best early nectar and pollen sources for bees and other small insects.

AMERICAN GERMANDER (Tveten)

WILD ONION

AMERICAN GERMANDER (*Teucrium canadense*)
Mint Family (Lamiaceae)

Bloom Period: March–November

Description: Upright, hairy perennial to 3 ft (1 m), usually lower; stem solitary, 4-angled, branched in upper portion. Plants usually forming dense colonies from creeping rhizomes. **Flower** ¾ in. (2 cm) long, fragrant, pale pink or lavender with purple spots, 2-lipped; upper lip very short and deeply notched into 2 small, toothlike segments; lower lip 3-lobed, the middle lobe broad, flat; stamens 4, projecting from between cleft of upper lip, prominently curved downward. Flowers numerous, congested in dense, elongating spikes. **Leaves** 2¼–4 in. (5.7–10 cm) long, ¾–1½ in. (2–3.8 cm) wide, opposite, stalked, densely hairy on lower surface; margins usually toothed.

Habitat: Rich, wet soils or mud in pastures, meadows and thickets and along edges of swales, marshes, canals, streams or lakes. Throughout except western portion of PH.

Note: Another common name for this plant is *wood sage*. The scientific name honors Teucer, an ancient king of Troy.

WILD ONION (*Allium canadense* var. *mobilense*)
Lily Family (Liliaceae)

Bloom Period: April–May

Description: Low, upright, slender, clumped, smooth perennial from small bulb; stem absent, but flowering stalk 8–24 in. (2–6 dm) high. **Flower** about ¼ in. (6 mm) high, pale to dark-pink, scentless, the 6 segments petallike, thin, cupped. Flowers many, stalked, in solitary cluster at top of slender, leafless stalk. **Leaves** 6–18 in. (15–45 cm) long, less than ⅛ in. (3mm) wide, 2 or more from bulb, soft, shiny, flat with prominent groove down middle.

Habitat: Sandy, rocky or, rarely, on limestone or in clay soils of prairies, rangelands, stream banks, edges and openings of woodlands. In NE, SE, NC, SC.

Note: Like other *Allium*s, wild onion has a mild flavor and odor. It can be eaten raw or used as flavoring. Medicinally, the wild onions have been simmered into a syrup and taken for colds, croup and pneumonia. Some tribes of Indians reportedly applied the crushed plant to the stings of bees and wasps, which almost instantly relieved the pain.

DRUMMOND WILD ONION

PLAINS POPPY-MALLOW (Darby)

DRUMMOND WILD ONION (*Allium drummondii*)
Lily Family (Liliaceae)

Bloom Period: March–May

Description: Upright to somewhat sprawling, smooth perennial 4–12 in. (1–3 dm) high; flowering stems and leaves from cluster of small bulbs; bulbs covered with fine, meshlike netting. **Flower** ¼–⅜ in. (6–9 mm) high or long, white, pink or reddish, the 6 segments all petallike. Flowers 10–15, unequally stalked and forming a loose cluster at summit of leafless stem. **Leaves** to 12 in. (3 dm) high or long, to ⅛ in. (3 mm) wide, usually 3 or 4 per bulb, conspicuously creased along midrib, entire.

Habitat: Calcareous or limestone soils of plains, prairies, along hills and slopes. Throughout.

Note: This is the most common species of wild onion in Texas, and like the other onions, is edible and quite tasty. The flowers of Drummond wild onion are attractive, especially the darker colored ones, and can be used in border or group plantings.

PLAINS POPPY-MALLOW (*Callirhoë alcaeoides*)
Mallow Family (Malvaceae)

Bloom Period: March–May

Description: Upright or somewhat sprawling perennial herb to 18 in. (45 cm); stems several, unbranched or few-branched. **Flower** about 1¾ in. (45 mm) across, pink or white; petals 5, somewhat cupped, unevenly cut at tip, swirled in bud; stamens numerous, united basally and forming short column. Flowers few, at tips of long stalks from leaf axils. **Leaves** 2–3⁹⁄₁₆ in. (5–9 cm) long, 1⅝–4 in. (4.1–10 cm) wide, alternate, mostly long-stalked, the blade lobed or cut to base, the segments again slenderly lobed; upper leaves short-stalked or stalkless.

Habitat: Mostly calcareous clay soils in prairies. In NC.

Note: This species is rather local in distribution, but where found, large areas are often covered with these plants. The shell-pink flowers are most conspicuous and attractive in early spring. The plants do well in cultivation, being easily started from root divisions or seeds. The poppy-mallows are cross-pollinated mainly by bees, which get pollen on their backs from old flowers while seeking nectar from newly opened ones.

WINE-CUP

WINE-CUP (*Callirhoë involucrata*)
Mallow Family (Malvaceae)

Bloom Period: February–July
Description: Low, sprawling or trailing, hairy perennial; stems widely spreading, vinelike, 2–3 ft. (6–9 dm) long. **Flower** 1½–2⅜ in. (3.8–6 cm) across, dark purplish-red or wine, solitary on long stalks from leaf axils; petals 5, deeply cupped, white near base; stamen column whitish or yellowish. **Leaves** 1–2 in. (2.5–5 cm) long, 1⅛–2⅜ in. (3–6 cm) wide, merely angled to parted toward base into 5 or 7 narrow segments, the segments toothed, cut, lobed or parted.
Habitat: Sandy or gravelly soils on hillsides, in prairies, open woodlands, thickets and scrublands. In all except NE, SE, FW.
Note: Wine-cups, which are also known as *poppy-mallow*, are pollinated mainly by bees seeking the nectar. A European member of the mallow family, the marshmallow (*Althaea officinales*), exudes a sticky sap from its roots which is used in the making of commercially sold confectionary marshmallows.

TULIPÁN DEL MONTE (*Hibiscus cardiophyllus*)
Mallow Family (Malvaceae)

Bloom Period: Throughout year
Description: Upright, hairy perennial herb to 3 ft. (1 m) or more from somewhat woody base; stems solitary to few, leafy to top. **Flower** 2–3⅛ in. (5–8 cm) across, crimson to deep rose-red, long-stalked, solitary from leaf axils; petals 5, wide-spreading or somewhat cupped; stamens united at base, forming short column. **Leaves** 1⅛–3⁹⁄₁₆ (3–9 cm) long, alternate, long-stalked, the blade deeply notched at base, pale on lower surface; margins wavy to variously toothed.
Habitat: Well-drained loams, chalky or rocky soils in brushy pastures, chaparral, along boulders and ledges on hillsides and slopes. In CT, PH, ST, FW.
Note: The hardiness and long bloom period of this plant make it excellent for cultivation, and the red flowers nestled among the silvery, heart-shaped leaves make a striking display.

SALT MARSHMALLOW

SALT MARSHMALLOW (*Kosteletzkya virginica* var. *althaefolia*)
Mallow Family (Malvaceae)

Bloom Period: June–November

Description: Upright, robust, hairy perennial herb to 4½ ft. (1.5 m) or more; stems usually several and often forming clump, branched. Plants somewhat shrublike, with coarse, shaggy hairs throughout. **Flower** to 3½ in. (89 mm) wide, pale pink to rose-pink; petals 5, swirled in bud, opening wide; stamens united into long, slender column. Flowers solitary or few in terminal or axillary clusters. **Leaves** 1⅛–6 in. (3–15 cm) long, alternate, stalked; blade gray-green, rough, densely hairy; lower leaves notched at base.

Habitat: Wet soils, often saline, in ditches, along shores, in brackish or nearly fresh marshes, swamps or tidal pools. In SE, CT.

Note: Salt marshmallow much resembles a lovely rose-colored hibiscus. Many cultivated ornamental plants occur in this family, as well as the cotton plants (*Gossypium* spp.) and garden okra (*Hibiscus esculentus*).

MALVALLA (*Malvalla lepidota*)
Mallow Family (Malvaceae)

Bloom Period: Throughout year

Description: Low, sprawling or trailing, hairy herbaceous perennial; stems few to several, branched, to about 16 in. (4 dm) long. Plant silvery when young, conspicuously dotted throughout with small, scurfy scales mixed with star-shaped hairs. **Flower** to 1¼ in. (32 mm) across, pink, white or yellowish; petals 5, cupped, covered with star-shaped hairs on outer surface where exposed in bud. Flowers stalked, solitary from leaf axils. **Leaves** to about 1⅜ in. (35 mm) long, alternate, slender-stalked, the blade roughly triangular, veined from base, broader near base and somewhat lobed, the lobes irregularly toothed; margins in mature leaves with obviously enlarged ribbing following leaf outline.

Habitat: Dry, gravelly soils in clay flats and on limestone hillsides and mountain slopes. In PH, FW.

Note: Until recently, this plant was classified under the name *Sida lepidota* var. *depauperata*. Certain characteristics separate the two genera, however: the *Malvalla*s have conspicuously ribbed leaf margins; veins extending upward from base of leaf; and star-shaped hairs covering the exposed portion of the petals while still in bud.

ROCK ROSE

BRACTED SIDA (Hanasham)

ROCK ROSE (*Pavonia lasiopetala*)
Mallow Family (Malvaceae)

Bloom Period: Throughout

Description: Upright, somewhat shrubby, densely hairy perennial to 2 ft. (6 dm); stem usually solitary, branched. **Flower** to 1½ in. (38 mm) across, solitary on slender stems from leaf axils; petals 5, wide-spreading; stamens united basally into slender column. **Leaves** 1–2½ in. (25–63 mm) long, alternate, stalked; margins coarsely toothed or somewhat lobed.

Habitat: Dry, rocky, usually calcareous soils in open woodlands or brushlands. In EP, ST.

Note: The flowers of rock rose are an especially attractive shade of rose, and the plants are a worthy addition to the wildflower garden. They can be used for hedges or backgrounds, producing flowers throughout the year. The genus is named for Spanish botanist José Pavón (1750–1844), who worked primarily with plants from South America.

BRACTED SIDA (*Sida ciliaris*)
Mallow Family (Malvaceae)

Bloom Period: Throughout year

Description: Mostly widely spreading or sprawling, hairy, herbaceous perennial from tough, woody base; stems several, to 12 in. (3 dm) high or long, branched. **Flower** to 1¼ in. (32 mm) across, rose to purple or salmon, yellow or white, darker at base; petals 5, somewhat cupped to broadly spreading, swirled in bud. Flowers few, in dense cluster from upper leaves; clusters closely subtended by upper leaves and conspicuously fringed, leaflike bracts. **Leaves** to 1⅛ in. (29 mm) long, alternate, long-stalked, narrow, the blade toothed in tip portion; stalk of blade united to stalk of adjacent flower cluster.

Habitat: Sandy or clayey-loam soils in prairies, pastures, mesquite thickets, scrub oak woodlands, chaparral, and on clay flats. In CT, ST.

Note: This species of *Sida* can be identified by the long hairs on both the leafstalks and narrow bracts. The clusters of flowers are quite showy and the plants deserve greater use in cultivation.

CLAW

ND MEADOW-BEAUTY

DEVIL'S-CLAW (*Proboscidea louisianica*)
Unicorn-Plant Family (Martyniaceae)

Bloom Period: June–September

Description: Upright to sprawling, coarse, unpleasantly scented annual 1–3 ft. (3–9 dm) high, commonly lower; stem solitary, opposite-branched. Plant covered with glandular hairs and sticky to the touch. **Flower** to 2¼ in. (5.7 cm) long, pinkish to pale lavender or dull white, mottled or spotted with purplish and yellow, somewhat trumpet-shaped, 5-lobed at rim. Flowers 1 to 20 in open spikes (racemes), with only 1 or 2 open at once. **Leaves** to 12 in. (3 dm) wide, almost round, opposite, long-stalked; margins entire to shallowly lobed and usually wavy.

Habitat: Sandy soils of meadows, cultivated fields, playas, abandoned areas, and stream and river banks. In all except NE.

Note: Devil's-claw, also known as *ram's horn* and *unicorn plant*, is named for its oddly shaped fruit, a capsule tipped by a long, curved beak. When dry, the capsule splits and the beak becomes two hooks or claws that readily attach to animals which thereby disperse the seeds. The young seedpods are often pickled and eaten like okra.

MARYLAND MEADOW-BEAUTY (*Rhexia mariana*)
Melastoma Family (Melastomataceae)

Bloom Period: May–September

Description: Upright, slender, somewhat delicate perennial to 28 in. (7 dm); stems solitary to few, branched, unequally 4-angled in basal portion with 2 wide, rounded sides and 2 narrow, flat or indented ones. **Flower** 1–2 in. (2.5–5 cm) across, dark pink to white; petals 4, spreading flat, attached near top of urn-shaped structure, soon falling; stamens 8, the anthers narrow, long, conspicuously curved. Flowers few to several in terminal clusters. **Leaves** to 2⅜ in. (6 cm) long, opposite; margins finely toothed, the teeth bristle-pointed.

Habitat: Wet or moist, rich loam or sandy soils in meadows, savannahs, bogs, seepage areas, ditches or along edges of ponds, marshes or stream banks. In NE, SE, SC.

Note: The flowers of Maryland meadow-beauty are somewhat similar to the pink evening primrose (*Oenothera speciosa*), but the fruit is quite distinctive. The small capsules are shaped much like a miniature, long-necked urn or pitcher, with four bristle-like lobes at the rim.

TRAILING FOUR-O'CLOCK

(Wesby)

TRAILING FOUR-O'CLOCK (*Allionia incarnata*)
Four-o'clock Family (Nyctaginaceae)

Bloom Period: April–October

Description: Low, trailing or sprawling perennial densely covered with sticky hairs; stem much-branched at base, the branches many, forked, to 3 ft. (9 dm) long, often tinged with red. **Flower** to ¼ in. (6 mm) long, dark pink to magenta, occasionally white; petals absent; sepals 3, appearing petallike, one-sided. Flowers in cluster of 3, together appearing as a solitary flower; each cluster to 1 in. (25 mm) across, short-stalked, borne in axils of leaves, subtended by deeply lobed bract which later encloses fruit. **Leaves** ½–1½ in. (13–38 mm) long, opposite, with one of the pair larger than the other, short-stalked, thick, conspicuously covered with sticky hairs, usually entire; margins wavy.

Habitat: Dry sandy, gravelly or calcareous soils in full sun in open areas on hills, flats or valleys. In all except NE, SE, NC, SC.

Note: Flowers of this plant open in the morning and remain open for most of the day instead of opening in late evening and closing by midmorning, as do most members of the family. Also called *umbrella-wort, trailing allionia* and *hierba de la hormiga,* or "ant weed."

PURPLE SPIDERLING (*Boerhaavia purpurascens*)
Four-o'clock Family (Nyctaginaceae)

Bloom Period: May–November

Description: Upright, usually rough-hairy annual 8–20 in. (2–5 dm) high; stem much-branched from lower portion, the branches slender and covered with brown glands and sticky hairs. **Flower** to about ³⁄₁₆ in. (5 mm) long, pink; stamens 2 or 3, exserted. Flowers in dense clusters at tips of long, wiry, forking, upright stalks. **Leaves** to 1⅛ in. (3 cm) long, to ¾ in. (2 cm) wide, opposite, slender-stalked, the blade somewhat triangular, thin, bright green on upper surface, or often purplish, pale below, brown-dotted; margins entire to wavy.

Habitat: Dry, gravelly soils of plains, disturbed places, hillsides and brushlands. In FW.

Note: The generic name of this plant honors the Dutch physician Boerhaave. The common name refers to the many slender branches which give the plant a "leggy" or "spidery" appearance. Flowers on an individual plant of purple spiderling are not particularly showy, but when the plants occur en masse, as they frequently do, the blooms make a striking display.

WILD FOUR-O'CLOCK

SCARLET MUSK-FLOWER (Wesby)

WILD FOUR-O'CLOCK (*Mirabilis nyctaginea*)
Four-o'clock Family (Nyctaginaceae)

Bloom Period: April–November

Description: Upright, slender, smooth perennial herb 1–3 ft. (3–9 dm) high; stems usually solitary, swollen at joints, with forking branches. **Flower** ½–⅝ in. (13–15 mm) across; petals absent; sepals 5, petallike, dark pink to purplish. Flowers 3–5 in cluster, surrounded by greenish, leaflike bracts which become enlarged, papery and colored as fruit matures. **Leaves** 2–4¾ in. (5–12 cm) long, opposite; upper ones stalkless.

Habitat: Dry, sandy, gravelly or calcareous soils in prairies, along hillsides, slopes, railroad tracks and edges of woodlands. In NE, NC, EP, PH.

Note: The individual flowers of wild four-o'clock are not very showy, but often a number of plants form small colonies that are most attractive. The flowers open late in the afternoon and drop off early the next morning, but the bracts become rose-colored with age and are frequently mistaken as flowers.

SCARLET MUSK-FLOWER (*Nyctaginia capitata*)
Four-o'clock Family (Nyctaginaceae)

Bloom Period: April–November

Description: Semi-upright to straggling, grayish-green, rather unpleasantly scented herbaceous perennial; stem much-branched from base, jointed. Plants usually have conspicuously sticky hairs almost throughout. **Flower** 1–1⅛ in. (2.5–3 cm) long, pink to dark red, with strong musky fragrance; petals absent; sepals united into long, very slender, tubular shape, abruptly expanded into 5 lobes at rim; anthers long, threadlike,
. prominently exserted. Flowers 5–18, forming terminal cluster at ends of forked branches; each cluster subtended by leaflike bracts. **Leaves** 1½–3½ in. (3.8–9 cm) long, opposite, long-stalked, thick and copiously covered with sticky hairs, especially when young; margins entire or wavy.

Habitat: Sandy, loamy or calcareous soils in fields and along rocky slopes. In all except NE, SE, NC, SC.

Note: Flowers of this plant open in the cool of the evening and close the next morning in the hot sun. Although it is a showy wildflower, the strong and rather offensive scent makes it less desirable for garden plantings. It is also commonly known as *devil's-bouquet*.

273

SCARLET GAURA (Miller)

SHOWY PRIMROSE

SCARLET GAURA (*Gaura coccinea*)
Evening-Primrose Family (Onagraceae)

Bloom Period: May–September
Description: Upright, somewhat hairy perennial to 3 ft. (1 m); stems solitary or many and forming clumps, woody at base, leafy. Herbage gray-green. **Flower** about ½ in. (13 mm) across, white becoming dark pink, fragrant, the 4 petals all spreading upward; stamens 8, long, conspicuous, pointing downward. Flowers numerous, borne in slender spike (raceme) at end of leafless stalk. **Leaves** ½–2½ in. (13–63 mm) long, to ⁹/₁₆ in. (15 mm) wide, alternate, stalkless, crowded; margins entire to occasionally toothed or lobed.
Habitat: Sandy soils of almost all habitats except dense woodlands. In PH, EP, FW.
Note: The delicate fragrance and intense whiteness of the evening-opening flowers attract numerous moths, the primary pollinators of these plants. The common names *wild honeysuckle* and *bee blossom* refer to the fragrance of the plant and its use by insects and especially bees.

SHOWY PRIMROSE (*Oenothera speciosa*)
Evening-Primrose Family (Onagraceae)

Bloom Period: March–July, occasionally in fall
Description: Upright to sprawling perennial to 1½ ft. (45 cm); stems solitary or several from base, branching in upper portion. Plants spread underground to form extensive colonies. **Flower** to 3 in. (7.6 cm) across, dark rosy pink to white; petals 4, broad, delicate in texture, forming shallow cup. Flowers may open in morning or evening, depending upon populations. Buds nodding, becoming erect as flowers open. **Leaves** 2–3 in. (5–7.6 cm) long, alternate, entire, lobed or cleft near base; margins cut into narrow lobes, variously toothed or wavy.
Habitat: Various soils in prairies, open woodlands, ungrazed pastures and plains. In all except western portion of PH.
Note: Showy primrose is easily raised from fall-sown seed and is often seen in cultivation. Almost all of the evening primroses are known as "buttercups," from the "cupping" of the petals and the abundant butter-colored pollen left on the face when the flower is smelled. Also called *Mexican primrose* and *amapola*.

ROSE PRICKLY POPPY

ROUGE-PLANT (Washy)

ROSE PRICKLY POPPY (*Argemone sanguinea*)
Poppy Family (Papaveraceae)

Bloom Period: February–May

Description: Upright, smooth but prickly annual, biennial or short-lived perennial to 48 in. (12 dm); stems solitary to few, branched in upper portion. Plant has whitish coating easily rubbed off. **Flower** 2⅜–3½ in. (6–9 cm) across, pink to rosy-lavender, often white; petals 4–6, cupped; stamens 150 or more. **Leaves** 2–6 in. (5–15 cm) long, alternate, stalkless, bluish-green, the veins conspicuously blue; lower leaves deeply lobed almost to midrib; margins with prickle-tipped teeth.

Habitat: Various soils in disturbed areas, cultivated fields, rangelands and chaparral plains. In CT, EP, ST, FW.

Note: Rose prickly poppy is usually found in colonies that often cover several acres. The plants cannot be transplanted with any success but can be raised from seed and should be used more in cultivation. If these poppies are used as cut flowers, their stems should be seared over an open flame immediately after cutting.

ROUGE-PLANT (*Rivina humilis*)
Pokeweed Family (Phytolaccaceae)

Bloom Period: March–December

Description: Upright to sprawling and vinelike, smooth, bushy herbaceous perennial 12–60 in. (3–15 dm) high from thick root; stem solitary, much-branched, the branches slender. **Flower** to ¼ in. (6 mm) across, pinkish-rose to greenish or whitish; petals absent; sepals 4, petallike. Flowers several to numerous, in upright or drooping spikes. **Leaves** 1–6 in. (2.5–15 cm) long, ½–3⁹⁄₁₆ in. (1.3–9 cm) wide, alternate, stalked, the blade bright green, broadly rounded at base, the margins wavy.

Habitat: Dry or moist, usually shaded soils in brushlands, chaparral, openings and edges of woodlands, on rocky hillsides, floodplains or along stream banks. In all except NE, SE, PH.

Note: Rouge-plant usually forms small colonies that are quite showy when the plants are flowering and fruiting. The fruit is a small berry that turns bright red as it matures. Often the berries start ripening at the base of a spike while flowers are still opening at the tip portion. The berries yield a red dye. Also called *pigeonberry, inkberry* and *small pokeweed*.

SKYROCKET (Cheatham)

STANDING CYPRESS

SKYROCKET (*Ipomopsis aggregata*)
Phlox Family (Polemoniaceae)

Bloom Period: May–October

Description: Rather stiffly upright, coarse, hairy biennial to 6 ft. (2 m); stem firm, unbranched, sparsely leaved. Herbage of plant has rather unpleasant or "skunky" smell. **Flower** ¾–1¼ in. (2–3.2 cm) long, dark pink to bright red, with yellowish mottling, 5-lobed at rim, the lobes pointed, spreading flat. Flowers numerous, in small clusters scattered along upper portion of stem. **Leaves** 1–2 in. (2.5–5 cm) long, alternate, mostly near base of plant; blade divided into very narrow segments.

Habitat: Dry sandy or rocky soils on slopes, shrubby brushland and open woodlands. In FW.

Note: Widely scattered throughout the western portion of the state, skyrocket is one of the more common wildflowers. It is easily grown from seed and does well in native plantings. Also called *red gilia* and *fire pink*.

STANDING CYPRESS (*Ipomopsis rubra*)
Phlox Family (Polemoniaceae)

Bloom Period: June–August

Description: Strictly upright, slender biennial 2–6 ft. (6–18 dm) high; stem unbranched or branching if injured. **Flower** to 1¼ in. (32 mm) long, red, with orangy or yellowish spots inside; petals 5, united at base and somewhat tubular, widely and abruptly flaring at rim and appearing flat. Flowers numerous, forming long, thick spike, opening from tip of stem downward, long-lasting. **Leaves** ³⁄₁₆–1¼ in. (5–32 mm) long, in small basal rosette and also crowded along stem, alternate, the blade deeply divided into 11–17 threadlike segments and appearing feathery or fernlike.

Habitat: Dry sandy or gravelly soils, sun or part shade, in pastures, fields, gravel pits or woodland edges. Throughout.

Note: This is a spectacular plant for the garden and easily raised from fall-sown seed. The plants are highly prized as cut flowers, lasting a week or more. Rarely, a yellow-flowered form will be found, the flowers speckled inside with red. Other common names include *flame flower, Indian plume* and *Texas star*.

POINTED PHLOX

POINTED PHLOX (*Phlox cuspidata*)
Phlox Family (Polemoniaceae)

Bloom Period: February–May

Description: Delicate annual 2¼–6 in. (6–15 cm) high; stem slender, usually branched in upper portion. **Flower** ½–¾ in. (13–20 mm) across, light to rosy pink or purplish, sweetly fragrant, trumpet-shaped, 5-lobed at rim, the lobes spreading flat, narrowed at base, wider and sharp-pointed at tip. Flowers numerous or with only few opening at one time, forming terminal clusters. **Leaves** to 1¼ in. (33 mm) long, ¼ in. (6 mm) wide, stalkless, opposite in lower portion of plant, becoming alternate and narrower in upper portion; margins entire.

Habitat: Sandy or loamy soils in grasslands, prairies and open oak woodlands. In all except PH, FW.

Note: The state's three varieties of pointed phlox differ mainly in leaf width and flower size. Pointed phlox readily reseeds and usually forms extensive colonies. It is frequently found growing with sandwort, blue-eyed grass, Indian paintbrush and yellow star-grass.

DRUMMOND PHLOX (*Phlox drummondii* subsp. *wilcoxiana*)
Phlox Family (Polemoniaceae)

Bloom Period: February–June

Description: Low, upright annual 4–20 in. (1–5 dm) high, covered with sticky hairs; stem may be unbranched or branched in lower portion. **Flower** to 1 in. (25 mm) wide, scarlet to dark velvety red, trumpet-shaped, the tube very slender, abruptly flaring into 5 wide-spreading lobes at rim. Flowers numerous, congested into loose, somewhat flattened terminal cluster. **Leaves** 1–3 in. (25–76 mm) long, averaging 7 times as long as wide, usually opposite in lower portion of stem becoming alternate and somewhat broader in upper portion, entire.

Habitat: Deep, sandy soils in disturbed or abandoned areas, pastures, hillsides and woodland openings. In SC, CT, ST.

Note: This plant does not perform well in cultivation, primarily because of its specific requirement for a deep, sandy soil. It is named for Thomas Drummond, a Scottish botanist who collected in the southern portion of Texas in 1833–34.

PRAIRIE PHLOX

ABERT WILD BUCKWHEAT (Cheatham)

PRAIRIE PHLOX (*Phlox pilosa*)
Phlox Family (Polemoniaceae)

Bloom Period: April–May

Description: Slender, upright, perennial to 2 ft. (6 dm), covered with gland-tipped hairs, sticky to the touch. Stem usually solitary, sometimes branching in upper portion. **Flower** to ¾ in. (2 cm) long, 1¼ in. (32 mm) across, pale pink to lavender or purple, sweetly fragrant, tubular, 5-lobed at rim, the lobes wide-flaring and appearing almost flat. Lobes narrowed at base, broad at tip and often abruptly sharp-pointed. Flowers numerous, borne in an open terminal cluster. **Leaves** to 5 in. (12.7 cm) long, ⅜ in. (1 cm) wide, becoming broader in upper portion of stem, opposite, stalkless, fringed with hairs.

Habitat: Sandy or clay soils along dry slopes, fencerows, in open meadows and woodlands. In NE, SE, NC, SC, CT.

Note: The common name of *downy phlox* is perhaps more appropriate for this plant, as it is rarely found on prairies. It is a hardy plant and a desirable addition to wildflower gardens. The phloxes are, for the most part, pollinated by small bees and butterflies. *Phlox* is derived from the Greek word *phlogos* meaning "a flame," hence, "reddish," perhaps best describing species other than our more common ones, which are generally of more pinkish or magenta hues.

ABERT WILD BUCKWHEAT (*Eriogonum abertianum*)
Knotweed Family (Polygonaceae)

Bloom Period: Almost all year

Description: Upright or spreading hairy annual to 20 in. (5 dm); stems few to several, widely branched. Plant covered with silky, woolly hairs. **Flower** very small, ⅛–³⁄₁₆ in. (3–5 mm) long; sepals pettallike, white to pale yellow, often becoming rose or reddish; petals absent. Flowers clustered in a densely hairy, stalked cup at tip of stem; flowering stem often much-branched and forming large, showy cluster. **Leaves** ⅜–1½ in. (1–3.8 cm) long, ⅜–1⅛ in. (1–3 cm) wide; basal leaves numerous, very long-stalked; upper leaves narrow, stalkless or nearly so.

Habitat: Sandy or gravelly soils on flats, slopes, hillsides or open grasslands. In FW.

Note: When first flowering, this plant is a low rosette of leaves with a few flowers in the center. Later the stems elongate. The plants are very variable in size and in hairiness, depending on the local environment and time of year. This species is named for a 19th century American collector, James William Abert. The cultivated buckwheat (*Fagopyrum sagittatum*) is in this family.

CURL-TOP SMARTWEED

CURL-TOP SMARTWEED (*Persicaria lapathifolia*)
Knotweed Family (Polygonaceae)

Bloom Period: May–December

Description: Upright to somewhat sprawling, smooth annual to 6 ft. (2 m); stems solitary or few, much-branched, greenish, conspicuously sheathed at the swollen joints, the sheath brittle, strongly ribbed, fringed with bristles when young. **Flower** to ⅛ in. (3 mm) long, light to dark pink or rose, 4- or 5-parted or -lobed at rim, each lobe with anchor-shaped veins near tip. Flowers numerous, densely congested in slender, upright or nodding spike with only one or few flowers open at once. **Leaves** 2–12 in. (5–30 cm) long, ⅛–2 in. (1–5 cm) wide, alternate, stalked, long-pointed at both ends, thickly dotted with small glands on lower surface.

Habitat: Moist or muddy soils, or in shallow water, in disturbed areas, along banks of streams, ponds, lakes and ditches. Throughout.

Note: Curl-top smartweed is a common plant in wet areas, reaching its flowering peak in late summer and early fall. It and other smartweeds are an important food for ducks, and its flowers are visited by numerous species of small insects. A leaf tea was formerly used for its laxative and fever-reducing properties.

SHAGGY PORTULACA (*Portulaca mundula*)
Purslane Family (Portulacaceae)

Bloom Period: May–December

Description: Somewhat upright or flatly sprawling or trailing, succulent, hairy annual; stem usually solitary, much-branched, to 6 in. (15 cm) long. Plants form low mounds or spread flat and matlike. **Flower** about ½ in. (1.3 cm) across, dark rosy-red to purplish; petals 5, cupped. Flowers 2–8, crowded in densely hairy cluster subtended by whorl of 6–10 leaves. **Leaves** to ⅝ in. (1.6 cm) long, very narrow or somewhat threadlike, alternate, numerous, the blade thick. Small tufts of hairs occur in axils, the hairs white, woolly, conspicuously kinky.

Habitat: Sandy or gravelly soils in pastures, chaparral, flats, arroyos and along slopes, in open saline sands and along beaches. In all except NE.

Note: Shaggy portulaca usually forms large colonies and can be quite showy, especially when occurring in barren sandy areas. The flowers open fully only in bright sunlight, but usually several are open at once on each plant and they often form a solid swath of color, making the ground appear rosy-red. In southern portions of the state, the plants may live through the winter, producing flowers during periods of warm weather. Seeds are scattered from tiny capsules which open near the top by a lidlike structure. The plants readily self-seed, so usually only one planting is necessary. Also called *moss rose*.

285

PHEASANT'S-EYE

SCARLET CLEMATIS   (Miller)

PHEASANT'S-EYE (*Adonis annua*)
Crowfoot Family (Ranunculaceae)

Bloom Period: February–June

Description: Upright, smooth annual 8–24 in. (2–6 dm) high; stems solitary or few, much-branched. **Flower** about ¾ in. (2 cm) across, dark red with darker, almost black center, solitary and terminal; petals 6–8, cupped, somewhat finely cut at tip, soon falling; stamens many; pistils many. **Leaves** ¾–2 in. (2–5 cm) long, alternate, numerous, rather densely crowded on plant, the blade finely parted or divided into very narrow segments.

Habitat: Sandy or clay soils in prairies, pastures, rangelands and open bottomlands. In NE, NC, SC.

Note: Pheasant's-eye is a cultivated plant from Europe which has become established in the flora of the central and eastern portions of our state. The plants are easily started from seed and readily reseed each year. The flowers wilt almost immediately when cut and are not useful for floral arrangements.

SCARLET CLEMATIS (*Clematis texensis*)
Crowfoot Family (Ranunculaceae)

Bloom Period: March–July

Description: Low-climbing or sprawling herbaceous or slightly woody vine; stems slender, very leafy, 15–20 ft. (45–60 dm) long, climbing by twisting leafstalks. **Flower** ¾–1⅛ in. (2–3 cm) long, bright red or scarlet; petals absent; sepals petallike, thick in texture, united at base, 4-lobed at tips, the lobes slightly recurved. Flowers in clusters of 1–7 on stalks from leaf axils. **Leaves** opposite, stalked, the blade divided into 4 or 5 pairs of leaflets; leaflets usually 2- or 3-lobed.

Habitat: Rocky calcareous soils on shaded cliffs, slopes and ledges along moist ravines, streams and river bottoms. In NC, EP.

Note: The fruit of scarlet clematis consists of a feathery ball of plumed seeds which is very showy. Frequently sold by nurseries, scarlet clematis does fairly well in cultivation. It is very effective when allowed to cover a fence, trellis, small brush pile or stump. A tea from the dried, chopped stems has been reported as a treatment for headache in general, but especially for migraine. A tincture was formerly used as a counterirritant.

FINE-LEAF BLUETS

TEXAS PAINTBRUSH

FINE-LEAF BLUETS (*Hedyotis nigricans*)
Madder Family (Rubiaceae)

Bloom Period: April–November

Description: Upright to sprawling, smooth, delicate perennial 2–20 in. (5–50 cm) high from stout taproot; stems slender, solitary or few from base and forming clump, opposite-branched in upper portion. **Flower** to ⅜ in. (1 cm) long; pink, purplish, or occasionally white; trumpet-shaped, 4-lobed at rim. Flowers few to numerous, in clusters at ends of stiff branches. **Leaves** ⅜–1⅝ in. (1–4.1 cm) long, very narrow and threadlike, opposite, essentially stalkless, often with clusters of smaller leaves in axils; margins often rolled toward lower surface.

Habitat: In dry or moist sandy or calcareous soils of prairies, woodlands, rocky hillsides and slopes. Throughout.

Note: Represented in Texas by three varieties, the species is highly variable but well distributed throughout the state. *H. nigricans* is so named because the leaves turn black as they dry. *Prairie bluets* is another common name.

TEXAS PAINTBRUSH (*Castilleja indivisa*)
Figwort Family (Scrophulariaceae)

Bloom Period: May–June, sporadically until fall

Description: Upright, hairy annual or biennial to 16 in. (4 dm); stems usually several from base and forming clumps, unbranched. **Flower** to 1 in. (25 mm) long, whitish or greenish, tubular, very slender, 2-lipped, subtended by conspicuous red-tipped, leaflike bracts. Flowers and bracts numerous, the whole forming showy terminal spike. **Leaves** 1–4 in. (2.5–10 cm) long, alternate, stalkless, narrow, entire or sometimes with few lobes near base.

Habitat: Moist sandy loams in prairies, pastures and on hillsides, but especially along roadsides. In all except PH, FW.

Note: Texas paintbrush gets its common name from a resemblance to a ragged brush dipped in paint. The roots of the plant grow until they touch the roots of other plants, frequently grasses, then they penetrate the roots of the "host" plant and obtain a portion of their needed nutrients; hence, they are considered semiparasitic. This is our only annual species of *Castilleja*; the other eight species which occur in the state are all perennials. The genus name honors the Spanish botanist Juan Castillejo. Also called *Indian paintbrush*.

PINK PLAINS PENSTEMON (Young)

FOXGLOVE (Gatlin)

PINK PLAINS PENSTEMON (*Penstemon ambiguus*)
Figwort Family (Scrophulariaceae)

Bloom Period: May–August

Description: Upright, essentially smooth, somewhat woody perennial to 20 in. (5 dm); stems few to several, much-branched and moundlike. **Flower** ⅝–1⅛ in. (16–29 mm) long, dark pink to white, the throat lined with red, tubular, abruptly 2-lipped; upper lip deeply 2-lobed, somewhat reflexed; lower lip deeply 3-lobed, slightly projecting forward. Flowers few to several, in terminal clusters. **Leaves** mostly about ⅜–1 in. (9–25 mm) long, threadlike in width, opposite; margins entire.

Habitat: Sandy soils in plains, rangelands and on hillsides and slopes. In EP, ST, PH, FW.

Note: A large, almost woody plant, pink plains penstemon forms large clumps or mounds and is very showy. The plants are worthy of cultivation, producing an almost solid mass of flowers throughout the spring and summer. Plants may be propagated by root division or seed.

FOXGLOVE (*Penstemon cobaea*)
Figwort Family (Scrophulariaceae)

Bloom Period: May–June

Description: Upright, hairy perennial to 24 in. (6 dm); stems solitary or several and forming clump. Plants usually found in colonies. **Flower** 1¼–2¼ in. (32–58 mm) long, usually pink tinged with reddish-purple or lavender and streaked with darker lines, tubular but widely inflated, 2-lipped, broadly open and 5-lobed at rim; lower lip without hairs within; stamens 5, one of them bearing no pollen but bearded for most of its length with yellow hairs. Flowers few to numerous, arranged in clusters around stem, forming terminal spike. **Leaves** to 3¼ in. (83 mm) at midstem, opposite, stalked in basal portion of plant, becoming smaller and stalkless toward summit of stem; margins usually sharply toothed.

Habitat: Loamy or rocky soils of prairies and along bluffs, slopes and edges of creeks. In all except FW.

Note: Foxglove is a most beautiful wildflower easily raised from seed. The botanist Thomas Nuttall discovered it in Arkansas over a century ago and named it after its striking resemblance to the Mexican genus *Cobaea*. The early settlers knew it as *balmony*, and brewed a tea from the leaves as a laxative. Also called *fairy thimbles, wild belladonna, dewflower* and *beardtongue*.

HAVARD PENSTEMON (Tveten)

LOOSE-FLOWERED PENSTEMON

HAVARD PENSTEMON (*Penstemon havardii*)
Figwort Family (Scrophulariaceae)

Bloom Period: April–June

Description: Strictly upright, smooth perennial 3–6 ft. (1–2 m) high; stems usually several from base and forming clump, unbranched. Herbage covered with a whitish coating which will come off when rubbed. **Flower** ¾–1⅛ in. (2–3 cm) long, red, straight and narrowly tubular, shallowly 2-lipped at rim; upper lip 2-lobed, projecting past lower lip; lower lip 3-lobed; sterile stamen not "bearded." Flowers few to several, in stalked clusters from upper leaf axils, forming long terminal spike. **Leaves** 2–4 in. (5–10 cm) long, 1–2¾ in. (2.5–7 cm) wide, opposite, thick; margins entire.

Habitat: Rocky, gravelly or sandy soils of plains, deserts, hillsides and mountain slopes. In FW.

Note: Havard penstemon is endemic to the hills and mountain slopes of western Texas. The long spikes of scarlet flowers stand tall above low clumps of blue-green foliage, making a most attractive display. This plant is much used by various species of hummingbirds.

LOOSE-FLOWERED PENSTEMON (*Penstemon laxiflorus*)
Figwort Family (Scrophulariaceae)

Bloom Period: March–June

Description: Upright to somewhat leaning or sprawling perennial 1–2½ ft. (3–7 dm) high; stems one to few, slender, may be branched in upper portion. **Flower** ¾–1¼ in. (2–3.2 cm) long, pale pink to white, tubular, 2-lipped, narrow; upper lip deeply 2-lobed, lower lip 3-lobed, spreading. Flowers few, in long-stalked clusters, the stalks paired, opposite, from upper leaf axils. **Leaves** to 4 in. (10 cm) long, ¾ in. (2 cm) wide, opposite, stalkless and clasping stem at base of blade; blade thin, conspicuously toothed on margins.

Habitat: Sandy or gravelly soils of prairies, pastures, abandoned fields and open woodlands. In all except PH, FW.

Note: The word *penstemon* is derived from two Greek words meaning "five" and "stamen," and refers to a unique fifth stamen present in this genus. Most other members of the figwort family bear either two or four stamens, but the penstemons have four regular stamens and a fifth stamen usually much broader than the others and covered with brightly colored hairs. This hairy or "bearded" stamen gives the genus the common name *beardtongue*.

DAKOTA VERVAIN

ROSE VERVAIN

DAKOTA VERVAIN (*Verbena bipinnatifida*)
Vervain Family (Verbenaceae)

Bloom Period: Throughout year

Description: Low, trailing or creeping hairy perennial 6–18 in. (15–45 cm) high; stems 4-angled, branching from base, rooting at lower joints (nodes). Plants often form matlike colonies, covering large areas. **Flower** to ⅜ in. (1 cm) across, purple, lavender or pink, trumpet-shaped, 5-lobed at rim, hairy on outside. Flowers numerous, in rounded, terminal clusters which become elongated during flowering. **Leaves** ¾–2½ in. (2–6.3 cm) long, opposite, stalked, the blade cut or lobed into numerous narrow segments.

Habitat: Dry sandy or calcareous soils in abandoned areas, prairies, pastures, on hillsides and slopes. Throughout.

Note: Dakota vervain is an attractive plant for the garden, the finely cut foliage adding a lacy background to the balls of purple flowers. The flowers are especially rich in nectar and attract many species of butterflies and other insects. Also called *small-flowered verbena*.

ROSE VERVAIN (*Verbena canadensis*)
Vervain Family (Verbenaceae)

Bloom Period: February–June

Description: Upright to sprawling, creeping, hairy perennial 6–16 in. (15–40 cm) high; stem 4-angled, branched, rooting at lower joints (nodes) and forming large, dense mats of plants. **Flower** ½–¾ in. (1.3–2 cm) across, purple to lavender or rose, with darker center, sweetly fragrant, trumpet-shaped, 5-lobed at rim. Flowers many, in solitary, terminal cluster. Cluster short and dense at first, becoming elongated in fruit. **Leaves** 1–3½ in. (2.5–9 cm) long, opposite, stalked, the blade deeply cut, lobed, toothed or entire.

Habitat: Sandy or rocky soils in fields, prairies, pinelands, open woodlands and railroad embankments. In all except western portion of PH.

Note: One of the showiest *Verbena*s, rose vervain frequently forms extensive masses and is intensely fragrant. An early bloomer and rich in nectar, it is heavily used by early-emerging or overwintering butterflies and moths. The plants are easily cultivated and make excellent bedding or border plants, blending equally well with cultivated species or other wildflowers.

TEXAS VERVAIN

(Myers)

TEXAS VERVAIN (*Verbena halei*)
Vervain Family (Verbenaceae)

Bloom Period: February–December

Description: Upright, rather smooth, delicate, slender-branched perennial to 2½ ft. (7 dm); stem solitary or several from base, 4-angled, grooved, branched in upper portion. **Flower** about ¼ in. (6 mm) across, pink, bluish-lavender or rarely white, trumpet-shaped, 5-lobed at rim. Flowers numerous, forming long, very slender spikes either terminal or from leaf axils. **Leaves** ¾–3⅛ in. (2–8 cm) long, to 1½ in. (38 mm) wide, opposite, stalked, the blade varying from deeply to shallowly cut or lobed in lower portion of plant to toothed or entire in upper portion of plant.

Habitat: Various soils in abandoned areas, fields, meadows, pastures, prairies, rocky hillsides and woodlands. Throughout.

Note: Since early times, Texas vervain, or *slender vervain*, as it is sometimes called, has been considered an important medicinal herb and a powerful charm against witches. A related species, English vervain, was regarded as a holy herb in the Old World, particularly by the Druids.

BLUE FLOWERS

SNAKE-HERB (Johnston)

LOW RUELLIA

SNAKE-HERB (*Dyschoriste linearis*)
Acanthus Family (Acanthaceae)

Bloom Period: April–July

Description: Rather stiffly upright, coarsely and stiffly hairy perennial 7¼–12 in. (18–30 cm) high; stems 4-angled, few to several, usually unbranched. **Flower** ⅝–1⅜ in. (16–35 mm) long, bluish-purple or lavender, dark-spotted in throat, hairy outside, somewhat tubular, 2-lipped; upper lip unlobed; lower lip deeply 3-lobed. Flowers stalkless, from upper leaf axils. **Leaves** ⅝–2 in. (16–50 mm) long, opposite, stalkless, rather rigid; margins fringed with hairs.

Habitat: Dry sandy, rocky or commonly calcareous soils on grassy slopes, silty flats, along bluffs, cap rock, ravines or open brushlands or woodlands. In NC, SC, CT, EP, FW.

Note: Snake-herb looks very much like *Ruellia* spp. and the plants may be easily confused. The two may be separated in the field by examining the tubes of the flowers. Snake-herb has very short tubes, while the flowers of *Ruellia* have conspicuously long, slender tubes.

LOW RUELLIA (*Ruellia humilis*)
Acanthus Family (Acanthaceae)

Bloom Period: April–October

Description: Upright to somewhat sprawling, clumped, rather stout, conspicuously hairy perennial to 32 in. (8 dm), commonly much lower; stems usually several in clump, prominently 4-angled, branched. Branches slender, often lying on ground. **Flower** 2–3⅛ in. (5–8 cm) long, to ¾ in. (2 cm) across, lavender to purplish-blue, usually with darker markings in throat, trumpet-shaped, deeply 5-lobed at rim. Flowers few, in clusters from middle and upper leaf axils. **Leaves** to 3⅛ in. (8 cm) long, 1¾ in. (4.5 cm) wide, opposite, essentially stalkless, somewhat crowded on stem; blade leathery, blunt or wedge-shaped at base and extending onto stalk, blunt or sharp-pointed at tip, densely hairy on veins and margins.

Habitat: Dry sandy or clayey soils in old fields, prairies, savannahs, open forests and slopes. In all except PH, ST, FW.

Note: Low ruellia has several distinct varieties. The ruellias are commonly referred to as "wild petunias" and are attractive plants worthy of wildflower plantings, doing equally well in full sun or part shade.

VIOLET RUELLIA

SHAGGY STENANDRIUM (Simpson)

VIOLET RUELLIA (*Ruellia nudiflora*)
Acanthus Family (Acanthaceae)

Bloom Period: March–December

Description: Upright to semisprawling perennial to 28 in. (7 dm) from somewhat woody base; stem solitary, branching in upper portion. Plant densely hairy when young, becoming almost entirely smooth with age. **Flower** to 2⅛ in. (55 mm) long, 1½ in. (38 mm) across, lavender to purple, trumpet-shaped, deeply 5-lobed at rim, conspicuously curved, opening about sunrise, then falling from plant in early afternoon. **Leaves** generally to 2⅜ in. (6 cm) long, 1⅛ in. (3 cm) wide, opposite, stalked; blade gray-green, prominently net-veined on lower surface; margins curled or wavy-toothed. Summer leaves to 4¾ in. (12 cm) long, much smaller in upper portion of plant.

Habitat: Heavier sands or clays in abandoned areas, pastures, prairies, openings, edges of woodlands and thickets. In all except PH.

Note: This plant's showy flowers are produced in the summer in loose, terminal clusters; smaller clusters of nonopening, self-fertilizing flowers are produced in the spring. Both types produce seed. Ruellias are commonly called "wild petunias," but the true wild petunia from which the cultivated petunia was derived belongs to the Solanaceae, or nightshade family.

SHAGGY STENANDRIUM (*Stenandrium barbatum*)
Acanthus Family (Acanthaceae)

Bloom Period: March–June

Description: Low, dwarfed, densely hairy perennial to 2⅜ in. (6 cm); stems several, forming small mounds or tufts. Plants conspicuously covered with soft, white, straight hairs. **Flower** to ⅝ in. (16 mm) long, purple, funnel-shaped, 5-lobed and wide-spreading at rim. Flowers few to several, densely clustered in short spikes among the foliage. **Leaves** to 1½ in. (3.8 cm) long, to 5⁄16 in. (8 mm) wide, opposite, crowded, narrowed at base, the margins entire.

Habitat: Dry limestone or clay soils on flats, plains, rocky hillsides, mountain slopes and ridges. In FW.

Note: While these plants are small, the flowers are very conspicuous in early spring as they open against a stark background of the barren, often gravelly or rocky sites they normally inhabit. With a little moisture, the plants continue to flower for some time and are excellent additions to a rock garden, or in edgings or borders.

ERYNGO (Miller)

SHOWY BLUE-STAR

ERYNGO (*Eryngium leavenworthii*)
Parsley Family (Apiaceae)

Bloom Period: July–September

Description: Upright, rather slender, prickly annual 20–40 in. (5–10 dm) high; stem leafy, branched in upper portion with the branches broadly spreading. Almost the entire plant some shade of purple. **Flower** minute, purple; petals 5; stamens dark-blue, long, slender, protruding. Flowers numerous, mingled with small, spiny bracts and congested in elongated, terminal, head-like cluster; cluster to 1 in. (25 mm) across, subtended by conspicuously spiny-tipped bracts. **Leaves** to 2⅜ in. (6 cm) long and ¾ in. (2 cm) wide, stalkless and clasping stem at base; blade deeply parted, the segments edged and tipped with stiff spines.

Habitat: Clay or limestone soils of plains, prairies and grasslands. In all except ST, FW.

Note: Few plants can rival eryngo for beauty in late summer, when it forms sheets of brilliant purple across fields and prairies. Gathered when the flowers are freshly opened, and hung upside down to dry, this plant will keep its dark purple color for several months, making it quite useful in dried arrangements.

SHOWY BLUE-STAR (*Amsonia illustris*)
Dogbane Family (Apocynaceae)

Bloom Period: March–June

Description: Stiffly upright, smooth perennial to 4 ft. (12 dm) from woody roots; stems stout, usually several and forming clump. **Flower** ¾–1 in. (2–2.5 cm) across, pale to dark blue, tubular, deeply 5-lobed at rim with lobes spreading flat. Flowers numerous, loosely congested in terminal cluster. **Leaves** to 4 in. (10 cm) long, 1⅛ in. (3 cm) wide, alternate, thick, firm, the upper surface dark green and shiny.

Habitat: Moist or wet soils of meadows, low woodlands, floodplains, edges of marshes or swamps, in streams or ditches. In NE, SE, NC, SC.

Note: Normally growing in a very moist situation, blue-star often does well in cultivation in loose, rich soils with a little extra moisture. Seed may be sown or clumps divided in the fall. The species *A. ciliata* is common on limestone and chalky hills in western Texas.

MEADOW ASTER

BASKET FLOWER

MEADOW ASTER (*Aster pratensis*)
Sunflower Family (Asteraceae)

Bloom Period: September–November

Description: Stiffly upright, slender, hairy perennial commonly 20–32 in. (5–8 dm) high from woody base; stem stiff, brittle, solitary, unbranched or with few stiffly upright branches in upper portion. **Flower** head to 1½ in. (38 mm) or more across; ray flowers 15–25, purple or violet; disk flowers yellow, numerous. Heads few on plant, at ends of stem and branches. **Leaves** ⅜–1⅛ in. (1–3 cm) long, alternate, stalkless, firm; lower leaves usually dried and withered by flowering time; upper leaves not reduced in size, extending up stem to head.

Habitat: Sandy or sandy loam soils in prairies, meadows, open woodlands and woodland borders. In all except PH, EP, FW.

Note: Meadow aster is one of the more attractive asters, the flower heads large and showy. The genus *Aster* is from the Greek word *asteros* meaning "star," and is descriptive of the common form of the flower heads. The species name *pratensis* is a Latin word meaning "pertaining to or growing in a meadow." This is a most poetic name for this plant but is not particularly accurate, as its most common habitat is woodland openings and edges.

BASKET FLOWER (*Centaurea americana*)
Sunflower Family (Asteraceae)

Bloom Period: May–August

Description: Upright, smooth annual 1½–5 ft. (4.5–15 dm) high; stem solitary, grooved or ridged, thick, leafy, much-branched in upper portion. **Flower** head 1½–3⅛ in. (3.8–8 cm) across, dark lavender to pink, rarely white, fragrant, solitary at ends of upper branches; ray or outer flowers absent; disk flowers numerous, included in a cup or basketlike structure of green prickly margined bracts (phyllaries). Stem swollen or enlarged beneath flower head. **Leaves** to 2½ in. (6.3 cm) long, alternate, stalkless, entire or shallowly toothed.

Habitat: Sandy or clayey loams of abandoned sites, closely grazed pastures and edges of fields, but most commonly on prairies. Throughout.

Note: One of our showiest and most common wildflowers, basket flower is easily cultivated and makes an excellent cut flower for bouquets. The seeds are often sold in nursery catalogues under the names *powderpuff* or *sweet sultan*. This plant looks quite similar to the thistles, but lacks their prickly characteristics.

CHICORY (Myers)

TEXAS THISTLE

CHICORY (*Cichorium intybus*)
Sunflower Family (Asteraceae)

Bloom Period: June–October

Description: Mostly upright to occasionally sprawling, smooth perennial 8–40 in. (2–10 dm) high from deep taproot; stems solitary or few, branched in upper portion, the branches short, stiff or rigid. Plant contains milky sap. **Flower** heads about 2 in. (5 cm) across; ray flowers about 15, blue, 5-toothed and squared at tip; disk flowers absent. Heads solitary at tips of spreading, leafless branches, or stalkless in axils of leaves. **Leaves** 3–10 in. (7.6–25 cm) long, alternate, stalkless, variously lobed or toothed; upper leaves reduced to very small bracts.

Habitat: Various soils, mostly in disturbed areas, edges of cultivated fields and along roadsides. In NC, PH.

Note: Chicory is a native of Europe that has escaped from cultivation in this country and is rapidly becoming established among our native flora. The bright, true blue of the flowers is beautiful in wildflower plantings, but each flower remains open for only one day. The large roots of this plant are commonly roasted, ground and mixed with coffee or used alone as a coffee substitute. This genus also provides us with endive (*C. endivia*), a popular garden vegetable used in salads or as a potherb.

TEXAS THISTLE (*Cirsium texanum*)
Sunflower Family (Asteraceae)

Bloom Period: May–July

Description: Upright, bristly-spiny, woolly biennial or perennial 2–5 ft. (6–15 dm) high; stem solitary, much-branched in upper portion. **Flower** heads to 1½ in. (38 mm) across, pink to rose-purple, solitary at tips of long, woolly, almost leafless stalks; ray flowers absent; disk flowers numerous, held in cup of small, prickly tipped bracts (phyllaries). **Leaves** 4–9 in. (10–22.5 cm) long, alternate, numerous, clasping stem at base, dark green and smooth on upper surface, the lower surface felted with whitish hairs. Blade with 3–9 triangular or rounded lobes on each side, each lobe irregularly spiny-toothed. Basal leaves larger, forming winter rosette; upper leaves smaller.

Habitat: Sandy or clayey loam in abandoned areas, disturbed sites, pastures and prairies. In all but NE, SE.

Note: Texas thistle is especially attractive to butterflies and other insects. Larvae of the painted-lady butterfly feed on the foliage. Goldfinches eat the seeds and also use the silky fluff of the ripened seeds to line their nests.

MISTFLOWER (Tveten)

MISTFLOWER (*Eupatorium coelestinum*)
Sunflower Family (Asteraceae)

Bloom Period: July–December

Description: Semi-upright to sprawling perennial to 2 ft. (6 dm); stems solitary or several and forming clump, rather weak, branched in upper portion. Plants usually form large colonies from long, slender, thickened roots. **Flower** head about ¼ in. (6 mm) across, blue to purplish-blue; ray flowers absent; disk flowers 40–50; styles threadlike, conspicuously protruding. Heads numerous and borne in dense, flat-topped terminal clusters. **Leaves** ¾–2¾ in. (2–7 cm) long, ¾–2 in. (2–5 cm) wide, opposite, stalked, the blade widest at base, triangular or heart-shaped, conspicuously veined, wrinkled on both surfaces; margins sharply toothed.

Habitat: Sandy soils in seeps, marshy areas and along edges of shady streams or ponds. In all except ST, PH, FW.

Note: Mistflower is highly prized in the wildflower garden as a border or specimen plant. The flowers are often so numerous on the plant that it becomes an almost solid sheet of color. It is especially good for attracting late-season butterflies. Also called *blue boneset*.

NARROW-LEAF GAYFEATHER (*Liatris mucronata*)
Sunflower Family (Asteraceae)

Bloom Period: August–December

Description: Stiffly upright to widely spreading smooth perennial 12–32 in. (3–8 dm) high from large round corm; stems few to numerous and forming clump, from corm, unbranched, often reddish in color. **Flower** head to ¾ in. (18 mm) long, purple; ray flowers absent; disk flowers 3–6 per head, purple. Heads numerous, from axils of upper leaves, densely congested in long, slender terminal spike. Flowers open from top of spike downward. **Leaves** 2–4 in. (5–10 cm) long, to ³⁄₁₆ in. (5 mm) wide, alternate, somewhat crowded, progressively smaller from base of plant, becoming small bracts in flowering portion of stem.

Habitat: Well-drained gravelly, sandy or calcareous soils in prairies, plains, cuestas, edges and openings of woodlands, on hillsides and slopes. In NC, SC, CT, PH, EP, ST.

Note: The gayfeathers are among our most attractive late-summer and early-fall wildflowers. Easily grown from fall-transplanted corms, they do very well in cultivation and under favorable conditions will grow tall and lush. The roots or corms of *Liatris* have been employed in treating sore throat and rattlesnake bite, the latter usage giving the plant the common name *button snakeroot*.

BLAZING STAR

BLAZING STAR (*Liatris squarrosa*)
Sunflower Family (Asteraceae)

Bloom Period: June–September
Description: Stiffly–upright perennial 12–24 in. (3–6 dm) high
with several to numerous stems rising from large, bulblike
corm. **Flower** heads to 1⅛ in. (3 cm) long and broad, short-
stalked; ray flowers absent; disk flowers 25–40, rose-purple or
magenta, tubular. Heads few to many, surrounded by several
leaflike bracts, loosely congested in leaf axils along upper portion of stem and forming terminal spike. Flowers open from top
of stem downward. **Leaves** to 10 in. (25 cm) long, ¼ in. (6 mm)
wide in basal portion of plant, becoming progressively smaller
until small bracts in flowering portion of stem.
Habitat: Sandy or clayey soils in open uplands and along woodland edges or clearings. In NE, SE, SC.
Note: Blazing star is easily cultivated and is an excellent plant for
the wildflower garden. It is especially attractive to butterflies
and other insects. The species name means "rough" or "scruffy"
and refers to the spreading tips of the small bracts subtending
the heads.

SKELETON PLANT (*Lygodesmia texana*)
Sunflower Family (Asteraceae)

Bloom Period: April–October
Description: Upright, slender, smooth perennial herb to 2 ft. (6
dm) from fleshy root; stems usually several, sparsely branched,
brittle, practically leafless. **Flower** head 1⅝–2 in. (4.1–5 cm)
across, solitary, terminal, fragrant; ray flowers 8–12, lavender,
pale bluish or rose, sharply cut at squarish tip into 3–5 minute
lobes; disk flowers absent; styles dark lavender, conspicuously
erect in center. Only one head blooms at a time on the stem
and lasts for only a few hours in the morning. **Leaves** 4–6 in.
(10–15 cm) long, mostly in basal rosette, the blade entire or
with few short lobes. Upper leaves reduced to mere scales.
Habitat: Dry sandy loam, clayey or calcareous soils, in openings,
on limestone hills or slopes, but especially on prairies. In all except NE, SE, SC.
Note: Texas skeleton plant is a most attractive addition to the
wildflower garden and is easily started from fall-sown seed.
Other common names include *purple dandelion*, *flowering
straw* and *milk pink*.

TANSY ASTER (Simpson)

OYSTER PLANT (Young)

TANSY ASTER (*Machaeranthera tanacetifolia*)
Sunflower Family (Asteraceae)

Bloom Period: May–October

Description: Low, upright to widely spreading or sprawling annual herb 4–16 in. (1–4 dm) high; stems solitary or several from
base, densely leafy, much-branched and often forming clumps
or mounds. Herbage is glandular-hairy and sticky to the touch.
Flower head 1¼–2½ in. (32–63 mm) across, not crowded, solitary at tip of leafy stem; ray flowers 15–25, very narrow, red-
violet to purple; disk flowers numerous, yellow, becoming
reddish-brown. **Leaves** 2–5 in. (5–12.5 cm) long, alternate,
spine-tipped, the blade deeply cut or divided into numerous
narrow segments and appearing fernlike; upper leaves becoming smaller, less divided to merely toothed.

Habitat: Sandy soils on plains, hillsides and slopes, often in disturbed areas. In PH, FW.

Note: Tansy aster is one of the showiest western wildflowers and
is much used in cultivation. The common name is from the resemblance of the leaves to the true tansy (*Tanacetum* spp.). It is
often sold by seedsmen under the name *Tahoka daisy*. Also
called *dagger-flower* because of its sharp-pointed leaves.

OYSTER PLANT (*Tragopogon porrifolius*)
Sunflower Family (Asteraceae)

Bloom Period: May–June

Description: Stiffly upright, stout, smooth biennial from deep
taproot; stems solitary or few, sparingly branched in upper portion, very tough. **Flower** head 2–4 in. (5–10 cm) across; ray
flowers 8–120, blue to dark-violet; disk flowers absent. Heads
solitary at ends of branches, the branches swollen and hollow
just beneath head. Long, slender bracts subtend each head.
Leaves to 12 in. (30 cm) long, very narrow and grasslike, tapered
to fine point, alternate, stalkless and basally clasping stem.

Habitat: Various soils in disturbed areas, edges of cultivated fields
and along roadsides. In NC, FW.

Note: The fruit of oyster plant is most conspicuous and almost
as striking as the flowers. Each seed is tipped with feathery
bristles, with numerous seeds congested into a round, fluffy,
beige-colored ball. The roots of this plant may be boiled and
eaten and the leaves may be eaten either cooked or in salads. A
native of Europe, oyster plant is becoming widely established in
our flora. Also known as *salsify*.

WESTERN IRONWEED

WESTERN IRONWEED (*Vernonia baldwinii*)
Sunflower Family (Asteraceae)

Bloom Period: July–October

Description: Upright, stout, coarse, hairy perennial 2–5 ft. (6–15 dm) high; stems usually several and forming clump, sometimes few-branched in flowering portion. Plants spread by underground runners and form small colonies. **Flower** head to ½ in. (13 mm) high; ray flowers absent; disk flowers 18–34 per head, purple to purple-rose; each head surrounded by several purplish-green leaflike bracts bending outward at sharp-pointed tips. Heads many, stalked, the whole forming large, compact terminal cluster. **Leaves** 3¼–6 in. (8.3–15 cm) long, ¾–2⅜ in. (2–6 cm) wide, alternate, stalkless; margins sharply toothed.

Habitat: Rich loamy, sandy or clay soils of prairies, plains, rocky hillsides and slopes, openings and edges of woodlands and low, open areas. In all except ST, FW.

Note: Western ironweed is one of our most robust and drought-resistant perennials and is especially showy in overgrazed pastures or rangelands where its bitter-tasting foliage prevents it from being browsed by cattle. The genus is named for William Vernon (d. 1711), an English botanist who collected in North America.

WOOLLY IRONWEED (*Vernonia lindheimeri*)
Sunflower Family (Asteraceae)

Bloom Period: May–August

Description: Upright, slender, usually densely woolly perennial 8–32 in. (2–8 dm) high; stems usually several and forming clumps, branched only in upper portion, covered with gray, woolly hairs. **Flower** head ⁵⁄₁₆–½ in. (8–12 mm) high; ray flowers absent; disk flowers 20–60 per head, purple. Each head surrounded by several rows of small, felty-hairy leaflike bracts. Heads many, stalked, the whole forming large terminal mass. **Leaves** 1½–5 in. (3.8–12.5 cm) long, narrow, alternate, stalkless, rather thick, gray-green on upper surface, densely white-woolly on lower surface; margins turned under.

Habitat: Rocky calcareous soils in open areas, brushlands, on hillsides and slopes. In NC, EP, FW.

Note: All of the ironweeds are most attractive plants and should be used more in cultivation. Many insects are attracted to these plants, seeking both the nectar and pollen. The roots of the ironweeds have reportedly been used to "purify" the blood, to reduce fevers and, by some peoples, as an aphrodisiac and a snakebite-cure.

AIN MUSTARD

E TWIST-FLOWER

MOUNTAIN MUSTARD (*Sisymbrium linearifolium*)
Mustard Family (Brassicaceae)

Bloom Period: March–November

Description: Tall, upright, slender, smooth perennial herb 20–60 in. (5–15 dm) high; stem usually solitary, branching above base. Plant covered with whitish coating easily removed by rubbing. **Flower** to 1½ in. (3.8 cm) across; petals 4, lavender, conspicuously veined, narrowed at base. Flowers many, densely congested in elongating terminal spikelike raceme. **Leaves** 2–4 in. (5–10 cm) long, alternate, tapered at base; margins entire. Lowest leaves usually withered or missing in older plants.

Habitat: Rocky soils in open brushland, along hillsides, mountain slopes, ledges and in rock crevices. In FW.

Note: Mountain mustard is widespread in the mountainous areas of western Texas, flowering almost continuously throughout the season. Many species of this genus have been introduced into our country and often become a problem to ranchers or farmers. The native species such as this one are rarely so prolific and present no problem.

LYRE-LEAF TWIST-FLOWER (*Streptanthus carinatus*)
Mustard Family (Brassicaceae)

Bloom Period: March–April

Description: Upright, smooth, succulent annual 1–2 ft. (3–6 dm) high; stems solitary or few, branched above base and upwards. Herbage has whitish, waxy coating which rubs off easily when plant is handled. **Flower** purplish or white with purple markings; petals 4, narrow, twisted, with wavy or crinkled edges. Petals surrounded by purplish, urn-shaped structure narrower at tip than in middle. Flowers few to numerous, in elongating terminal spike. **Leaves** about 4 in. (1 dm) long, alternate; lower leaves stalked, variously lobed; upper leaves stalkless, lobed at base with the lobes clasping stem.

Habitat: Dry sandy or gravelly soils in canyons or along dry creek beds, on slopes or at bases of hillsides and mountains. In FW.

Note: This purple-flowered member of the mustard family is quite showy when in bloom, with the large, purplish "urn" almost as conspicuous as the petals. It is endemic to the western portion of the state, but is usually found in widely scattered colonies.

VENUS'S LOOKING-GLASS

ERECT DAYFLOWER

VENUS'S LOOKING-GLASS (*Triodanis perfoliata*)
Bluebell Family (Campanulaceae)

Bloom Period: April–July

Description: Upright to sprawling hairy annual to 24 in. (6 dm); stem solitary, angled, mostly unbranched. **Flower** to ¾ in. (2 cm) across, purplish to bluish-violet, deeply 5-lobed with the lobes spreading rather flat. Flowers one to several in cluster with the clusters forming slender terminal spike. Lower flowers set seed but do not open and are not showy. **Leaves** to 1 in. (25 mm) across, alternate, the blade roundish, deeply notched at base and clasping stem, shallowly lobed or the margins with shallowly rounded teeth.

Habitat: Dry, poor, usually sandy soils in prairies, old fields, disturbed areas, pastures and edges of woodlands. In all except PH.

Note: This genus is sometimes placed with the genus *Specularia*. The name of the European plant, *S. speculum-veneris*, is a Latin derivative meaning "mirror of Venus," which refers to its flat, black, shiny seeds. The Cherokee steeped the roots of Venus's looking-glass along with parts of other plants, and drank the infusion for indigestion.

ERECT DAYFLOWER (*Commelina erecta*)
Spiderwort Family (Commelinaceae)

Bloom Period: May–October

Description: Upright or somewhat sprawling, thin, succulent, slender-stemmed perennial to 24 in. (6 dm) or higher. **Flower** 1 in. (2.5 cm) or more across, blue, closing early in day; petals 3, with 2 petals of equal size and the third quite inconspicuous or absent. Buds several, clustered in boat-shaped terminal spathe with flower stalks elongating and emerging from spathe and flowers opening one at a time. **Leaves** to 6 in. (15 cm) long, 1 in. (2.5 cm) wide, alternate, mostly in basal cluster, flat or grooved along midrib, hairy on upper surface, somewhat rough to the touch.

Habitat: Sandy or clayey soils in almost all habitats including limestone slopes, open pinelands, abandoned pastures, stream banks, thickets or woodlands. Throughout.

Note: The Swedish botanist Linnaeus named this plant for the three Commelin brothers, Dutch botanists, two of whom were very productive in their field. The third brother published nothing and was relatively unknown. Linnaeus used the flower's three petals to represent the traits of the three brothers.

PRAIRIE SPIDERWORT

OHIO SPIDERWORT (Tveten)

PRAIRIE SPIDERWORT (*Tradescantia occidentalis*)
Spiderwort Family (Commelinaceae)

Bloom Period: February–July

Description: Upright to somewhat sprawling, smooth perennial to 32 in. (8 dm); stem straight, sometimes branching, with 2–6 joints. Plant covered with whitish "bloom" which comes off when plant is handled. **Flower** to 1½ in. (38 mm) long, blue, occasionally white or rose; petals 3, equal in size; stamens 6, feathery; anthers 6, bright gold. Flowers in clusters, lasting for only a few hours in the mornings. **Leaves** to 20 in. (5 dm) long, to ¾ in. (2 cm) wide, alternate, stalkless, thick, firm, usually folded lengthwise; margins entire.

Habitat: Sandy or rocky soils in disturbed areas, prairies, plains and openings in woodlands and thickets. Throughout.

Note: Supposedly the leaves and flowers of this plant can be eaten raw or boiled, but the root contains the poisonous substance saponin and should be avoided. The species name *occidentalis* is from the Latin word *occidental*, meaning "western" or "westerly."

OHIO SPIDERWORT (*Tradescantia ohioensis*)
Spiderwort Family (Commelinaceae)

Bloom Period: February–May

Description: Upright to sprawling, smooth, clump-forming perennial 2½–3 ft. (7.5–9 dm) high; stem with 3–8 joints, containing gluey sap. Herbage has whitish coating which comes off when rubbed. **Flower** about 1½ in. (38 mm) across, from white through darkest blue or rose; petals 3, all alike; sepals 3, leaf-like, usually with tuft of hair at tip; stamens 6, conspicuously covered with hairs. Flowers in clusters, emerging from 2 leaf-like bracts folded lengthwise. Flowers last only a few hours in the morning. **Leaves** to 18 in. (45 cm) long, 1¾ in. (4.5 cm) wide, alternate, stalkless, folded and clasping stem at base, long-pointed in tip portion; margins entire.

Habitat: Clay soils in abandoned areas, meadows, prairies and woodland openings. In all except PH, FW.

Note: The spiderworts were named in honor of John Tradescant, who served as gardener to Charles I of England. Tradescant started plants from seed sent to him from America, and today, spiderwort is still commonly cultivated in English gardens.

HAIRY CLUSTER-VINE

HAIRY CLUSTER-VINE (*Jacquemontia tamnifolia*)
Morning-Glory Family (Convolvulaceae)

Bloom Period: July–October

Description: Hairy annual vine, at first upright, becoming elongated and trailing or twining; stems solitary or few, to 7 ft. (2.3 m) long. **Flower** ½–¾ in. (1.3–2 cm) across, blue, funnel-shaped, 5-angled. Flowers several to many in dense cluster, the cluster terminal on long stalk from leaf axil, the flowers opening one to few at a time in cluster. **Leaves** 1¼–4¾ in. (3.2–12 cm) long, ¾–3½ in. (2–8.9 cm) wide, alternate, long-stalked, the blade usually notched at base.

Habitat: Moist sandy soils in disturbed areas, along open edges of cultivated fields, streams or roadsides. In NE, SE, SC.

Note: The small, bright blue flowers of this vine are intermixed with numerous hairy bracts to form a conspicuous cluster that is quite showy. The plants are hardy, easily raised from seed and a welcome addition to gardens. The flowers, which are swirled in the bud, usually remain open a little longer in the day than other members of the morning-glory family. If the weather is cloudy or cool, they sometimes remain open all day. This is the only species of *Jacquemontia* that grows in Texas.

GROUND PLUM (*Astragalus crassicarpus*)
Legume Family (Fabaceae)

Bloom Period: March–July

Description: Upright to widely sprawling, hairy perennial; stems to 2 ft. (6 dm) high or long, usually several, spreading from center and forming clump or circle. **Flower** to 1 in. (25 mm) long, purple, lilac, cream-colored or greenish-white; upper petal or banner extending forward, upright at tip; the lower petals (keel) tipped with purple or pink. Flowers few to several in terminal cluster at ends of branches. **Leaves** 1⅜–6 in. (3.5–15 cm) long, the blade divided into 15–33 leaflets.

Habitat: Clayey or rocky soils of prairies, brushlands, hillsides, slopes and edges of woodlands. In NC, CT, PH, EP, FW.

Note: The fruit or "plum" of this plant is round, thick and succulent, becoming reddish or purplish when mature. It is reported to be edible, tasting similar to the pod of green garden peas. Another common name for the plant is *Indian pea*.

SLIM-POD MILK-VETCH

SLIM-POD MILK-VETCH (*Astragalus leptocarpus*)
Legume Family (Fabaceae)

Bloom Period: March–May

Description: Low, weakly upright, slender, delicate annual 6–14 in. (15–35 cm) high or long; stems few to several, from common root. **Flower** to ½ in. (13 mm) long, magenta to darkest purple; petals 5, the upper petal or banner erect, with large, conspicuous white spot or "eye" at base; side petals (wings) often white-spotted to near tip. Flowers few to several, congested in short, roundish terminal cluster. **Leaves** to 2¾ in. (7 cm) long, the blade divided into usually 11–17 leaflets, each leaflet to ⅜ in. (1 cm) long, thick-textured, green, smooth.

Habitat: Various soils in open areas, prairies, pastures, along hills, slopes and woodland edges. In all except PH, EP, FW.

Note: Although this plant is an endemic, it is quite abundant and conspicuous in the areas where it occurs. The plants may grow singly, but more often form large showy colonies. Often the flowers begin opening before the leaves are fully developed and appear as solid patches of dark purple. Milk-vetch is often mistaken for the true vetches (*Vicia* spp.), but has a grooved fruit pod and lacks the tendrils of the vetches.

WOOLLY LOCOWEED (*Astragalus mollissimus*)
Legume Family (Fabaceae)

Bloom Period: March–July

Description: Low, upright to sprawling, robust, densely hairy, short-lived perennial to 1 ft. (3 dm); stem usually much-branched at base and forming clump. Herbage with long, silky hairs. **Flower** to 1 in. (25 mm) long, reddish-purple to lavender or creamy; upper petal (banner) upright; lower petals often lighter in color. Flowers numerous, forming long spikes from leaf axils. **Leaves** to 6 in. (15 cm) long, alternate, the blade divided into 11–35 leaflets; each leaflet ¾–1½ in. (20–38 mm) long, densely covered with silvery hairs.

Habitat: Dry sandy or gravelly soils of high prairies, rangelands, hills and mesas. In PH, FW.

Note: Woolly locoweed contains the toxic principal lococine and is one of several species of plants which can cause death to cattle and horses when eaten. Animals show a nervous derangement and display irrational and spasmodic movements, appearing "loco" or "crazy."

WILD BLUE INDIGO (Wesby)

BUTTERFLY PEA

WILD BLUE INDIGO (*Baptisia australis*)
Legume Family (Fabaceae)

Bloom Period: April–May

Description: Upright, robust, smooth perennial 2–4 ft. (6–12 dm) high from woody base; stem solitary, much-branched in upper portion and bushy. Herbage pale bluish-green. **Flower** to about 1 in. (25 mm) across, blue; petals 5, the upper petal or banner erect. Flowers few to numerous, not subtended by conspicuous leaflike bracts as in some species, congested in dense, upright terminal spikelike raceme 4–16 in. (1–4 dm) long. **Leaves** alternate, short-stalked, the blade divided into 3 leaflets, with each leaflet 1½–3⅛ in. (3.8–8 cm) long.

Habitat: Clay soils of prairies and plains. In NC and eastern portion of PH.

Note: This is our only blue-flowered *Baptisia*. The plant's juice turns purple upon exposure to air. It is a fair substitute for true indigo in making a blue dye and is still used for dying wool for weaving. In late fall, the above-ground portion of the plant turns silvery-gray, breaks off at ground level and tumbles about in the wind.

BUTTERFLY PEA (*Centrosema virginianum*)
Legume Family (Fabaceae)

Bloom Period: March–November

Description: Sprawling, trailing, usually vigorously twining herbaceous vine; stems usually branched, to 6 ft. (2 m) long. **Flower** to 1½ in. (3.8 cm) long, purplish to pale lavender, in upside down position; petals 5, the largest or banner usually wider than long, wide-spreading, notched at tip. Flowers one to few, in clusters from leaf axils. **Leaves** 1⅛–4 in. (3–10 cm) long, alternate, long-stalked, the blade divided into 3 leaflets; each leaflet to 2½ in. (6.3 cm) long.

Habitat: Sandy soils of old fields, fencerows, openings and edges of woodlands and thickets. In all except PH, FW.

Note: Butterfly pea is a delicate vine readily recognized by the "upside down" flowers; normally the blooms of this family have the upper petal or banner in an upright or uppermost position. This attractive vine is easily propagated by seed or root division.

PURPLE DALEA

(Keeney)

PURPLE DALEA (*Dalea lasiathera*)
Legume Family (Fabaceae)

Bloom Period: March–June

Description: Upright or sprawling smooth perennial from woody roots; stems several, from base, to 12 in. (3 dm) high or long. **Flower** to ⅝ in. (16 mm) long, purple to rosy-violet; petals 5, irregularly attached; upper petal almost round; side and lower petals strongly curved. Flowers usually 12–18, arranged in loose or moderately dense terminal spike. **Leaves** ¾–1⅜ in. (20–35 mm) long, alternate, bluish-green, gland-dotted beneath, the blade divided into 7–13 small leaflets.

Habitat: Dry, rocky, calcareous soils in brushlands, chaparral, edges and openings of woodlands, on hillsides and slopes. In all except NE, SE, SC, CT.

Note: This genus was named in honor of Samuel Dale, an 18th century English botanist. Usually inhabiting dryish soils, the *Dalea*s are useful in the wildflower garden as ground covers or in "problem" spots where other plants do not grow well.

BEARDED DALEA (*Dalea pogonathera*)
Legume Family (Fabaceae)

Bloom Period: March–November

Description: Low, upright to sprawling or trailing, rather delicate, smooth perennial herb; stems many from base, slender, to 12 in. (3 dm) long. **Flower** to ⅜ in. (1 cm) long, purple or purple-violet to pale lavender; petals 5, irregularly arranged. Flowers numerous, congested in dense, elongating, silky-hairy clusters from leaf axils. **Leaves** ⅜–¾ in. (1–2 cm) long, alternate, stalked, the blade divided into 5 or 7 bluish-green, gland-dotted leaflets.

Habitat: Various soils in prairies, plains, rangelands, chaparral and on hillsides and slopes. In all except NE, SE, SC.

Note: In areas where common, bearded dalea is considered a good forage plant for some species of wildlife. The petals of the *Dalea*s are uniquely placed at different levels on the floral cup rather than in a regular "flower" pattern. A common Spanish name is *hierba del corazón*, meaning "herb of the heart."

SLENDER BUSH CLOVER

ANNUAL LUPINE (Cheatham)

SLENDER BUSH CLOVER (*Lespedeza virginica*)
Legume Family (Fabaceae)

Bloom Period: July–October

Description: Strictly upright, slender, leafy perennial 1–5 ft. (3–15 dm) high; stems solitary or few from base and clumped, occasionally branched in upper portion. **Flower** about ¼ in. (6 mm) long, blue-purple to purple; petals 5, the upper petal erect, the side petals about as long as lower petals. Flowers numerous, in small clusters crowded along upper portion of stem, the clusters shorter than subtending leaves. Nonopening (cleistogamous) flowers present in clusters with open flowers. **Leaves** alternate, numerous and crowded along stem; blade divided into 3 leaflets with each leaflet ½–1½ in. (13–38 mm) long, rather blunt at tip.

Habitat: Dry, sandy soils of pastures, fields, fencerows, thickets and woodlands. In all except PH, ST, FW.

Note: The legumes are very important in improving soil fertility, and the seeds of many species are important to wildlife, especially dove and quail.

ANNUAL LUPINE (*Lupinus concinnus*)
Legume Family (Fabaceae)

Bloom Period: March–May

Description: Low, upright or somewhat sprawling, hairy winter annual 1⅝–6 in. (4.1–15 cm) high; stems unbranched or much-branched from base and becoming moundlike. Plant densely hairy throughout. **Flower** to ½ in. (1.3 cm) long; petals 5, reddish-purple; upper petal or banner upright, with white central spot. Flowers few, loosely clustered in elongated terminal spike sometimes shorter than the leaves. **Leaves** ⅜–¾ in. (1–2 cm) long, alternate, numerous, long-stalked, the blade divided to base into 5–8 segments with each segment to 3/16 in. (5 mm) wide, both surfaces densely covered with long hairs.

Habitat: Sandy, gravelly or rocky soils in grassy areas along mountain slopes above 4,500 feet elevation. In FW.

Note: Annual lupine is designated one of our state wildflower species although it is not common here nor particularly showy. It is found most frequently on the lower slopes of the Franklin Mountains, near El Paso.

D BLUEBONNET

BIG BEND BLUEBONNET (*Lupinus havardii*)
Legume Family (Fabaceae)

Bloom Period: January–June

Description: Upright, hairy winter annual to 32 in. (8 dm), sometimes to as much as 4 ft. (12 dm); stem branched, the branches slender and usually strictly upright. **Flower** to ½ in. (13 mm) long, purple-blue; petals 5, the upper petal or banner with creamy-white spot at base becoming yellow and finally red after pollination. Flowers numerous, in slender terminal spike to 18 in. (45 cm) long. **Leaves** alternate, stalked, the blade divided into usually 7 leaflets, each leaflet to ¾ in. (20 mm) long or longer.

Habitat: Gravelly, fine talus or alluvial soils in deserts or valleys and on hills and mountain slopes. In FW.

Note: Big Bend bluebonnet, also called *Chisos bluebonnet*, is much taller and has more vigorous growth than our other bluebonnets, with flowers a much darker blue. The genus name is from the Latin word *lupus* meaning "wolf." In early times it was thought these plants robbed the soil of its nutrients. It is now known that legumes actually enrich the soil through the symbiotic bacteria in the root nodules which fix atmospheric nitrogen into organic compounds used later by other plants.

DUNE BLUEBONNET (*Lupinus plattensis*)
Legume Family (Fabaceae)

Bloom Period: April–May

Description: Upright, hairy perennial herb to 20 in. (5 dm); stems unbranched or branched from base and forming clump. **Flower** to ½ in. (13 mm) long; petals 5, dark-blue or purplish; upper petal or banner upright or almost so, with bright white spot at base. Flowers many, somewhat loosely congested into elongated terminal spike to 10 in. (25 cm) long. **Leaves** large, numerous, alternate, stalked, clustered near base, the blade completely divided into 7–10 narrow segments, sparsely hairy or smooth on upper surface.

Habitat: Deep sandy soils of dunes or open areas. In PH.

Note: Extremely rare in Texas, dune bluebonnet is more common in states across our northwestern borders. It is a lovely plant, forming small colonies on dunes and in rangelands in the extreme northwestern portions of the Panhandle. Like other species of *Lupinus* found in Texas, it, too, is a state wildflower.

SANDYLAND BLUEBONNET

TEXAS BLUEBONNET

SANDYLAND BLUEBONNET (*Lupinus subcarnosus*)
Legume Family (Fabaceae)

Bloom Period: March–April

Description: Upright or sprawling hairy winter annual 6–16 in. (15–40 cm) high; stem unbranched or few-branched from base, the branches often partially lying on ground. **Flower** to ½ in. (13 mm) long; petals 5, bright blue; upper petal strictly upright, with white center which usually turns purplish in age or after pollination; side petals (wings) much-inflated when young. Flowers several, loosely congested in terminal spike. Buds with yellowish-gray or brownish hair, forming rounded tip to spike, not conspicuous from a distance. **Leaves** to 1 in. (25 mm) long, alternate, long-stalked, clustered at base of plant, the blade divided to base into usually 5 narrow segments or leaflets, essentially smooth on upper surface.

Habitat: Loose, deep, sandy soils in abandoned areas, rangelands, openings and edges of thin woodlands. In NE, SE, SC, ST.

Note: Sandyland bluebonnet is endemic to Texas. In 1901 it was adopted as the state flower, but because it is the less showy of the two most common species (*L. texensis* being the other common one), by popular demand it was decided to make all *Lupinus* taxa occurring naturally in Texas the state flower. This was done in 1971, thus ending the dispute as to the *real* state flower.

TEXAS BLUEBONNET (*Lupinus texensis*)
Legume Family (Fabaceae)

Bloom Period: March–May

Description: Upright to sprawling, hairy winter annual 6–16 in. (15–40 cm) high; stem usually branched from base. Plant forms rosette of leaves in the fall and blooms the following spring. **Flower** ⅜–⅝ in. (10–16 mm) long, intoxicatingly fragrant; petals 5; upper petal with white spot at base turning wine-red or purplish after pollination; side petals flat, not cupped or appearing inflated when viewed from the front. Flowers many, in dense terminal spike, the tip pointed, conspicuously silvery-white. **Leaves** alternate, mostly basal, long-stalked, the blade divided into usually 5 leaflets, the leaflets to 1 in. (25 mm) long, to ½ in. (13 mm) wide.

Habitat: Gravelly, sandy, sandy-clay or calcareous soils in plains, brushlands, flats, pastures, on hillsides and slopes. In all except PH, FW.

Note: Texas bluebonnet and sandyland bluebonnet (*L. subcarnosus*) are the only two *Lupinus* species endemic to Texas, the others having wider distribution into adjacent states and Mexico. This species is widely planted by the highway department in its roadside-beautification and erosion-control programs. 337

LOCOWEED (Wesby)

PURPLE PRAIRIE CLOVER (Tveten)

LOCOWEED (*Oxytropis lambertii* var. *articulata*)
Legume Family (Fabaceae)

Bloom Period: April–July

Description: Upright, hairy perennial herb to 14 in. (35 cm); stems several and forming tuft or clump. Herbage densely covered with silvery hairs. Plants often forming colonies from underground runners. **Flower** ½–1 in. (1.3–2.5 cm) long, purple-red, lavender, rose or almost white, fragrant; petals 5; lower 2 petals (keel) extending into sharp, upright point. Flowers 10–25, forming dense, elongated terminal racemes on leafless stalks. **Leaves** 1½–12 in. (3.8–30 cm) long, alternate, clustered at base of plant, the blade divided into 9–19 leaflets, each leaflet to 1½ in. (3.8 cm) long.

Habitat: Sandy, rocky limestone or calcareous soils of prairies, plains, rangelands, rocky outcrops and open forests. In NC, PH, EP.

Note: Locoweed is highly toxic and is one of the most dangerous plants to livestock found on the western rangelands. Grazing animals will readily eat the plants, with often fatal results. It is a beautiful plant when flowering and forms spectacular clumps of color as a garden specimen.

PURPLE PRAIRIE CLOVER (*Petalostemum purpureum*)
Legume Family (Fabaceae)

Bloom Period: June–July

Description: Upright, smooth to grayish-hairy perennial 1–3 ft. (3–9 dm) high; stems usually several from woody base, slender, grooved lengthwise, occasionally branching in upper portion. **Flower** about ¼ in. (6 mm) long, purple-rose or reddish-lavender; petals 5, irregularly placed; stamens 5, the pollen golden-yellow. Flowers numerous, densely congested in short-stalked terminal spikes, the spikes elongating as flowers open. **Leaves** 1⅛–2 in. (3–5 cm) long, alternate, stalked, numerous, the blade divided into usually 5 leaflets, each leaflet to ¾ in. (2 cm) long.

Habitat: Sandy soils of prairies, plains and mountain slopes. In NC, PH, FW.

Note: The *Petalostemum*s are often placed in the genus *Dalea*, but may be separated on the basis of having only five stamens while the *Dalea*s have more. Purple prairie clover is a highly nutritious forage and is readily eaten by all livestock. New growth is particularly high in protein.

TALL SCURFY PEA (Darby)

INDIAN BREADROOT (Cheatham)

TALL SCURFY PEA (*Psoralea cuspidata*)
Legume Family (Fabaceae)

Bloom Period: April–May

Description: Upright to somewhat sprawling herbaceous perennial 6–24 in. (1.5–6 dm) high from thick roots; stems few to several, branched in upper portion. Almost entire plant dotted with small glands. **Flower** ½–¾ in. (1.3–2 cm) long, light blue to purplish-blue or violet; petals 5, the upper petal (banner) upright. Flowers numerous, congested in long terminal spikes, each flower subtended by a conspicuously gland-dotted bract. **Leaves** alternate, short-stalked, the blade divided to base into 3–5 segments or leaflets, each leaflet 1–2 in. (2.5–5 cm) long.

Habitat: Sandy, clayey, calcareous, often rocky soils of prairies, plains, cedar brushlands, chaparral, hillsides and slopes. In NC, PH, EP.

Note: While the root of this plant is not as large as *P. hypogaea*, it is edible and was probably eaten during periods of food shortage. After drying, the roots could be pounded into a flour and baked into cakes.

INDIAN BREADROOT (*Psoralea hypogaea*)
Legume Family (Fabaceae)

Bloom Period: April–June

Description: Low, hairy perennial from tuberous root; stems absent or very short. Plant covered with whitish hairs throughout. **Flower** ⁵⁄₁₆–½ in. (8–13 mm) long, pale-lavender to purple; petals 5, upper petal upright. Flowers densely congested in roundish cluster on short stalks from base of plant. **Leaves** at ground level, long-stalked, the blade divided to base into 3–7 separate segments or leaflets, each leaflet 1–2 in. (2.5–5 cm) long, ⅛–⅜ in. (4–9 mm) wide.

Habitat: Dry sandy, usually calcareous soils of prairies, plains, hillsides and slopes. In NC, PH, EP.

Note: The large, tuberlike root of this plant is edible and was an important food source for Western Indian tribes and early explorers. The tuber may be eaten raw, boiled, or sliced and dried for later use as a flour or thickening for soups. Other common names include *prairie potato*, *pomme blanche* and *pomme-de-prairie*, the last two names French and meaning "white apple" and "prairie apple," respectively.

SCURFY PEA

LINDHEIMER TEPHROSIA (Cheatham)

SCURFY PEA (*Psoralea tenuiflora*)
Legume Family (Fabaceae)

Bloom Period: May–July

Description: Upright or somewhat sprawling, smooth to hairy perennial 8–24 in. (2–6 dm) high; stem solitary, much-branched with the branches widely spreading. Herbage covered with tiny, dark-colored glandular dots. **Flower** to ⁵⁄₁₆ in. (8 mm) long, violet-blue; petals 5; upper petal or banner almost round. Flowers numerous, congested in slender, upright or drooping, terminal spikelike raceme. **Leaves** alternate, stalked, the blade divided to base into 3–5 leaflets; each leaflet 1⅛–2 in. (3–5 cm) long, ³⁄₁₆–½ in. (5–13 mm) wide, gland-dotted on both sides.

Habitat: Sandy or rocky soils in prairies, ungrazed pastures, openings and edges of woodlands. In all except NE, SE, ST.

Note: This plant gets its common name from the small, scalelike glands which cover the stem and leaves and give it a rough or scaly look. Scurfy pea, also known as *wild alfalfa*, is not readily eaten by livestock until grazing pressure forces its use. It is rather drought-resistant and adds much beauty to the late-season rangelands.

LINDHEIMER TEPHROSIA (*Tephrosia lindheimeri*)
Legume Family (Fabaceae)

Bloom Period: March–October

Description: Upright or trailing, grayish-hairy perennial from woody tuberous root; stems solitary to several, extremely tough, angled, zigzag, to 3 ft. (1 m) or more, many-branched. **Flower** to about ¾ in. (2 cm) long, purple-rose; petals 5, upper petal broad, erect, with small white spot at base. Flowers numerous, loosely arranged in terminal spikelike raceme opening upward. **Leaves** to 10 in. (2.5 cm) long, alternate, velvety-hairy, the blade divided into 7–13 leaflets, each leaflet about 1⅛ in. (3 cm) long, pointed at tip, conspicuously white-margined.

Habitat: Well-drained sandy soils of open areas, prairies, plains, brushlands or chaparral. In SC, CT, EP, ST.

Note: Lindheimer tephrosia is an especially showy and attractive legume common in southern and central Texas. It is excellent as a ground cover or trellis plant. It needs practically no care after becoming established and the large flowers continue to open throughout the season. The plants can be propagated by root division or, more easily, from seed. Seeds of tephrosia are eaten by various forms of wildlife, and the crushed roots were reportedly used by some Indian tribes as an insecticide and fish poison. The plants contain an alkaloid and were once much used medicinally. The roots and young growth are especially potent.

WINTER VETCH

BLUEBELLS

WINTER VETCH (*Vicia dasycarpa*)
Legume Family (Fabaceae)

Bloom Period: April–August

Description: Weakly upright to sprawling, trailing or climbing annual or biennial; stems solitary or few, slender, weak, often brittle, to 3 ft. (1 m) long. **Flower** about ¾ in. (2 cm) long, violet and white, or lavender to rose-colored, or solid white; petals 5, the upper petal upright, side petals spreading. Flowers 5–20, crowded, forming one-sided curved spike. **Leaves** alternate, the blade divided into 5–10 opposite pairs of narrow leaflets, each leaflet ½–1 in. (1.3–2.5 cm) long. Threadlike tendrils present at tip of leaf.

Habitat: Various soils in disturbed sites, edges of fields and especially along roadsides. In NE, SE, NC, SC.

Note: Winter vetch is a European plant which was widely used in this country as a cover crop and soil builder before the development of inexpensive commercial fertilizers. It is still occasionally used as a high-protein component in winter pastures. The plants often spread onto the roadsides from nearby fields or rangelands and form large, thick, solid masses, the stems covering all nearby vegetation.

BLUEBELLS (*Eustoma grandiflorum*)
Gentian Family (Gentianaceae)

Bloom Period: June–September

Description: Upright, smooth, usually short-lived perennial to 28 in. (7 dm), the herbage covered with a whitish coating easily rubbed off; stems usually branched in upper portion. **Flower** to 2½ in. (6.3 cm) high, to 4 in. (10 cm) across, varying from blue-purple prominently marked in center with darker purple, to white, or white tinged with purple or yellow; petals 5, united at base, deeply cupped. Flowers on slender stalks, several, and forming large terminal cluster. **Leaves** to 3⅛ in. (8 cm) long, 1¼ in. (3.2 cm) wide, opposite, stalkless and clasping stem at base, noticeably 3-veined.

Habitat: Moist areas in prairies, fields and around ponds or tanks. In all except NE.

Note: Bluebells is one of our most beautiful wildflowers and also does exceptionally well under cultivation in a moist, sunny site. The cut flowers last for several days; however, gathering the flowers inhibits the plants' normal propagation from seed. (Seeds are available commercially.) Also called *purple prairie gentian* and *lira de San Pedro*.

TEXAS STORK'S-BILL (Worthington)

BLUE WATERLEAF

TEXAS STORK'S-BILL (*Erodium texanum*)
Geranium Family (Geraniaceae)

Bloom Period: February–April

Description: Low annual herb branched from base, the branches either lying flat on ground or turned upward at tips. Branches frequently forking and elongating during flowering, eventually becoming up to 20 in. (5 dm) long. **Flower** to 1 in. (25 mm) or more across, reddish-purple, the 5 petals wide-flaring or flattened, short-lived. Flowers in clusters from leaf axils, with usually 1 or 2 flowers open in cluster at a time. **Leaves** to 1⅜ in. (35 mm) long, opposite or alternate, long-stalked, deeply veined and appearing wrinkled; margins shallowly to deeply lobed, the lobes bearing rounded teeth.

Habitat: Rocky or sandy calcareous soils of hillsides, disturbed areas, prairies and other open areas. In all except NE, SE.

Note: This plant gets its common name from the fruit, which develops from a long-beaked pistil somewhat reminiscent of a bird's beak. When mature, the pistil splits at the base into five sections, with each section coiling upward toward tip and flinging the seed outward.

BLUE WATERLEAF (*Hydrolea ovata*)
Waterleaf Family (Hydrophyllaceae)

Bloom Period: September–October

Description: Upright, stout, spiny aquatic perennial to 30 in. (76 cm); stems solitary or several from base and clumplike, usually branching in upper portion. Plants form large colonies from thick roots. **Flower** to 1½ in. (38 mm) across, light to dark blue, funnel-shaped, deeply 5-lobed at rim, the lobes spreading flat. Flowers numerous, arranged in several few-flowered clusters and forming large terminal and axillary clusters. Clusters from axils often long-stalked. **Leaves** 1–2½ in. (25–63 mm) long, to 1 in. (25 mm) wide, alternate, short-stalked or stalkless, subtended by conspicuous spine at base of stalk; margins entire.

Habitat: Mud of lake, pond, stream and swamp edges and in wet meadows, seeps and ditches. In NE, SE, SC.

Note: The family name comes from two Greek words, *hydro*, referring to water, and *phyll*, meaning "leaf" or "rich in leaves." *Ovata* refers to the shape of the leaves. Blue waterleaf is a common plant of the autumn landscape and an important source of pollen and nectar for late-season insects.

SAND-BELL (Cheatham)

BABY BLUE-EYES (Miller)

SAND-BELL (*Nama hispidum*)
Waterleaf Family (Hydrophyllaceae)

Bloom Period: March–November

Description: Upright to weakly sprawling, rough-hairy annual 4–20 in. (1–5 dm) high; stem solitary, much-branched at base or in upper portion, the branches forking. **Flower** 5/16–5/8 in. (8–16 mm) long, bright purple to pink, somewhat bell-shaped, 5-lobed at rim. Flowers in small clusters from axils of upper leaves. **Leaves** 3/8–2 in. (1–5 cm) long, to 5/16 in. (8 mm) wide, mostly alternate, the margins rolled toward lower surface.

Habitat: Sandy or gravelly soils in almost all habitats. In all except NE, SE.

Note: Sand-bells usually form small, showy clumps or mats with many purple flowers open at once, but the flowers fall rather easily if the plant is disturbed. The plants are very attractive when used in a rock garden or as a border in sandy soils.

BABY BLUE-EYES (*Nemophila phacelioides*)
Waterleaf Family (Hydrophyllaceae)

Bloom Period: March–May

Description: Upright to straggling, watery-stemmed, hairy annual to 28 in. (7 dm); stems often much-branched from base. **Flower** to 1 in. (25 mm) across, blue or purplish, frosted or whitish in center, solitary from leaf axils or in clusters at tip of stem; petals 5, somewhat cupped or wide-opening and appearing flat. **Leaves** 2 3/8–3 1/8 in. (6–8 cm) long, 1–2 in. (2.5–5 cm) wide, alternate, stalked, blue-green, the blade lobed or divided into 9–11 broad segments which are sometimes irregularly toothed.

Habitat: Sandy or occasionally clay soils in prairies, open, moist woodlands and bottomlands, semishaded edges of thickets and coastal brushlands. In SC, ST, CT, EP.

Note: The genus name *Nemophila* is from two Greek words meaning "lover of a wood or grove" and aptly describes the preferred habitat of this plant. Usually found in large masses, the dainty flowers form a lovely carpet of almost solid blue. Other common names include *large-flowered nemophila* and *flannel breeches*.

349

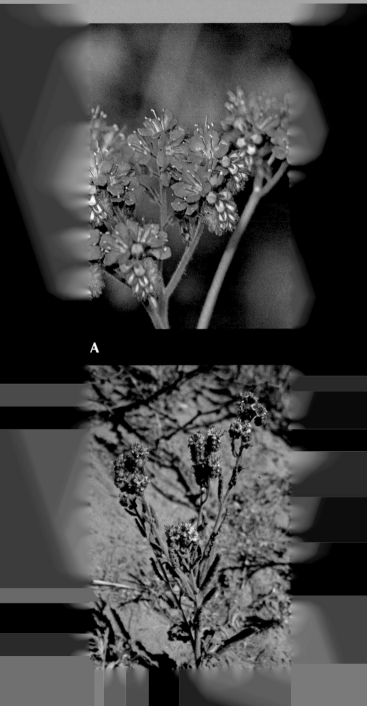

A

PHACELIA (*Phacelia congesta*)
Waterleaf Family (Hydrophyllaceae)

Bloom Period: March–June

Description: Upright, leafy annual or biennial to 3 ft. (1 m), with soft, sticky hairs; stem very brittle and breaking easily, branched in upper portion. **Flower** to ¼ in. (6 mm) across, blue to purplish, bell-shaped, deeply 5-lobed at rim; stamens 5, conspicuously protruding from flower. Flowers numerous, in slender, coiled clusters (racemes) which uncurl as the buds develop. **Leaves** to 4 in. (10 cm) long, 1½ in. (3.8 cm) wide, alternate, soft, deeply cut into irregularly toothed lobes and appearing ragged-looking

Habitat: Sandy, gravelly or rocky soils in prairies, edges of woodlands, fencerows and along stream banks. In all except NE, SE, SC.

Note: This is a most attractive wilding, easy to grow from seed and well worth cultivation. Usually found in large colonies or masses, it makes quite a visual display. The blooming season can be extended with adequate moisture. It is also known as *blue-curls*, *spider flower* and *wild heliotrope*.

GYP BLUE-CURLS (*Phacelia integrifolia*)
Waterleaf Family (Hydrophyllaceae)

Bloom Period: March–May

Description: Upright, stout, hairy, unpleasantly scented annual or biennial to 28 in. (7 dm) most often much lower; stem solitary, leafy, reddish, usually unbranched. Herbage covered with glandular hairs and sticky to the touch. **Flower** about ¼ in. (6 mm) across and long, purplish, funnel-shaped, 5-lobed at rim; stamens 5, protruding. Flowers numerous, loosely congested along one side of coiled spike which uncurls as flowers open. **Leaves** to 3 in. (7.6 cm) long, to 1 in. (25 mm) wide, alternate, stalkless, the margins toothed, scalloped or shallowly lobed.

Habitat: Dry rocky or sandy soils, particularly gypsum or limestone, of plains, deserts, hillsides and lower mountain slopes. In PH, FW.

Note: *Phacelia* is from the Greek word *phakelos* meaning "bundle" or "fascicle" and refers to the coiled flower cluster. These coiled spikes and the protruding stamens are distinguishing characteristics of this genus.

PURPLE PHACELIA

HERBERTIA

PURPLE PHACELIA (*Phacelia patuliflora*)
Waterleaf Family (Hydrophyllaceae)

Bloom Period: February–May

Description: Low, weakly upright or sprawling, delicate, densely hairy annual to 12 in. (3 dm); stems solitary or few from base, branched. **Flower** to 1 in. (25 mm) across, lavender to purplish-violet, usually white in center; petals 5, shallowly cupped to wide-spreading. Flowers several, in loose, curled spike which uncurls as flowers open. **Leaves** ⅜–4 in. (1–10 cm) long, ⅜–1⅝ in. (1–4.1 cm) wide, alternate, mostly stalkless, the blade toothed, lobed or variously divided into segments.

Habitat: Sandy soils in prairies, fields, openings and edges of woodlands and along stream banks. In all except NE, PH.

Note: Purple phacelia is very similar to baby blue-eyes (*Nemophila phacelioides*) and the two are often confused. However, the flowers of baby blue-eyes are solitary while the flowers of purple phacelia are in coiled clusters. The word *patuliflora* means "spreading flowers" and aptly describes the broad, almost flat, mature flowers of this plant.

HERBERTIA (*Alophia drummondii*)
Iris Family (Iridaceae)

Bloom Period: March–May

Description: Upright, delicate, smooth perennial to 12 in. (3 dm) from deep, globelike bulb. **Flower** about 2 in. (5 cm) across, petallike segments 6; outer 3 segments broad, wide-spreading, heavily spotted with violet outlined with purple in basal portion; inner 3 segments much smaller, blackish-violet in basal portion, violet near tip. Flowers solitary or 2 or 3 at tip of leafless stem, emerging from a broad, sheathing, leaflike bract. **Leaves** to 12 in. (3 dm) long, alternate, mostly basal, narrow and grasslike, folded together for most of length.

Habitat: Sandy or clay soils in prairies, meadows, grasslands and other open areas. In SE, SC, CT.

Note: Herbertia is endemic to the southern portion of Texas but is usually abundant where found, forming large areas of almost solid blue.

PURPLE PLEAT-LEAF

SOUTHERN IRIS

PURPLE PLEAT-LEAF (*Eustylis purpurea*)
Iris Family (Iridaceae)

Bloom Period: May–October

Description: Upright, delicate, smooth perennial to 30 in. (76 cm) from shallow-rooted bulb. Plants thinly scattered in colonies. **Flower** to 2 in. (5 cm) across, velvety purplish in outer portion, yellowish spotted with reddish-brown toward center; petallike segments 6, the outer 3 large, broadly rounded in tip portion; inner 3 much smaller, cupped. Flowers few to several at tip of slender, zigzag stem with 1 flower opening at a time, withering usually by noon. **Leaves** 18–24 in. (45–60 cm) long, to ¾ in. (2 cm) wide, alternate, mostly basal, narrow and grasslike, flat or folded together for part of length, conspicuously veined.

Habitat: Dry, sandy soils of prairies and open woodlands. In all except PH, EP, FW.

Note: Purple pleat-leaf, while most attractive in the wild, does not make a good cut flower due to the short period the flowers remain open. They do make interesting garden plants, however, and are easily raised from fall-sown seed scattered in sandy soils.

SOUTHERN IRIS (*Iris virginica*)
Iris Family (Iridaceae)

Bloom Period: April–May

Description: Upright to sprawling, smooth perennial to 3 ft. (1 m) from stout, creeping root. Stem solitary, unbranched or few-branched in upper portion. Plants often form extensive colonies. **Flower** to 3 in. (76 mm) long, pale blue with darker streakings, fragrant; petallike segments 6; outer 3 segments to 1½ in. (38 mm) wide, drooping downward, the middle portion yellow, hairy; inner 3 segments upright or spreading; style parted into 3 segments, the segments petallike, spreading, covering anthers, recurved at tips. Flowers one to few, emerging from green leaflike terminal bract. Flower stalk arches downward and deposits ripening seeds on ground or in water. **Leaves** to 30 in. (76 cm) long, to 1¼ in. (3.2 cm) wide, alternate, mostly basal, sheathing stem at base.

Habitat: Rich moist or wet soils or in shallow water of marshes, swamps, streams and ditches. In NE, SE, SC.

Note: Southern iris is an ideal plant for edges of ponds, lily pools, drainage ditches or even around dripping faucets. The substance known as orrisroot is mainly from the dried and powdered roots of an iris (*I. florentina*) native to France. The fragrant powder is much used in medicines and in the making of sachets, perfumes and other cosmetics.

DOTTED BLUE-EYED GRASS

HENBIT

DOTTED BLUE-EYED GRASS (*Sisyrinchium pruinosum*)
Iris Family (Iridaceae)

Bloom Period: April–May

Description: Upright or sprawling, clumped, delicate, smooth perennial 3½–12 in. (9–30 cm) high; stems slender, usually several, unbranched, flattened, not conspicuously winged as in some species. **Flower** to 1⅛ in. (3 cm) across, violet-purple to purple-blue, rarely white, the 6 segments all appearing petal-like, wide-spreading. Flowers usually 1 or a few in cluster at tip of stem, closing during overcast weather. **Leaves** to 9 in. (22.5 cm) long, ⅛ in. (3 mm) wide, basal, slender, grasslike and flattened like flower stem.

Habitat: Clay or sandy clay in open prairies, pastures, meadows, open woodlands and oak uplands. In all except PH, FW.

Note: These plants are usually found in abundance and can be spectacular on warm, sunny days where they cover entire pastures with almost solid sheets of blue. They are very beautiful used as borders in the wildflower garden. The *Sisyrinchium*s hybridize readily, often making species identification quite difficult.

HENBIT (*Lamium amplexicaule*)
Mint Family (Lamiaceae)

Bloom Period: Almost throughout year

Description: Upright or sprawling annual or biennial to 18 in. (45 cm); stems 4-angled or square, branched near base or from lower leaf axils. **Flower** ½–⅝ in. (13–16 mm) long, purple and pale lavender with darker markings, hairy, 2-lipped; upper lip upright and cupped; lower lip 3-lobed with the middle lobe deeply notched at tip. Usually 6–10 flowers in whorled clusters around stem; clusters subtended by leaflike bracts. Seed produced from earlier, unopening flowers. **Leaves** ½–1½ in. (13–38 mm) long, opposite, roundish, thick and conspicuously veined; margins coarsely toothed or scalloped. Lower leaves long-stalked; upper leaves stalkless and clasping stem.

Habitat: Almost all soils in lawns, gardens, cultivated and disturbed areas, low open ground, edges of fields and woodlands. Throughout.

Note: A native of Europe, henbit has become established throughout North America. It is frequently a troublesome "weed" in lawns and cultivated fields. An early source of nectar, it is visited frequently by bees and other small insects. It is also called *dead nettle*.

LEMON-MINT (D. Williams)

WILD BERGAMOT

LEMON-MINT (*Monarda citriodora*)
Mint Family (Lamiaceae)

Bloom Period: April–October
Description: Upright, aromatic annual or biennial to 32 in. (8 dm);
stems 4-angled, usually solitary, unbranched or branched in upper portion. **Flower** ½–¾ in. (13–20 mm) long, rosy-pink to purplish or white, dotted with purple, tubular in basal portion,
prominently 2-lipped; upper lip narrow, curved forward; lower
lip 3-lobed. Flowers numerous, in interrupted whorls around
stem and forming elongated spike. Each whorl subtended by
whitish or lavender leaflike bracts. **Leaves** 1⅛–2⅜ in. (3–6 cm)
long, about ⅝ in. (15 mm) wide, opposite, long-stalked; blade
entire or with few teeth.
Habitat: Sandy loams or rocky soils in pastures, prairies, plains,
savannahs and meadows. Throughout.
Note: Linnaeus named the genus *Monarda* in honor of Nicolas
Monardes, an early Spanish writer on medicinal plants. The
species name is from the Latin *citrus* meaning "lemon tree,"
and *odoro* meaning "having a fragrant smell." In this instance,
the entire plant has a noticeable fragrance of lemon. A delightful tea can be brewed from the dried leaves. The plant contains
a volatile oil from which citronellol is obtained, an aromatic
substance often used in perfumes. The dried and crushed leaves
also make a fair insect repellent when rubbed on the body.

WILD BERGAMOT (*Monarda fistulosa*)
Mint Family (Lamiaceae)

Bloom Period: May–July
Description: Upright, soft-hairy perennial to 5 ft. (15 dm); stems
square, mostly unbranched, commonly several from base and
forming clump. **Flower** ¾–1⅛ in. (2–3 cm) long, dark pink to
lavender, slenderly tubular, hairy, 2-lipped; upper lip with tuft
of hairs at tip; lower lip spreading, 3-lobed; stamens 2, long
and exserted. Flowers several, congested in dense, solitary, terminal cluster subtended by small, leaflike bracts often tinged
pink. **Leaves** 1⅛–4½ in. (3–11.4 cm) long, to 1½ in. (3.8 cm)
wide, opposite, pale green, short-stalked, coarsely toothed.
Habitat: Dry or moist rocky or sandy soils in meadows, openings
and edges of woodlands. In NE, SE, NC, SC.
Note: Wild bergamot, also called *beebalm*, is often cultivated, especially as a border or specimen plant. The entire plant is pleasantly aromatic. The dried flowers and leaves are used in sachets
and potpourris, while the fresh leaves are used to flavor foods
and to make teas. The Cherokee used a hot leaf tea to treat
heart trouble and fevers, and to induce restful sleep.

FALSE DRAGONHEAD

BEAUTIFUL FALSE DRAGONHEAD

FALSE DRAGONHEAD (*Physostegia digitalis*)
Mint Family (Lamiaceae)

Bloom Period: June–August

Description: Upright, stout, robust, smooth perennial to 6 ft. (2 m), frequently lower; stem solitary, prominently 4-angled, unbranched or sparsely branched in flowering portion. Plants form small colonies. **Flower** ¾–1 in. (2–2.5 cm) long, lavender to pale rose or whitish, spotted with reddish-purple; funnel-shaped, 2-lipped; upper lip wavy; lower lip 3-lobed, the middle lobe broad, notched at tip. Flowers numerous, forming dense terminal spike. **Leaves** to 8¾ in. (22 cm) long, to 3 in. (76 mm) wide, opposite, stalkless and partially clasping stem at base; blade thick, leathery; margins wavy or toothed in tip portion.

Habitat: Moist, usually sandy soils in prairies, ditches and meadows and along edges of marshes, open stream banks and moist woodlands. In NE, SE, SC.

Note: The species name of this plant comes from its resemblance to the genus *Digitaria*, which produces the potent drug digitalis. Almost all of the false dragonheads do well in the garden, being easily propagated by seed or root division. These plants are excellent for attracting numerous insects, especially butterflies. Hummingbirds frequently seek the nectar. Also called *lion-heart* and *obedient plant*.

BEAUTIFUL FALSE DRAGONHEAD (*Physostegia pulchella*)
Mint Family (Lamiaceae)

Bloom Period: April–June

Description: Upright, usually slender, smooth perennial to 56 in. (14 dm), commonly much lower; stem solitary, prominently 4-angled, unbranched or occasionally branched in flowering portion. Plants form colonies from underground runners. **Flower** ¾–1⅛ in. (2–3 cm) long, deep reddish-purple to lavender striped or spotted with purple, somewhat tubular, inflated, 2-lipped at rim; upper lip upright, unlobed; lower lip 3-lobed. Flowers numerous, opposite, stalkless, forming long, slender, terminal spikelike raceme. **Leaves** to 3⅛ in. (8 cm) long, opposite, stalkless and basally clasping stem, thick, firm, leathery; margins sometimes toothed in tip portion. Leaves become progressively smaller up stem.

Habitat: Moist sandy or clayey soils mostly in prairies, swales, depressions, ditches, floodplains or along edges of swamps and marshes. In NE, SE, NC, SC.

Note: The flowers of *Physostegia* may be moved up, down or sideways and will remain in those positions, giving this genus another of its common names, *obedient plant*. Beautiful false dragonhead is endemic to the eastern and central portions of the state, but where it occurs, it is usually abundant. It often forms long lines in ditches along highways.

SELF-HEAL (Koros)

BLUE SAGE (Myers)

SELF-HEAL (*Prunella vulgaris*)
Mint Family (Lamiaceae)

Bloom Period: April–June

Description: Upright to sprawling perennial to 24 in. (6 dm) but usually much lower; stems square, solitary or few from base, occasionally branched in upper portion. **Flower** to ¾ in. (2 cm) long, purple or violet and lavender, 2-lipped; upper lip upright, cupped; lower lip 3-lobed, drooping, fringed. Flowers several, densely clustered in squarish or roundish terminal spike which elongates after flowering. Each flower subtended by hairy, leaf-like bract. **Leaves** to 3½ in. (8.9 cm) long, ⅜–1½ in. (1–3.8 cm) wide, opposite, mostly long-stalked, thin, tapering at base, entire or obscurely toothed.

Habitat: Various soils in meadows, fields, gardens, pasturelands and along moist woodland edges. In NE, SE, SC.

Note: Self-heal is visited by bumblebees and especially by the clouded sulphur butterfly, which aids in fertilization. Another common name is *heal-all*, and, as these names imply, the plant is highly regarded for its medicinal uses. The Cherokee used an infusion for bathing bruises and burns, and to heal cuts. It was often used to flavor other medicines.

BLUE SAGE (*Salvia azurea* var. *grandiflora*)
Mint Family (Lamiaceae)

Bloom Period: May–November

Description: Upright to widely sprawling, hairy perennial to 5 ft. (15 dm); stems solitary or few from base, 4-angled especially in basal portion, branched in upper portion. **Flower** to 1 in. (25 mm) long, dark blue to pale blue or occasionally white, 2-lipped; upper lip upright, cupped, not lobed; lower lip 3-lobed, spreading. Flowers in small clusters, the clusters usually several and forming long, slender terminal spike. **Leaves** to 2 in. (5 cm) long, ½ in. (13 mm) wide, opposite, stalked; margins entire to irregularly toothed.

Habitat: Dry rocky, clayey or sandy soils in prairies, plains, flats, openings and edges of chaparral and pine-hardwoods, along embankments and oak-cedar slopes. In all except ST, FW.

Note: The sky-blue flowers of blue sage are striking in garden plantings, with the plants' height making them most effective for background use. The foliage of blue sage is not as aromatic as that of most of the mints, nor are the stems as prominently square. Culinary sage (*S. officinalis*) is a native of southern Europe and is frequently grown in this country as a garden plant.

MEALY SAGE (Wesby)

LYRE-LEAF SAGE

MEALY SAGE (*Salvia farinacea*)
Mint Family (Lamiaceae)

Bloom Period: March–November

Description: Upright to sprawling hairy perennial to 3 ft. (1 m) from woody root; stems usually numerous and forming clump, 4-angled or square. **Flower** to 1 in. (2.5 cm) long, purple or violet-blue, 2-lipped; upper lip 2-lobed, densely hairy with violet colored hairs on back; lower lip 3-lobed, much longer than upper lip. Flowers many, densely congested in whorls at intervals along upper portion of grayish, leafless stems. **Leaves** 1–3½ in. (2.5–8.9 cm) long, opposite, long-stalked; margins wavy to coarsely saw-toothed. Leaves usually plentiful in lower portion of plant.

Habitat: Dry, often rocky, calcareous or chalky soils in prairies, plains, chaparral, edges and openings of woodlands and on hillsides and slopes. In all except NE, SE, SC.

Note: The united sepals subtending the flowers of this plant are covered with whitish hairs, giving the flowers a "grayish" or "mealy" appearance. Highly prized for border plantings, mealy sage is often carried by nurseries.

LYRE-LEAF SAGE (*Salvia lyrata*)
Mint Family (Lamiaceae)

Bloom Period: April–June

Description: Strictly upright, hairy perennial 1–2 ft. (3–6 dm) high; stem solitary, 4-angled, unbranched or branched in flowering portion. **Flower** ¾–1¼ in. (20–32 mm) long, pale blue to violet, 2-lipped; upper lip short, not lobed; lower lip much larger, 3-lobed. Flowers numerous, in whorls around stem, forming interrupted terminal spike. **Leaves** to 8 in. (20 cm) long, mostly in basal rosette, stalked; blade of basal leaves entire to deeply cut or lobed with terminal lobe largest. Stem leaves opposite, of 1 or 2 pairs, small, stalkless, mostly entire. Winter leaves hairy, often purple-tinged.

Habitat: Sandy or occasionally clay or gravelly soils in meadows, clearings, lowlands, slopes and open woodlands. In NE, SE, NC, SC, CT.

Note: The distinctive, lyre-shaped leaves of this plant were once used by the Cherokee to brew a tea as a laxative and for colds, coughs and nervousness. It was also mixed with honey to make a syrup for asthma.

SKULLCAP (Wesby)

WILD HYACINTH (Wesby)

SKULLCAP (*Scutellaria drummondii*)
Mint Family (Lamiaceae)

Bloom Period: February–November

Description: Low, upright to somewhat sprawling, soft-hairy annual or short-lived perennial herb 8–12 in. (2–3 dm) high; stem solitary, 4-sided or square, much-branched at base and often forming clump. **Flower** to ½ in. (13 mm) long, blue-violet to purple, 2-lipped; upper lip short; lower lip 3-lobed, the middle lobe bearing conspicuous white spot dotted with purple, notched at tip. Flowers numerous, solitary in axils of upper leaves. **Leaves** ³⁄₁₆–¾ in. (5–20 mm) long, opposite, short-stalked; blade soft, rounded at tip.

Habitat: Various soils in prairies, chaparral, open plateaus, rocky slopes, flats, brushlands and shell beaches. In all except NE, SE.

Note: Both the common and genus names are derived from the small caplike structure which covers the seed during the fruiting period and remains on the plant long after the seed is gone. These plants are excellent for use in borders or rock gardens. Seeds should be sown in late fall.

WILD HYACINTH (*Camassia scilloides*)
Lily Family (Liliaceae)

Bloom Period: March–May

Description: Upright, smooth perennial 6–24 in. (1.5–6 dm) high, from small, deep bulb; flowering stem leafless, from bulb. **Flower** about 1 in. (25 mm) across, lavender to pale-blue, sweet-scented, the 6 segments all petallike, upright or widely spreading. Flowers numerous, stalked, loosely congested in elongated terminal cluster. **Leaves** 8–16 in. (2–4 dm) long, to ⅝ in. (16 mm) wide, alternate, grasslike, clustered in clump; blade thick, soft, the midrib prominently ridged.

Habitat: Sandy, rocky or alluvial soils of prairies, pastures, meadows, lowlands, hillsides, slopes, edges and openings of woodlands. In NE, NC, SC, EP.

Note: The bulbs of wild hyacinth were an important food source for Indians and early explorers. The genus name has its origin in the Indian name *quamash* or *camass*. The plants often form large colonies in the wild, but a few clumps in the wildflower garden are most showy and blend well with other wildings.

LANCE-LEAF LOOSESTRIFE (Darby)

AMELIA'S SAND-VERBENA (Hill)

LANCE-LEAF LOOSESTRIFE (*Lythrum lanceolatum*)
Loosestrife Family (Lythraceae)

Bloom Period: April–October

Description: Upright, smooth perennial to 5 ft. (15 dm); stems slender, brittle, 4-angled, usually branching in upper portion. Plants have numerous creeping basal offshoots, eventually forming large colonies. **Flower** about ½ in. (13 mm) across, purple, lavender-blue or reddish, solitary in axils of upper leaves; petals 4–6, spreading flat. **Leaves** to 2¼ in. (5.7 cm) long, about ½ in. (13 mm) wide. Lower leaves alternate; upper leaves opposite, much smaller, often folded against stem.

Habitat: Moist, usually periodically inundated swales or depressions in prairies or meadows, along edges of open marshes or swampy ponds, in roadside ditches and seepage areas. In all except PH, FW.

Note: This plant is considered to be a useful astringent in Mexico, but is not so popular north of the border. When rooted in rich, moist soils, the plants form nice clumps and produce flowers over a long period.

AMELIA'S SAND-VERBENA (*Abronia ameliae*)
Four-o'clock Family (Nyctaginaceae)

Bloom Period: March–June

Description: Upright to widely sprawling, rather coarse, densely hairy perennial to 24 in. (6 dm); stems solitary or few, usually much-branched. Plants have dense glandular hairs throughout and are sticky to the touch. **Flower** to ⅜ in. (1 cm) across, fragrant, lavender to violet-purple, trumpet-shaped, deeply and flatly 5-lobed at rim. Flowers numerous, forming rounded terminal clusters to 3 in. (7.6 cm) or more across. **Leaves** 1⅛–3⅛ in. (3–8 cm) long, ¾–2⅜ in. (2–6 cm) wide, opposite, long-stalked, the blade thick, the margins conspicuously and strongly wavy.

Habitat: Dry, deep, loose sands in live oak belts and edges and openings of live oak woodlands or motts. In ST.

Note: A most beautiful wildflower, this plant was named by Dr. C. L. Lundell for his wife, Amelia. Lundell has authored numerous papers and publications in agriculture and botany. He was founder and director of the Texas Research Foundation at Renner, and was founder of the herbaria at Southern Methodist University and Renner.

NARROW-LEAF SAND-VERBENA   (Worthington)

VIOLET WOOD-SORREL

NARROW-LEAF SAND-VERBENA (*Abronia angustifolia*)
Four-o'clock Family (Nyctaginaceae)

Bloom Period: May–July

Description: Sprawling or trailing, hairy annual herb; stems few to several, 4–20 in. (1–5 dm) long, branched, the branches stout or slender. Plant densely covered with glandular hairs and feeling sticky when touched. **Flower** to ¾ in. (2 cm) long, fragrant, purplish-red, trumpet-shaped, deeply and flatly 5-lobed at rim. Flowers numerous, congested in round cluster at ends of branches, usually closing by noon. **Leaves** ⅝–2 in. (1.6–5 cm) long, to 1⅛ in. (3 cm) across, opposite, slender-stalked, the blades variable in outline, the margins entire, wavy or, rarely, shallowly lobed.

Habitat: Deep, dry sandy or gypsum soils on dunes or plains. In FW.

Note: The sand-verbenas are especially lovely and many species do well in cultivation if sandy soils are present. The flowers are sweetly fragrant, adding to their attraction for garden plantings. The blossoms are visited by numerous small insects, especially butterflies.

VIOLET WOOD-SORREL (*Oxalis violacea*)
Wood-Sorrel Family (Oxalidaceae)

Bloom Period: March–May

Description: Low, delicate, somewhat succulent, smooth perennial 4–16 in. (1–4 dm) high from bulb. Plants spread from underground runners, forming small colonies. **Flower** to ¾ in. (2 cm) across, lavender to pinkish purple; petals 5, wide-spreading. Flowers several, in cluster at top of long, leafless stalk rising above the leaves. Flowers nodding in bud, closing at night and during cloudy weather. **Leaves** from bulb, long-stalked, the blade equally divided into 3 leaflets deeply notched at the tips, upper surface bright green, lower surface often reddish or purplish. Leaflets fold downward at night or during cloudy weather.

Habitat: Dry sandy or rocky soils in pinelands, open oak woods, prairies, on slopes and rock outcrops. In NE, SE, NC, SC.

Note: Violet wood-sorrel blooms in the spring along with several leaves, then again in the fall with no leaves being present. Leaves of this plant reportedly were chewed for their agreeable sour taste, but in large amounts can cause violent convulsions due to the presence of poisonous oxalic acid crystals. Brewed correctly, a mild tea is said to be good for the blood, and a cold leaf tea stops vomiting.

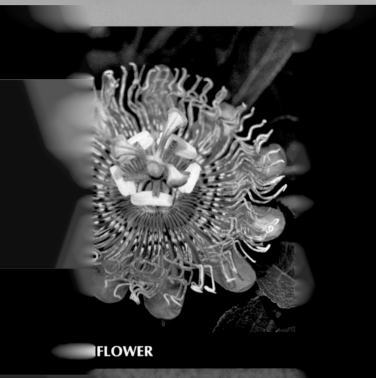

FLOWER

PASSIONFLOWER (*Passiflora incarnata*)
Passionflower Family (Passifloraceae)

Bloom Period: April–September

Description: Upright, sprawling, trailing or climbing herbaceous vine supported by tendrils from leaf axils; stem angled when young, to 25 ft. (7.5 m) long. **Flower** to 2½ in. (6.3 cm) across, lavender to purplish, solitary, short-stalked, from leaf axils. The 5 sepals and 5 petals much alike, subtending a fringe of wavy or crimped hairlike segments; stamens 5, united basally and forming long tube, 5-parted, wide-spreading in upper portion; pistil 3-parted, rising above stamens. **Leaves** 3–5 in. (7.6–12.7 cm) long and wide, alternate, stalked, with two conspicuous nectar glands on stalk near base of blade, the blade dark green above, whitish below, deeply 3-lobed.

Habitat: Various soils in pastures, old fields, fencerows, along stream banks and edges of woodlands and thickets. In NE, SE, NC, SC, CT.

Note: The fruit is a large berry, orange-yellow when ripe, 2–3 in. (50–76 mm) long, with edible pulp. The passionflowers comprise the food plant of several species of butterfly larvae.

SEA LAVENDER (*Limonium nashii*)
Plumbago Family (Plumbaginaceae)

Bloom Period: May–November

Description: Upright perennial 8–34 in. (2–8.5 dm) from woody roots; stem leafless, much branched from near middle. **Flower** about ¼ in. (6 mm) long, violet to lavender-blue; petals 5, usually remaining somewhat cupped. Flowers in 1- to 3-flowered clusters along one side of slender branches. **Leaves** 4–8 in. (10–20 cm) long, to 1¾ in. (45 mm) wide, in basal rosette, with stalks about as long as blade.

Habitat: Saline sands in grasslands, salt flats, along edges of brackish marshes and on shell beaches and dunes. In CT, ST.

Note: Sea lavender is one of the most common and conspicuous plants of the coastal area. When cut and dried, the flowers retain their purple tint for a long period, making them attractive material for winter bouquets. The scraped roots are reputed to cure canker sores and skin ulcers. The species *L. limbatum* is commonly found around saline flats and depressions in western Texas.

BLUE GILIA (Young)

WATER HYACINTH

BLUE GILIA (*Gilia rigidula*)
Phlox Family (Polemoniaceae)

Bloom Period: March–October
Description: Low, upright or sprawling, smooth or hairy perennial herb 4–12 in. (1–3 dm) high from stout, woody base; stems slender, much-branched, often clumplike. Plant somewhat sticky to the touch from glandular hairs. **Flower** to ¾ in. (2 cm) wide, blue to blue-violet, yellow in center around throat; petals 5, united at base to form short tube. Flowers stalked, solitary or few in cluster, from upper leaf axils. **Leaves** ½–1½ in. (13–38 mm) long, alternate, firm, entire or finely divided into 3–7 narrow segments; lower leaves crowded in rosette.
Habitat: Dry sandy, rocky or chalky soils of prairies, plains, slopes, brushlands and evergreen wooded areas. In PH, EP, ST, FW.
Note: The deep blue flower with conspicuous yellow center is distinctive and makes field identification of this plant easy. It is excellent in the wildflower garden and can be raised either from seed or young transplants. After the first prolific blooming in spring, flowers continue sporadically throughout the season. The genus was named for Felipe Gil, an 18th century Spanish botanist.

WATER HYACINTH (*Eichhornia crassipes*)
Pickerelweed Family (Pontederiaceae)

Bloom Period: April–July
Description: Low, aquatic perennial, free-floating or occasionally rooted in mud; roots long, feathery. Plants reproduce mostly from stolons. **Flowers** 1½–2½ in. (3.8–6.3 cm) long and broad, blue to bluish-purple, lasting a day or less; 6 petallike segments united at base into tube; upper 3 lobes prominently streaked with purple and the middle lobe with conspicuous yellow spot; lower 3 lobes lighter in color. Flowers many, forming spike exserted from leaflike spathe. **Leaves** 1¼–4¼ in. (3.2–10.8 cm) long, alternate, stalked, mostly in basal rosette; stalk to 10 in. (25 cm) long, spongy, conspicuously inflated at base, blade leathery, almost round.
Habitat: Water or mud in ditches, canals, ponds, streams, sloughs and lakes. In all except NC, PH, FW.
Note: A beautifully flowered plant, water hyacinth is a native of Brazil that has escaped and established itself so well it has become a noxious "weed," clogging waterways and destroying native vegetation. Also called *wampee*, *river-raft* and *water orchid*.

PICKERELWEED

CAROLINA ANEMONE

PICKERELWEED (*Pontederia cordata*)
Pickerelweed Family (Pontederiaceae)

Bloom Period: June–September

Description: Strictly upright, smooth, stout aquatic perennial 1–2 ft. (3–6 dm) high from creeping, rootlike rhizome rooted in mud beneath water and with leaves and flowering spike extending above water. **Flower** 5/16 in. (8 mm) long, violet-blue, funnel-shaped, 2-lipped; middle lobe of upper lip marked with 2 yellow spots. Flowers numerous, crowded in slender, elongating spike to 6 in. (15 cm) long, at tip of long stalk, each flower lasting for a day or less. **Leaves** from base, alternate, very long-stalked, thick, glossy, variable in shape but mostly longer than wide and deeply notched at base and forming long lobes on either side of leaf stalk. A solitary leaf occurs about midway on flowering stem.

Habitat: In shallow, quiet water along edges of sluggish streams or in margins of bogs, marshes, swamps or lakes. In NE, SE, SC, EP.

Note: This is a beautiful plant when in flower, and it attracts numerous insects seeking pollen and nectar. Plants often form large colonies.

CAROLINA ANEMONE (*Anemone caroliniana*)
Crowfoot Family (Ranunculaceae)

Bloom Period: February–April

Description: Upright, unbranched perennial to 12 in. (3 dm) high, from small, round, bulblike tuber and with slender rhizomes or stolons present. **Flower** to 1½ in. (38 mm) across, solitary, terminal on unbranched stalk; petals absent; sepals 10–30, petallike, white, pink, purplish or blue with the outer row wine-purple on lower surface. Flowers close at night and during cool or cloudy weather. **Leaves** mostly at base, stalked, the blade deeply divided or lobed, the segments ½–1½ in. (13–38 mm) long. One whorl of much smaller leaves on stem below flower.

Habitat: Sandy or loamy soils in prairies, old fields, pastures, along fencerows and in open woodlands. In all except ST, FW.

Note: *Anemone* is derived from the Greek word *anemos* meaning "wind"; the flowers supposedly open with spring breezes. The plant contains anemonin, a poison which affects the nervous system. Some Indian tribes attributed great healing powers to the roots, however, and used them in treating wounds.

BLUE LARKSPUR

SMALL BLUETS

BLUE LARKSPUR (*Delphinium carolinianum*)
Crowfoot Family (Ranunculaceae)

Bloom Period: April–July

Description: Upright, slender perennial to 3 ft. (1 m) from cluster of shallow, tuberlike roots; stem straw-colored or bluish in upper portion, branched or unbranched. **Flower** to 1¼ in. (32 mm) long, dark blue to blue-violet, sometimes whitish, short-stalked; sepals 5, petallike, the upper sepal with backward-projecting spur; petals 4, small, the upper 2 with spurs extending into upper sepal. Flowers few to several, opening upward in narrow, terminal spike. **Leaves** to 2¾ in. (7 cm) wide, alternate, stalked, the blade divided and lobed into numerous narrow segments; basal leaves often forming winter rosette, withering before flowers open with only the stem leaves remaining.

Habitat: Dry, sandy soils in fields, sand hills, open woodlands and brushlands. In all except PH.

Note: The fancied resemblance of the flower's spur to the spur of a lark gave this genus its common name. It gets the Spanish name of *espuela del caballero* from its resemblance to a horseman's spur.

SMALL BLUETS (*Hedyotis crassifolia*)
Madder Family (Rubiaceae)

Bloom Period: January–April

Description: Upright to somewhat sprawling, low, delicate winter annual 1¼–4¾ in. (3.2–12 cm) high; stems usually branched. Plants often form large colonies. **Flower** to ⁵⁄₁₆ in. (8 mm) across, blue-violet to lilac with darker throat, or rarely white, solitary, terminal on very slender stalks, trumpet-shaped, 4-lobed at rim. **Leaves** to ⅜ in.(1 cm) long, less than ¼ in. (6 mm) wide, opposite, stalked, abruptly tapering at base. Blades of upper leaves many times longer than stalks.

Habitat: Sandy soils in abandoned fields, pastures, prairies, woodland openings and lawns. In all except PH, EP, FW.

Note: Among the first flowers of spring to bloom, small bluets often form large, showy patches of almost solid blue-violet in pastures and old fields, often blooming with field pansy and spring beauties. Other common names include *star-violet, innocence, angel-eyes* and *Quaker ladies*. Other plants of this family provide coffee and quinine; the cultivated gardenia is also a relative.

PURPLE GERARDIA

DOWNY PAINTBRUSH (Cheatham)

PURPLE GERARDIA (*Agalinis purpurea*)
Figwort Family (Scrophulariaceae)

Bloom Period: August–November

Description: Upright to sprawling annual to 4 ft. (12 dm) high, but usually much lower; stems solitary, commonly angled, much-branched in upper portion, with the branches slender, wiry and wide-spreading. **Flower** 1–1⅛ in. (25–30 mm) long, purplish to light pink, the throat lined with yellow, spotted with purple, and conspicuously bearded at base, short-tubular with 5 unequal, flaring lobes at rim. Flowers from axils of upper leaves. **Leaves** to about 1½ in. (38 mm) long, to ⅛ in. (3 mm) wide, opposite, stalkless, occasionally with clusters of tiny leaves in axils.

Habitat: Moist, sandy soils in bogs, meadows, prairies, low or upland grasslands and open pinelands. In NE, SE, SC.

Note: The flowers of purple gerardia are visited frequently by various bees and butterflies, especially the sulphur and buckeye. The plant is a major food source of the fall broods of the buckeye larvae. (The early spring larvae feed on toadflax.) A decoction of the roots of this semiparasitic plant was once used for medicinal purposes.

DOWNY PAINTBRUSH (*Castilleja sessiliflora*)
Figwort Family (Scrophulariaceae)

Bloom Period: March–May

Description: Upright, low, hairy perennial herb to 12 in. (3 dm); stems few to several from base. **Flower** 1⅜–2⅛ in. (35–55 mm) long, purplish to pinkish or sometimes yellow, tubular, 2-lipped, the upper lip slender, beaked, longer than lower lip. Flowers exserted from purple- or pink-tinged, lobed calyx and subtended by bracts; bracts shorter than leaves with pair of long, narrow lateral lobes, green or sometimes pink-tinged. Flowers and bracts numerous, the whole forming showy terminal spike. **Leaves** 1–2 in. (2.5–5 cm) long, alternate, stalkless, the lower leaves very narrow, upper ones usually with narrow lobes.

Habitat: Dry rocky, gravelly or sandy soils on plains and along wooded hillsides and slopes. In PH, EP, FW.

Note: As with other paintbrushes, this plant is semiparasitic on other plants and is almost impossible to transplant to the garden, but can be started easily from fall-sown seed in appropriate soils. The plants are excellent when used to form a solid border or to form clumps among other plants.

TEXAS TOADFLAX

SNAPDRAGON VINE (Wesby)

TEXAS TOADFLAX (*Linaria texana*)
Figwort Family (Scrophulariaceae)

Bloom Period: March–May

Description: Upright, slender, delicate, smooth annual or winter biennial to 28 in. (7 dm); stems usually solitary or occasionally few, with small rosettes of short, trailing, sterile branches at base. Plants usually form colonies. **Flowers** ½–⅝ in. (13–16 mm) long, pale blue to violet, fragrant, 2-lipped; upper lip short, erect, 2-lobed; lower lip spreading, 3-lobed, with curved, slender spur at base. Flowers few to many, in terminal spike. **Leaves** to 1½ in. (38 mm) long, thin, linear, smooth and alternate on stem; opposite, thicker and much smaller on basal branches.

Habitat: Usually dry, sandy soils in abandoned areas, meadows, pastures, old fields and open areas of woodlands. Throughout.

Note: Texas toadflax is pollinated by moths, bees and butterflies. The leaves and stems are eaten ravenously by larvae of the spring brood of the buckeye butterfly. A similar but smaller-flowered species with fewer flowers open along the spike is *L. canadensis*, which is usually found in even sandier soils.

SNAPDRAGON VINE (*Maurandya antirrhiniflora*)
Figwort Family (Scrophulariaceae)

Bloom Period: April–December

Description: Climbing, trailing or extensively twining, smooth, delicate herbaceous vine; stems solitary or few, slender, much-branched, to 3 ft. (1 m) or more. **Flower** ⅝–1 in. (16–25 mm) long, violet to purple or rarely whitish, shortly tubular, 2-lipped; upper lip 2-lobed; lower lip 3-lobed and with raised ridge or hump partially closing throat. Flowers solitary from leaf axils. **Leaves** 2–10 in. (5–25 cm) long, alternate, long-stalked, the blade mostly triangular-shaped, often lobed at base.

Habitat: Sandy or rocky soils of dry salt marshes, beaches, dunes, limestone hills or bluffs. In NC, CT, EP, ST, FW.

Note: Climbing snapdragon responds well to cultivation and makes an attractive vine that quickly covers a mesh or wire support. The uniquely shaped flowers are often borne in profusion and continue for a long period. Our cultivated garden snapdragon (*Antirrhinum majus*) is a closely related species native to the Mediterranean region.

PURPLE GROUND-CHERRY

(Tveten)

PURPLE GROUND-CHERRY (*Quincula lobata*)
Nightshade Family (Solanaceae)

Bloom Period: March–December

Description: Low, spreading or sprawling, scruffy-looking perennial; stems several, branched from base, to 1 ft. (3 dm) long. **Flower** ¾–1 in. (2–2.5 cm) across, violet or blue, bell-shaped, wide-flaring, appearing flat at rim, solitary, terminal on short stalks. Usually several flowers open at one time. **Leaves** 1½–4 in. (3.8–10 cm) long, ³⁄₁₆–1⅛ in. (5–30 mm) wide, narrowed at base into long, winged stalk, the blade cut, lobed, shallowly toothed or entire.

Habitat: Various dry soils in bare and disturbed sites, plains, barren slopes and hillsides. In PH, EP, ST, FW.

Note: Purple ground-cherry is closely related to the genus *Physalis*, with one of the most obvious differences being in the flowers: purple ground-cherry has upright purple flowers while flowers in the genus *Physalis* are yellow and hang downward, or "droop." When fully ripened and yellow, the fruit of purple ground-cherry is edible but not particularly tasty. It is occasionally used to make preserves and is an excellent addition to the rock garden, as it performs well in extreme drought.

SILVER-LEAF NIGHTSHADE (*Solanum elaeagnifolium*)
Nightshade Family (Solanaceae)

Bloom Period: March–October

Description: Upright, sparsely prickly perennial to 3 ft. (1 m), forming colonies from creeping roots. Stems solitary or few from base. Plant densely covered with star-shaped hairs and appearing silvery. **Flower** ¾–1⅛ in. (2–3 cm) across, violet to pale lavender or rarely white; petals 5, united at base, 5-lobed at rim and appearing star-shaped; anthers large, yellow. Flowers few, in clusters from leaf axils near ends of branches. **Leaves** to 6 in. (15 cm) long, 3 to 5 times longer than wide, alternate, long-stalked, gray-green, usually wavy-edged.

Habitat: Various soils in pastures, prairies, old fields, bottomlands and disturbed areas. Throughout.

Note: The fruit of this plant, a berry that is yellow or blackish when ripe, was used by Southwestern Indians in making cheese. The berries were also used to treat sore throat and toothache. Nightshade berries mixed with cream have reportedly been used as a cure for poison ivy. One can occasionally find small colonies of the white-flowered form, f. *albiflorum*.

LOVELL VIOLET

BIRD'S-FOOT VIOLET

LOVELL VIOLET (*Viola lovelliana*)
Violet Family (Violaceae)

Bloom Period: March–April

Description: Low, upright, often clumped, smooth perennial producing new plants from thick, underground root. Plants usually found in thin, scattered colonies. **Flower** to 1 in. (25 mm) across, dark lavender or violet, solitary, long-stalked, from root. Petals 5; upper 2 petals erect; lower 3 petals conspicuously bearded in throat, the middle or lowermost petal spurred at base. The long-stalked, seed-producing flowers do not open and are not showy, usually lying on ground, where pod opens. **Leaves** from root, with blade width ½ to nearly equal the length, long-stalked; blade broadly lobed in basal portion, elongated in tip portion.

Habitat: Dry or moist loams in openings and edges of thickets and deciduous woodlands. In all except NC, PH, ST.

Note: The fragrance of violets temporarily makes it impossible to smell them, thus the frequent reference to the violet scent as being "elusive." Most violets, including this one, do well in gardens, especially if given a cool, shady, semimoist area in rich soil.

BIRD'S-FOOT VIOLET (*Viola pedata*)
Violet Family (Violaceae)

Bloom Period: March–April

Description: Low, smooth, clumped perennial 4–10 in. (10–25 cm) high from a short, thick root. **Flower** to 1½ in. (38 mm) across, dark lavender to whitish, solitary; petals 5, flattened, pansylike; upper 2 petals smaller than lower 3, frequently flared backward; lowermost petal spurred at base; all petals without hairs or "beard"; stamens 5, orange-tipped and conspicuously protruding from throat. **Leaves** ¾–2 in. (2–5 cm) long, from root, smooth, long-stalked; blade almost round in outline, deeply divided to base into several narrow segments.

Habitat: Dry, upland, sandy or rocky soils in open pastures, woodlands and on hillsides and slopes. In NE, SE, CT.

Note: This is our largest-flowered native violet. In its most common form it has solid-colored petals, but occasionally one finds small colonies with the upper petals a dark, velvety purple and lower petals lavender. Bird's-foot violet does not reproduce vegetatively as do most other violets, but only by seed from the open, showy flowers. Picking these flowers hinders the plants' reproduction and distribution.

FIELD PANSY

FIELD PANSY (*Viola rafinesquii*)
Violet Family (Violaceae)

Bloom Period: February–April

Description: Upright or sprawling, slender, smooth annual to 8 in. (2 dm); stem usually solitary, branched or unbranched at base, leafy. **Flower** to 1 in. (2.5 cm) across, dark violet to pale lavender or white, with darker markings, yellow in throat; petals 5; upper 2 petals large, erect; lowermost petal spurred at base. Seed produced from both opening and nonopening flowers. **Leaves** to 1¼ in. (3.2 cm) long, alternate, stalked, with 2 conspicuous, deeply cut leaflike bracts at base of stalk; basal leaves long-stalked, roundish; stem leaves smaller, narrower; margins entire.

Habitat: Sandy soils in lawns, pastures, meadows and open woodlands. In all except CT, EP, ST, FW.

Note: In good years this little plant forms extensive colonies and abundantly covers an area with color. It often occurs along with spring beauties and bluets. The crushed roots have a pleasing fragrance of wintergreen, and various parts of the plant were once used medicinally. Also called *Johnny-jump-up, heartsease* and *cupid's-delight*.

GLOSSARY

Alkaline (soil). Having an exchangeable sodium content high enough to interfere with the growth of most crop plants.

Alternate. Arranged other than opposite or whorled; borne at different levels; situated between other organs or plant parts.

Annual. Growing from seed to maturity and dying in one year or season.

Annual (winter). Starting growth in the cooler winter months, and flowering the following spring.

Anther. The part of the stamen that bears the pollen.

Aquatic. Living in water.

Aromatic. Having a noticeable, not unpleasant scent; pungent. Often refers to crushed plant parts; not usually used in reference to flowers.

Arroyo. An eroded (usually deep) gully or dry stream- or river-bed in arid country.

Axil. The angle between any two structures or organs, as where a leaf or branch joins the stem.

Banner. The unpaired petal of the five petals in a flower of the legume family, usually the largest and uppermost.

Basal. Located at or relating to the base.

Beard. A zone of long, stiff hairs.

Berry. A fleshy or pulpy, nonopening fruit containing one to many seeds, the seeds without a stony covering.

Biennial. Requiring two years to complete the life cycle.

Bladder. A thin, usually transparent organ capable of being inflated or expanded.

Blade. The expanded portion of a leaf, petal, or other organ.

Bract. A reduced or modified leaf, most often occurring below or subtending a flower or inflorescence, sometimes brightly colored or petallike. May appear as a scalelike or threadlike structure.

Bristle. A very stiff hair or similar structure.

Bud. The structure which is the undeveloped stem or leaf, usually enclosed by scales. An unexpanded flower, subtended or sometimes enclosed by bracts or the calyx.

Bulb. A short underground bud surrounded by layers of thick, fleshy, modified leaves, as an onion.

Calcareous (soil). Containing a high percentage of calcium carbonate.

Calyx. The outer whorl of a flower; the sepals collectively, which may be separate or united and may be green or colorful and petallike.

Carnivorous. Flesh-eating; applied to those plants which trap and digest insects or other small organisms.

Chaff. Small, dry, thin scales or bracts.

Chalky (soil). A distinctive, cemented layer of caliche, usually exposed or near the surface.

Chaparral. Low, dense, usually thorny, scrubby growth consisting of shrubs, cacti and yuccas in the southern and southwestern portion of the state.

Clasping. Basal portion of a leaf or other organ partly or wholly surrounding the stem or other structure, but not united.

Cleistogamous. Applied to flowers, usually small and inconspicuous, which are self-fertilizing and never open.

Climbing. Reaching upward using the support of other plants or objects.

Cluster. A general term for a group of flowers or other plant parts.

Colony. A relatively dense stand or population of plants of one species more or less isolated from other stands.

Column. The structure formed by the union of the filaments in the mallow family.

Congested. Crowded; arranged or set close together.

Corolla. The inner whorl of a flower; the petals collectively, which may be separate or united; often colorful.

Creeping. Growing beneath or on the surface of the ground and rooting at nodes.

Cut. General term used for any dissection.

Decoction. The liquid obtained from boiling a medicinal plant in water.

Disk. Applied to the tubular, central flowers of the head in the sunflower family.

Endemic. Restricted to a limited geographic area.

Entire. Margins without teeth, lobes or incisions.

Erect. Pointing upward; upright. Somewhat perpendicular to a surface.

Escape. A cultivated plant growing and reproducing in the wild.

Exserted. Projecting out or extending beyond; not included.

Extract. A preparation containing the properties of the substance from which it was derived; usually obtained by evaporation.

Filament. Basal portion of stamen supporting anther, usually slender. Any threadlike structure.

Fleshy. Thick, succulent, appearing "juicy," although it may not be.

Flower. A structure consisting of associated plant parts which function as a reproductive unit. Often colorful and showy.

Fringe. Finely cut margins of leaf or petal; or margins having a row of hairs.

Fruit. The mature ovary and any associated parts which may be fused with it, normally containing seed.

Funnel-shaped. Tubular at the base, gradually flaring upward.

Gland. Small structure on or near a surface which secretes sticky or volatile oils or fluids.

Glandular. Bearing glands.

Glossy. Smooth, shiny or glistening; usually applied to a surface, as of a leaf.

Gyp (soil). Containing a large percentage of the mineral gypsum.

Hair. Any of the structures occurring on a plant which resemble in appearance the true hairs of animals; they may be microscopic or readily visible.

Head. Compact cluster of stalkless flowers or fruits. Used here only as an individual flower cluster of either ray or disk flowers (or both) of the sunflower family.

Herb. A plant without a persistent, above-ground woody stem, either annual or dying back to the ground each year.

Herbaceous. Having the characteristics of a herb.

Herbage. The green parts of a plant, mainly the stem and leaves.

Igneous (soil). Derived from rock which was formed from the cooling and solidification of magma.

Inflated. Bladderlike; appearing blown up; enlarged.

Infusion. The liquid extract obtained by steeping or soaking in water of plant parts, usually the herbage. Generally administered as a tea.

Introduced. Descriptive of a wild or cultivated plant brought in intentionally or unintentionally from another region, which has become established in the wild.

Joint. The place of connection of distinct structures; a node.

Keel. The two lower petals in the flowers of the legume family.

Larva. The second ("worm" or caterpillar) stage in the life cycle of a butterfly. (*Plural:* **Larvae**.)

Leaf. A unit of foliage.

Leaflet. One segment of a divided (compound) leaf, itself appearing as a small leaf.

Limestone (soil). Derived from sedimentary rock that is composed primarily of calcite.

Lip. The upper or lower portion of a calyx or corolla which has been partially divided into two parts.

Lobe. Any projection of a margin, often rounded, normally larger than a tooth.

Lobed. Having lobes.

Margin. The outer edge of a flattened or somewhat flattened structure, as of a leaf.

Nectar. A sweet liquid produced by plants and used as food by insects.

Nodding. Hanging or drooping downward.

Node. A place on a stem where branches, leaves, or flower stalks are attached; a joint.

Opposite. Two like parts connected at the same place but across from each other. Two structures, one occurring directly in front of the other, as a stamen opposite a petal.

Panicle. A branched inflorescence with the flowers in racemes.

Parasitic. A species which attaches to another species and obtains food from it without returning appreciable benefits.

Perennial. Living for more than two years.

Petal. One segment of a corolla.

Phyllary. One of a whorl of bracts subtending a flower cluster, as in the heads of the sunflower family.

Pistil. The female reproductive part of the flower containing the ovary, the style (if present), and the stigma.

Pollen. The male spores borne by the anther.

Raceme. An elongating unbranched inflorescence with flowers stalked and opening progressively from the base of the inflorescence upward.

Ray. The outer, flattened, petallike flowers in the flower head of the sunflower family.

Recurved. Curving or bending backward or downward.

Resaca. A former channel or course of a stream or river, usually containing water and forming a long, narrow lake.

Resin. A sticky, usually aromatic liquid produced by the glands of some plants.

Rhizome. An underground, horizontal, usually elongated stem producing roots and leafy stems at the nodes.

Ridged. Having lengthwise furrows or grooves.

Rim. The terminal border of a united calyx or corolla.

Root. A usually underground part of a plant which normally anchors the plant to the substrate and functions chiefly in obtaining water and minerals.

Rosette. A circular cluster of leaves radiating from the center at or near the ground.

Rough. Having a coarse texture; not smooth to the touch; may be due to hairs or any other unevenness.

Saline (soil). Containing sufficient soluble salts to impair productivity.

Scale. Any small, thin, nongreen, dry plant structure.

Seed. A fertilized ovule; an embryo and its immediate covering, normally capable of germination to produce a new plant.

Sepal. One segment of a calyx.

Smooth. Not rough to the touch. Used here as a general term to denote the absence of hairs.

Solitary. One. Alone; not forming part of a group or cluster.

Spike. Used here as a general term to describe an elongated group or cluster of flowers. Technically, an elongating, unbranched inflorescence with flowers unstalked and opening progressively from the base of the inflorescence upward.

Sprawling. Leaning over; lax.

Spreading. Flaring toward a flat or somewhat flat position. Not appressed or pressed together. Parting.

Spur. A tubular or saclike extension of a sepal or petal, usually containing nectar.

Stalk. A general term for the usually elongated structure connecting or supporting an organ or group of organs.

Stamen. Pollen-bearing male reproductive structure of a flower consisting of filament and anther.

Stem. The main stalk of a plant arising from the roots.

Stolon. A somewhat horizontal, above-ground, sometimes below-ground, stem or branch rooting at the tip of nodes and forming new plants.

Style. The portion of the pistil between the ovary and the stigma, often elongate, sometimes apparently absent.

Subtend. To be below and close to.

Succulent. Juicy and fleshy.

Swirled. Overlapping and appearing spiraled but not necessarily ascending.

Teeth. Any small marginal protuberances, usually regularly repeated.

Tendril. A modified portion of a stem or leaf, usually slender and coiling or twining and functioning as a support.

Terminal. At the end or tip.

Throat. The area at the junction of the tube with the rim in a united calyx or corolla.

Toothed. Having teeth.

Trailing. Lying on the ground and elongating but not rooting.

Trumpet-shaped. Tubular at the base, abruptly flaring in the upper portion.

Tube. The tubular, basal portion of a calyx or corolla. Any tubular structure.

Tubular. Circular in cross-section, hollow, nearly uniform in width, and usually longer than wide.

Tuft. A clump or cluster of stems, leaves, hairs, or other elongated structures, commonly densest at the base and spreading upward.

Twining. Supporting by wrapping around or encircling other plants or structures.

United. Fused together; not separate.

Urn-shaped. Enlarged at the base, contracted at the throat, and without a prominent rim.

Vein. An externally visible fibrous strand; a rib.

Veined. Having veins, especially conspicuous or numerous ones.

Wavy. Applied to margins with waves perpendicular to the plane of the blade.

Weed. A plant of rank, prolific, or obnoxious growth, usually growing to the detriment of a crop or more desirable species. An unwanted plant.

Whorl. A circular arrangement of structures arising from the same location.

Wing. A flattened membranous structure extending from an organ. One of a pair of lateral petals in some flowers of the legume family.

Woody. Having hard, persisting tissues.

Woolly. Having long, soft, more or less matted hairs.

ILLUSTRATED GLOSSARY

Floral Structures

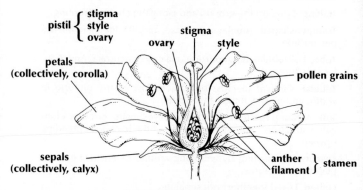

pistil { stigma, style, ovary }

petals (collectively, corolla)

sepals (collectively, calyx)

stigma

ovary

style

pollen grains

anther, filament } stamen

HYPOTHETICAL FLOWER

SOME COMMON CALYX OR COROLLA SHAPES

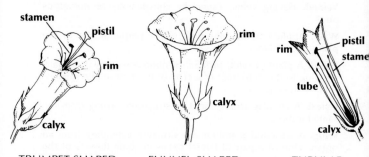

stamen

pistil

rim

calyx

TRUMPET-SHAPED
(stamens and pistil exserted)

rim

calyx

FUNNEL-SHAPED

rim

pistil

stamen

tube

calyx

TUBULAR
(stamens and pistil included)

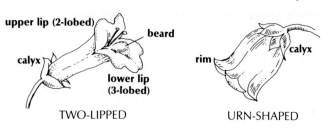

upper lip (2-lobed)

beard

calyx

lower lip (3-lobed)

TWO-LIPPED

rim

calyx

URN-SHAPED

GENERAL COROLLAS OF SOME FAMILIES

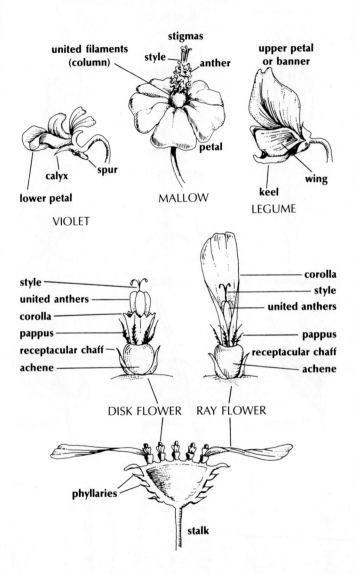

VIOLET

united filaments (column)

stigmas

style

anther

calyx

spur

lower petal

petal

MALLOW

upper petal or banner

wing

keel

LEGUME

style

united anthers

corolla

pappus

receptacular chaff

achene

DISK FLOWER

corolla

style

united anthers

pappus

receptacular chaff

achene

RAY FLOWER

phyllaries

stalk

HEAD (in section) (Sunflower Family)

Vegetative Structures

BLADE TIPS

Pointed

Rounded

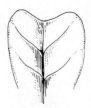

Notched

BLADE BASES

Tapering

Lobed

Notched

Sheathing

Clasping

Encircling

MARGINS

Entire

Toothed

Wavy

Fringed

Lobed

398

ARRANGEMENT

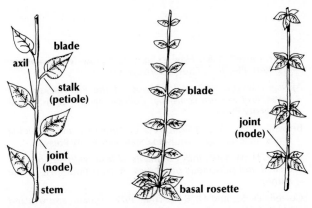

ALTERNATE LEAVES
stalked (petioled)

OPPOSITE LEAVES
stalkless (sessile)

WHORLED LEAVES
stalkless (sessile)

TYPES

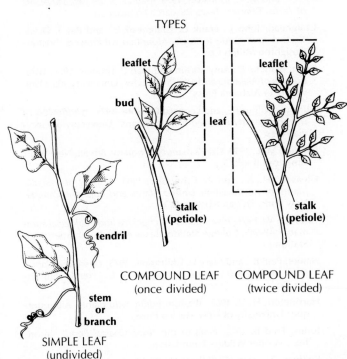

SIMPLE LEAF
(undivided)

COMPOUND LEAF
(once divided)

COMPOUND LEAF
(twice divided)

BIBLIOGRAPHY

Abbott, Carroll. 1982. *How to know and grow Texas wildflowers*. Kerrville, Tex.: Green Horizons Press.

Ajilvsgi, Geyata. 1979. *Wild flowers of the Big Thicket, east Texas, and western Louisiana*. College Station: Texas A & M University Press.

Brown, C. A. 1972. *Wildflowers of Louisiana and adjoining states*. Baton Rouge: Louisiana State University Press.

Burlage, H. M. 1968. *Index of plants of Texas with reputed medicinal and poisonous properties*. Austin: Published by the author.

Correll, D. S., and H. B. Correll. 1972. *Aquatic and wetland plants of the southwestern United States*. Washington, D.C.: Environmental Protection Agency.

———, and M. C. Johnston. 1970. *Manual of the vascular plants of Texas*. Renner: Texas Research Foundation.

Craighead, John J., Frank C. Craighead Jr., and Ray J. Davis. 1963. *A field guide to Rocky Mountain wildflowers*. Boston: Houghton Mifflin Co.

Dean, Blanche E., Amy Mason and Joab L. Thomas. 1973. *Wildflowers of Alabama and adjoining states*. University, Ala.: University of Alabama Press.

Duncan, Wilbur H., and Leonard E. Foote. 1975. *Wildflowers of the southeastern United States*. Athens: University of Georgia Press.

Fernald, M. L. 1950. *Gray's manual of botany*. 8th ed. New York: American Book Co.

Gleason, H. A., and A. Cronquist. 1963. *Manual of vascular plants of northeastern United States and adjacent Canada*. New York: D. Van Nostrand Co.

Gould, F. W. 1969. *Texas plants—a checklist and ecological summary*. MP-585. College Station: Texas Agricultural Experiment Station.

Hamel, Paul B., and Mary U. Chiltoskey. 1975. *Cherokee plants: Their uses, a 400 year history*. Sylva, N. C.: Herald Publishing Co.

Harrington, H. D. 1967. *Western edible wild plants*. Albuquerque: University of New Mexico Press.

Jones, Fred B. 1975. *Flora of the Texas Coastal Bend*. Sinton, Tex.: Welder Wildlife Foundation.

Kearney, Thomas H., Robert H. Peebles, *et al.* 1951. *Arizona flora*. Berkeley and Los Angeles: University of California Press.

Klots, Alexander B. 1951. *A field guide to the butterflies of North America, east of the Great Plains*. Boston: Houghton Mifflin Co.

Krochmal, A., Russell S. Walters, and Richard M. Doughty. 1971. *A guide to medicinal plants of Appalachia*. U.S. Department of Agriculture Pub. No. 400. Washington, D.C.: Government Printing Office.

McDougall, W. B., and Omer E. Sperry. 1951. *Plants of Big Bend National Park*. Washington, D.C.: Government Printing Office.

Mathews, F. Schuyler. 1927. *Field book of American wild flowers*. New York: G. P. Putnam's Sons.

Mooney, James, and Frans M. Olbrechts. 1932. *The Swimmer manuscript Cherokee sacred formulas and medicinal prescriptions*. Washington, D.C.: Government Printing Office.

Moote, Michael. 1979. *Medicinal plants of the Mountain West*. Santa Fe: Museum of New Mexico Press.

Muenscher, Walter C. 1939. *Poisonous plants of the United States*. New York: Macmillan Co.

Niering, William A., and Nancy C. Olmstead. 1979. *The Audubon Society field guide to North American wildflowers— eastern region*. New York: Alfred A. Knopf.

Parks, H. B. 1937. *Valuable plants native to Texas*. Bull. No. 551. College Station: Texas Agricultural Experiment Station.

Peterson, Roger Tory, and Margaret McKenny. 1968. *A field guide to wildflowers*. Boston: Houghton Mifflin Co.

Pyle, Robert M. 1981. *The Audubon Society field guide to North American butterflies*. New York: Alfred A. Knopf.

Radford, Albert E., Harry E. Ahles, and C. Ritchie Bell. 1968. *Manual of the vascular flora of the Carolinas*. Chapel Hill: University of North Carolina Press.

Reading, Robert S. 1960. *Arrows over Texas*. San Antonio: Naylor Co.

Rechenthin, C. A. 1972. *Native flowers of Texas*. U.S. Department of Agriculture. Temple, Tex.: Soil Conservation Service.

Rickett, H. W. 1967. *Wild flowers of the United States: the southeastern states*. New York: McGraw-Hill.

———. 1969. *Wild flowers of the United States: Texas*. New York: McGraw-Hill.

Shinners, L. H. 1972. *Spring flora of the Dallas and Fort Worth area*. 2nd ed. Fort Worth: Prestige Press.

Smith, Arlo I. 1979. *A guide to wildflowers of the Mid-South*. Memphis: Memphis State University Press.

Spellenberg, Richard. 1979. *The Audubon Society field guide to North American wildflowers—western region*. New York: Alfred A. Knopf.

Stevens, William Chase. 1948. *Kansas wild flowers*. Lawrence: University of Kansas Press.

Taylor, Constance E. S., and R. John Taylor. 1983. *The goldenrods (Solidago-Asteraceae) of Oklahoma and Texas*. Department of Biology, Southeastern Oklahoma State University, Durant, Okla. Unpublished manuscript (photocopy).

Turner, B. L. 1959. *The legumes of Texas*. Austin: University of Texas Press.

Warnock, Barton H. 1970. *Wildflowers of the Big Bend Country, Texas*. Alpine, Tex.: Sul Ross State University.

―――. 1974. *Wildflowers of the Guadalupe Mountains and the sand dune country, Texas*. Alpine: Sul Ross State University.

―――. 1977. *Wildflowers of the Davis Mountains and Marathon Basin, Texas*. Alpine: Sul Ross State University.

Whitehouse, E. 1967. *Texas flowers in natural colors*. 3rd ed. Dallas: Dallas County Audubon Society.

Wills, M. M., and H. S. Irwin. 1961. *Roadside flowers of Texas*. Austin: University of Texas Press.

INDEX

405

409

413

Amarillo

PH

Lubbock

Abilen

El Paso   Odessa

FW   San Ang

Alpine   EP

Del

E—East
(NE)—Northeast
(SE)—Southeast
CT—Coastal Texas
SC—South Central
NC—North Central
ST—South Texas
EP—Edwards Plateau
PH—Panhandle
FW—Far West